AN ENGLISH ODYSSEY

For
Benedict, Christopher, Geoffrey and Richard
Graham and Sandii, Geoff and Colin

AN ENGLISH ODYSSEY

The Pendleburys
of Lancashire and London:
nine generations
of a working family

MARION CUTTING

An English Odyssey
The Pendleburys of Lancashire and London: nine generations of a working family

Copyright © Marion Cutting, 2012

The moral rights of the author have been asserted by her
in accordance with the Copyright, Designs and Patents Act 1988

First published by Palatine Books
an imprint of Carnegie Publishing Ltd
Carnegie House,
Chatsworth Road,
Lancaster LA1 4SL

www.carnegiepublishing.com

British Library Cataloguing-in-Publication data
A catalogue record for this book is available from the British Library

ISBN 978-1-874181-86-6

Typeset and designed by Carnegie Book Production, Lancaster
Printed and bound in the UK by Page Bros, Norwich

Contents

Acknowledgements

This story would never have been started without the nineteenth-century Pendlebury documents, and I am so very grateful to my Uncle Geoff for transcribing them so painstakingly before passing on the originals to me.

I would like to thank the following for kindly giving me permission to cite or reproduce material: Bristol Record Office (image 40762/5); Bury Archives (images b07849 and b16270); Barbara Chambers (Richard Pendlebury's attestation and war record and information from her regimental database); Anthony Claydon (information about East Knoyle); City of London, London Metropolitan Archives (material from the School Board for London and Board of Guardians); The County Archivist, Lancashire Record Office for permission granted on behalf of the current owners of Lancashire probate and Quarter Sessions records (WCW infra 1608 Raphe and Susanna Bury, WCW infra 1683 Isaac Pendlebury, WCW infra 1751 Francis Pendlebury, WCW infra 1796 Nathan Pendlebury and WCW infra 1821 Francis Pendlebury); Dover Publications; Professor Ralph R. Frerichs (part of 'Cary's New and Accurate Plan of London and Westminster, the Borough of Southwark and parts adjacent' 1818 and part of 'Cruchley's New Plan of London, improved to 1846' from his website http://www.ph.ucla.edu/ epi/snow.html); Alan Godfrey (a section of Sheet 76, Southwark and Waterloo 1872); Guildhall Library (information on mariners); Dr Jonathon Healey (unpublished paper delivered at the 2008 Economic History Society annual conference); John Higson (early Radcliffe Sunday schools); Helen Jewell (transcription of inventories of Ralph and Susannah Pendlebury); Lancashire Parish Register Society (records of the parish registers of Bury and Radcliffe); Manchester Archives and Local Studies (image from the Parish Register of St Mary's Radcliffe); Mexborough and District Heritage Society (Mexborough connections); Museum of London (image 004745); Old-Maps (permission to publish a section of the map, Lancashire and Furness, 1848–1851, 1:10,560 scale); La Trobe Australian Manuscripts Collection, State Library of Victoria, Melbourne, Australia (citation of material from two unpublished diaries by Archibald Gilchrist and Richard Moffat); Radcliffe Library (information on Coggra Fold); Southwark Local History Library (image P4414); Surrey History Centre (image 7556/3); Phil Parker Ltd (information about the saxophone horn and the euphonium); Trade Union Congress (images of Pink's strike and of washerwoman); University College London, Special Collections; Wombwell Heritage Group (images of Wombwell).

Britain's archives are a national treasure. I am indebted to the enthusiasm and knowledge of staff at: the Barnsley Archives and Local Studies Department (Joan

Adams); Bury Reference and Information Services (Adam Carter) and Archives (Donna Hardman); the City of London, London Metropolitan Archives; the Docklands Museum London; Doncaster Archives; Huddersfield Library Local Studies (Barbara Hinchliffe); Lancashire Record Office; the Library of the London School of Economics; Liverpool Record Office; Lloyds Register Information Services; Manchester Archives and Local Studies; the Mexborough and District Heritage Society; the National Archives (Public Record Office); the Roman Catholic diocese of Westminster; the Surrey Record Centre; and Westminster City Archives.

Several internet sources have proved invaluable in providing me with a genealogical framework although it has not been practical to cite a detailed reference for each piece of information used. One is the Lancashire On-Line Parish Clerks' website (http://www.lan-opc.org.uk) which allowed me to search the early Radcliffe and Bury parish records from home. Another is Ancestry's on-line research facility (http://www.ancestry.co.uk) for its provision of electronic access to datasets on births, deaths and marriages in London and elsewhere, and to the census records. In addition, I have made extensive use of Officer's *Purchasing Power of British Pounds from 1264 to Present* (2009), an on-line facility for comparing the value of money between 1264 and 2009 (http://www.measuringworth.com); all the equivalent values cited in terms of the retail price index and the index of average earnings are taken from this source. The original text of many early books on Lancashire that would otherwise be difficult to trace can be found in the Internet Archive (http://www.archive.org).

I owe much to Anna Goddard and the staff of Carnegie Press, with a very special thank you to Alistair Hodge who has edited this manuscript and designed its layout with care and scholarship.

I might have abandoned this research had it not been for the encouragement and interest of my friends, particularly Marian who read a later draft and persuaded me it was worth publishing. And it has given me great pleasure to be introduced through my research to distant cousins whom I did not know I had: to Jane, descendant of Joseph Barron and Ann Pendlebury; and to Vivien, Peter, John and Barry, all of whom still live in Yorkshire as did their third great-grandfather, Henry Pendlebury, whose letters and escapades bring so much fun to this story. I thank them for their generosity in sharing their information and ideas with me. In particular, I owe so much to Barry and Pam who spent many hours reading though my writing and painstakingly re-checking my use of parish registers and census material; they provided me with new information about the family and lovely insights into Yorkshire dialect and customs. This book is enriched by their hard work, sense of humour and enthusiasm for all things Pendlebury.

As with all such projects, despite every effort at accuracy of fact and interpretation, it is possible that some errors of detail or judgement have found their way into the book. For any such lapses I apologise and take full responsibility.

Marion Cutting, April 2012

Introduction

T HIS is the story of the Pendlebury family and, more specifically, of Ralph and Dyna Pendlebury and their descendants. It begins in 1594, in the small village of Radcliffe, Lancashire, and ends in London a few years after the death of Thomas Pendlebury in 1900. It traces the lives of alehouse-keepers, cotton workers, parish clerks, soldiers, messengers, warehouse-men and carmen. It sets their fortunes within the social and religious upheavals of the 1600s, the growth of the Lancashire cotton trade during the 1700s, and the explosion of industry, trade, emigration and urban poverty that characterised nineteenth-century Victorian London. In so doing, it recalls villages, neighbourhoods and lifestyles that have long since disappeared. It tells, too, of robust women who not only raised large families but also struggled to find ways of earning money to provide the basic necessities for themselves and their children.

The account falls naturally into three parts. The first part (Chapters 1–7) takes place in the cotton heartland of Lancashire and the story is drawn from parish records, contemporary accounts and the wills and probate documents that were left behind by the Pendlebury family. The second part (Chapters 8–17) moves to London with Richard Pendlebury's enlistment in the army, his injuries at the Battle of Corunna in 1809 during the Peninsular Wars, and his residence close by the Chelsea Royal Hospital. It recounts the adventures of his son Tom and of Tom's family and friends in the lively but poverty-stricken and crowded streets of Southwark, through the warehouses of Cannon Street, the pubs of London, the tobacco trade and snuff-making, to deaths from cholera and from lead poisoning. This part draws not only upon contemporary accounts, newspaper articles and public health reports but also, most tellingly, upon the Pendlebury documents. These documents, preserved by chance and hidden away for over a hundred years in a cardboard box at the back of a cupboard, consist mainly of the letters that passed backwards and forwards between Tom Pendlebury and his friends, family and employers. This correspondence tells a story of good times and bad times, of love and of family disputes, of travel and unemployment, of entertainment and of death, as people weave their way between Lancashire and London, and London and Wiltshire, via India,

Scotland and Yorkshire. Educated traders and sea-captains feature within these documents, but for the most part their words are those of ordinary working men and of steadfast but barely literate women.

The third and final part of the book (Chapters 18–21) begins after the death of Tom Pendlebury in 1863. It traces the story of his widow Jane, who married twice again, and of his son Thomas Pendlebury who was plucked from the poor streets of Southwark by the School Board for London and sent to one of the very first Industrial Schools. It describes how Thomas later became a carman in the London Docks, and a strong trade unionist and brass band player, before his death from an industrial injury in 1900.

Original sources cited here for the first time include several wills and probate documents dating to the seventeenth, eighteenth and nineteenth centuries, diaries and other records, and the Pendlebury papers themselves. These papers date between 1833 and 1900 and include nearly 100 letters and a number of receipts and other documents. There are twelve letters from Joseph and Ann Barron in Yorkshire, thirteen letters from the Wolstenholmes in Radcliffe (Lancashire), seven from Henry Pendlebury in Yorkshire, and ten from various members of the Harding family in Wiltshire and Liverpool besides several from Robert Milner (a Yorkshire trader with a business in London) and Robert Jaques (an ex-East India Company captain and entrepreneur). The original phonetic spelling and sentence formation have been retained in the transcription of these nineteenth-century letters, so that the dialect of the ordinary working people of London, Lancaster and Wiltshire can still resonate through their written word.

Over 600 people – Pendleburys, Wolstenholmes, Hardings, Hollambys and their many relations – have been traced during the course of researching this book. From these, the names of a few key people in the long line between Ralph and Dyna Pendlebury (who married in 1594) and Thomas Pendlebury (who died in 1900) have been selected for inclusion in the simplified family trees that are located at the beginning of each of the early chapters, with the name of the person who is the focus of the ensuing text shown in bold.

Every effort has been made to ensure the accuracy of the family lineage. However, in the very early years, when parish records are sometimes patchy and corroborative documents lacking, phrases such as 'most probably' or 'possibly' occasionally creep in before statements about who was the father, wife or child of whom. But although this may be necessary in the interests of accuracy at the beginning of this story, it is no longer so once the parish registers become more complete, and individual births, deaths and marriages can be matched against the extended families named in detailed legacies. There is no doubt, for example, that Francis (1680–1751) was the third great-grandfather of Thomas (1859–1900).

Recorded history is largely concerned with men, with the landowners, the office holders and the main breadwinners. But among the Pendlebury men who have inevitably come to dominate this story can be found a few very special women. Notable among these is Gussy (née Barnard), who worked in a tobacconist shop and died of cholera in 1849. Then there is Jane (née Harding), who struggled to provide for herself and her very young children after she was widowed in 1863. Every bit as remarkable is Elizabeth (née Hollamby) who was born illegitimate in an east London workhouse, fostered and brought up in one room in Bermondsey by a leather-worker and his wife, and left a widow at the age of 36 with six young daughters to raise. She lived to the age of 80 and was the author's great-grandmother.

Through their documents and their letters, the following pages trace the lives and thoughts of one very 'ordinary' family over a period of 300 years and more. It is perhaps their very 'ordinariness' that makes this history so unusual. Titles, high office and wealth play no part. Instead, these pages reveal the fortunes, the recreation and the thoughts of the kind of individuals whom history so often overlooks: the innkeeper, the cotton worker, the parish clerk, the foot soldier, the messenger, the shopkeeper and the women who raised young children against all the odds. There is fun, too, the 'flearups' in Lambeth Marsh and the comfort of steadfast friendship. The lives of these very ordinary Pendleburys now begin to unfold.

A section of a map of Lancashire, 1796, drawn for John Aikin, showing the area around Radcliffe, Bury and Manchester.

CHAPTER ONE

Radcliffe and Bury in Lancashire

Ralph Pendlebury married **Dyna Allens** in 1594

Isaac Pendlebury (1606-1683)

Nathan (1646–1725), innholder

Francis (1680–1751), parish clerk, weaver

James (1718–1750), weaver

Francis (1745–1820), parish clerk, yeoman

Richard (1787–1831), whitster, soldier

Tom (1810–1863)
messenger, tobacconist, warehouseman

Henry (1823–1888)
waterman, glass mould maker

Thomas (1859–1900),
carman in London Docks

The Pendlebury line, 1594–1900:
Ralph and Dyna Pendlebury to Thomas Pendlebury

The earliest Pendleburys

The story of this Pendlebury family begins in 1594 in Lancashire, in the village of Radcliffe, about five miles north of Manchester. In June of that year Raüffe Pennellberi's marriage to Dyna Allens was recorded in the register of the parish church of St Mary the Virgin, Radcliffe. ('Raüffe' and 'Pennellberi', spelt variously in the early texts, are from now on standardised as 'Ralph' and 'Pendlebury'.) From Ralph and Dyna can be traced a direct line of descent down to their fifth and sixth great-grandsons, Tom (1810–63) and

Thomas (1859–1900), whose letters and papers feature in the nineteenth-century Pendlebury documents that appear later in this account.

There were, of course, Pendleburys living in the area around Radcliffe well before 1594. The name 'Pendlebury' was probably derived from the Celtic *Penul* (a hill) and *Bri* or *Beri* (strong). One of the earliest records of its use is found in a grant, made by King John in 1199, of 'one carucate of land called Peneburi', to 'Elias, son of Robert'.[1]* One carucate was a significant amount of land, as the number and rank of the witnesses to the grant show. The name continues to appear in early documents in association with places within a few miles of Radcliffe. There is, for example: Thomas, son of Ellis de Pendlebury (c.1200); Adam de Pendlebury (1320s); Robert, son of Robert de Pendlebury (1334); Henry, son of Robert de Pendlebury (1363); Roger Pendlebury of Westhoughton (killed in a dispute in 1532); and Roger and Ralph Pendlebury (named in 1574 in an agreement about a messuage, windmill and 40 acres of land in Westhoughton).[2] These individuals invariably belonged to the landed classes, for early texts speak of ownership, taxes and the high politics of king and church. Until quite late in history written records remain largely silent about the great majority of the population, the craftsmen, labourers and women, and certainly those without land or power. The process by which the name Pendlebury came to be more commonly adopted is therefore unrecorded. It was only in 1538, when local churches were first required to keep the records of births, deaths and marriages, that the names of ordinary people began to be written down on a regular basis.

It is little surprising, therefore, that Ralph Pendlebury's history prior to his marriage to Dyna in 1594 remains obscure. Two references to individuals with the name Pendlebury are, however, worth mentioning. They concern Lawrens Pendilbury from Ince (14 miles from Radcliffe) and Elys Pendilbury (or Penhulbery) from Over Hulton (9 miles from Radcliffe) who appeared as witnesses in two court cases arising from events that took place in 1491–92 and 1521–22 respectively. Their names are found in the records of the Duchy Court of Lancaster, tucked away among tales of disputes about lands, houses, boundaries, tithe crops and trespass, and amid charges of forceful eviction, rape and murder. They are worth mentioning because the two cases in which they were involved offer glimpses of early Lancashire society at a time when Ralph Pendlebury's father and grandfather would have been growing up. They hint at co-dependent relationships between freeholders, tenants, servants and Church

---

* The numbered endnote references appear at the end of the book, between pages 227 and 236.

dignitaries; they also show a justice system already seeking to regulate violence through recording, in pain-staking detail, the conflicting sworn accounts of the plaintiffs, defendants and witnesses, before passing judgement.

The first reference appears in the reign of Henry VII (1485–1509). In about 1492 (the exact year is unknown as the month is not recorded and under the old-style Julian calendar, in use in Britain until September 1752, the new year began not on 1 January but on the following Lady Day, 25 March), Lawrens Pendilbury, yeoman, appeared in the Duchy Court of Lancaster in an action brought by Thomas Gerrerd against his more powerful neighbour Sir Thomas Gerrerd.[3] Lawrens was on the side of the defendant, Sir Thomas. At the heart of the case lay a dispute over the ownership of Ince Moss, then in the possession of Thomas but claimed by Sir Thomas as part of his own estate. Sir Thomas maintained that as its drainage needed improving he had requested 'his' priest at Ashton Chapel to ask in church for volunteers to dig a ditch. About 50 tenants, neighbours and servants, Lawrence Pendlebury among them, turned up with spades and shovels and marched on to Ince Moss. The ditch they were digging was a substantial one: the transcript describes the ditch as being 40 'roods' in length.* When they had finished their work, they were rewarded with meat and drink. Not surprisingly, Thomas the plaintiff's version was rather different. He told how Sir Thomas's ditch-digging gang, composed of 56 servants and tenants led by the chaplain, one gentlemen and eight yeoman (including Lawrens), not only invaded his property 'in most riotous manner' but also broke down fences and stole cattle and a horse. He described how the row between the two men had escalated during Easter week 1491 when Sir Thomas turned up in Wigan with '100 riotous people' threatening to drive Thomas and his men forcibly from the town if they dared to try to attend his (i.e. Sir Thomas's) church. Sir Thomas's attacks on Ince continued apace throughout the summer with three sorties of servants, tenants and dogs sent to attack Thomas's animals; on one occasion they 'bote and hurt them sore' and on another drove horses and mares into the 'myre and mosse'. In his defence, Sir Thomas concluded that he was only trying to regain what was rightfully his and that the accounts of his aggression had been much exaggerated by his enemies. The outcome of the hearing is not recorded, but Sir Thomas appeared in court on a number of further occasions, usually associated with riotous behaviour.

The second mention of a Pendlebury in the Duchy Court of Lancaster comes thirty years later during the reign of Henry VIII (1509–47) with the appearance, in about 1522, of Elys Penhulbury of Overhulton, aged 60 and

---

* Forty 'rods' (a linear length) is equivalent to 220 yards (or about 201 metres).

'sometime servant' to Roger Gorton of Westhougton.[4] Elys had been living in the Gorton household for 50 years and he now testified on behalf of Roger's widow Ellen in her action against John and Kathryn Harrison and others. The dispute was once again about property; and once again Sir Thomas Gerrard featured, though now as a Justice of the Peace enforcing law and order rather than as the villain of the piece. Ellen sought to regain possession of the manor of Westhoughton from the Harrisons. Her evidence, backed by witnesses who included Elys, was that her husband Roger had held the manor on a 19-year lease by virtue of the customary rent of 'id. called only a *goddes peny*, and id. for his entry in the lord's rental', that he had paid only three years before his death to the Abbot of Cockersand. At the time of his death, therefore, Roger still had 16 years of his tenancy to run. Ellen claimed the manor as '… it has been an *olde Anneyant* custom within the said lordship from time immemorial that if a man die within the said term his wife shall peaceably enjoy the said lands for the said term, if she remains unmarried, she paying and doing all the customs and services accustomed'. She had accordingly continued to live there until forcibly evicted by John Harrison and others acting at the behest of the freeholder, the Abbot of Cockersand. Elys Penhulberry and Richard France (of Aspull), gave a vivid description of this eviction. Suddenly, 'bedtymes of the nyght', they recounted, Harrison and 40 men in 'hernez' (presumably horsemen) descended on the house and used a ladder to break down the doors. Ellen and the other occupants, including Elys Penhulbery, were bundled out of the house and John and Kathryn Harrison installed in their place.

The violence did not stop there. Subsequent attempts by Ellen Gorton to regain her property led to further trouble. On one occasion '… The said Elyn knocked and called and then Katherine Henryson, … asked what she wanted and said she should not come in, she then opened a window and *kest forthe* at them scalding water, then she took an iron spit and thrust forth …' Not to be deterred, Ellen drove her plough on to the disputed estate a few days later, whereupon she was immediately attacked by Katherine Harrison and six of her friends and so badly assaulted and wounded that she required the rites of the Church. The abbot of Cockersand seems to have played a somewhat dubious part in all this; it was he who instigated the violent eviction of Ellen that led to the installation of John Harrison in her place; and Harrison just happened to be the Abbot's nephew. The abbot was clearly a force to be reckoned with in the area: Ellen explained that when he had ordered both sides to appear before him to settle the dispute a few months after her eviction, she and her supporters had been reluctant to appear before him 'for fear of the Abbot's displeasure'. Ellen won her case, and the Harrisons were fined and ordered to leave.

There is no knowing whether these two Pendleburys, Lawrence and Elys, were in any way related to Ralph Pendlebury because parish registers did not begin until 1538 and some of the earliest records are fragmentary. The first recorded male Pendlebury in the Lancashire parish records appears in 1563 with the marriage entry of Lawrence Pendleburie to Ellen Hoope in the church register of St Mary the Virgin, Leigh. Given that Leigh is little more than six miles from Ince, and that the name Pendlebury appears rarely in these early documents, it seems likely that this record refers to either the son or grandson of the Lawrence Pendlebury who gave evidence in support of Sir Thomas Gerrerd's claim to Ince Moss in 1492. Sadly, however, there is no way of establishing a connection between Lawrence and the later Ralph, although the dates are consistent with them being father and son.

A hundred or so years after Elys Pendlebury was appearing at the Duchy Court in Lancaster in support of his mistress Ellen Gorton, Ralph and Diana Pendlebury were married in Radcliffe. It would probably have come as some surprise to Ralph and Dyna to have known that several of their descendants would benefit from the growth of a local cotton industry and become prosperous and literate leaders in their local church. Their great-grandson, Francis, was parish clerk of Radcliffe between about 1712 and 1745, and his son Nathan between about 1754 and 1786; and their great-great-great-grandson, Francis (son of James, 1718-50, and nephew of Nathan), was clerk between about 1795 and 1815. However, at the time that this story begins in the late sixteenth century, the Pendleburys were far from being figures of such probity. Instead, their lives were dominated by the alehouse and overshadowed by poverty and illegitimacy. Their world was almost unrecognisable from the one that would come to exist a century and a half later when the demand for cotton yarn and cloth began to dominate the economy and landscape at county, village and parish level.

Lancashire in the time of Ralph and Dyna

One account of mid-sixteenth-century Lancashire begins by describing the county as 'an obscure, remote, insular and backward corner of England' where a small population was scattered across wide areas of gorse and moorland interrupted only by the occasional small town. Accordingly, its people appeared to be inward-looking, poor and barbarous, living in a semi-feudal society dominated by a few extremely powerful local gentry who often maintained order through their own armed bands of liveried retainers. There were few churches and schools; and people seldom travelled, or married, outside their immediate locality.[5]

There is some truth in this description. Lancashire was certainly one of the more isolated parts of England during late medieval times. It lay near the geographical northern limit of the realm and had only ten seats in Parliament: two for the county and two each for the townships of Preston, Liverpool, Wigan and Lancaster. In over 200 years, Lancaster had sent not a single representative to Parliament. The county's integration with the rest of England was not helped by the fact that it was a county palatine, administered by the London-based Duchy of Lancaster rather than by the Council of the North.[6]

Administration was patchy. Manchester, for example, regularly appointed over 100 officers to regulate matters such as the keeping of the peace, the operation of the market, the quality of ale and the condition of the streets. This was a large number, given that the population of Manchester and Salford together is estimated to have been no more than about 5,000 in the mid-1600s (although this was treble what its population had been a century earlier in the 1550s).[7] Elsewhere, however, the lack of strong government meant that the routine maintenance of social order fell, by default, upon the local community: to the petty constables (an unpopular job sometimes imposed on the poor and powerless), the churchwardens and the overseers of the poor.[8]

The task of keeping the peace was made all the more onerous by the widespread poverty and illness that were facts of life for so many of the people of Lancashire. The 1590s were marked by economic and social depression, and life cannot have been easy for the likes of Ralph and Dyna and their young family. There were three consecutive years of bad harvests when rye had to be imported from Poland. Areas such as Radcliffe and Bury already depended on Manchester for their wealth, and that town was now struggling to compete with London for overseas markets amid the disruption caused by struggles with Spain and war with Ireland. As the price of basic commodities rose, a combination of low wages, a dearth of home-grown cereals and the high cost of imported grain and other essential food led to starvation and sickness. And sickness there was aplenty. As well as the devastating effects of typhus, typhoid and tuberculosis (commonly described as 'consumption'), and the endemic childhood illnesses of smallpox, scarlet fever, measles, whooping cough, diphtheria and the like, there were periodic bouts of plague. A particularly severe outbreak hit north-west England between 1597 and 1598 when the parish register of Penrith (about 90 miles from Radcliffe) recorded '... A sore plague in Richmond Kendal Penreth Carliell Apulbie [Appleby] and other places in Westmorland and Cumberland in the year of our god 1598 ...'[9] An inscription in the chapel at Penrith reads, '... Ex gravi peste, quod regionibus hisce incubuit, obierunt apud Penrith 2,260, Kendal 2,500, Richmond 2,200, Carlisle 1,196 ...'[10] Plague was again reported, in Manchester, in 1604–05 and remained an intermittent threat throughout this period.[11]

Perhaps the most serious crisis, however, came in 1622–23, when Ralph and Dyna's youngest son Isaac was little more than sixteen. A combination of a poor harvest and falling wool prices led to dreadful hardship and a sharp rise in deaths in Lancashire, Cumberland, Westmorland and parts of Scotland. The Mayor of York described the scarcity of corn in 1622 as 'greater than ever known in the memory of man';[12] outbreaks of plague, typhus, dysentery, smallpox and 'a malignant spotted fever' were reported between 1622 and 1624.[13] An analysis of over 80 parishes in Lancashire has shown that the number of burials in 1623 was more than twice the average for the decade.[14] And in Lancaster, burials rose to nearly four times the average, increasing during the plague months of August to October but peaking between October and January 1623–24, suggesting that typhus, 'a famine-related disease of the winter', was responsible. 'In cold and hungry winters the poor and starving huddled together for warmth and, remaining unwashed, provided perfect breeding conditions for the body lice which transmit typhus.'[15]

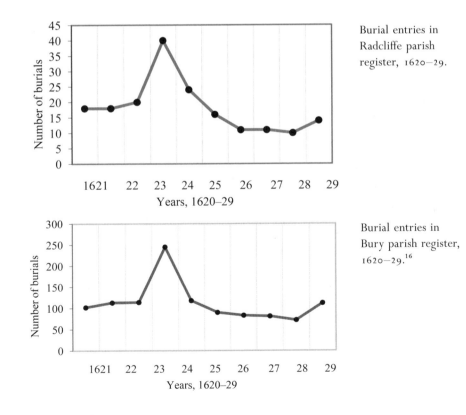

Burial entries in Radcliffe parish register, 1620–29.

Burial entries in Bury parish register, 1620–29.[16]

The 1623 crisis hit Radcliffe and Bury badly, though not as disastrously as some of the areas further to the north. The number of burials during that year doubled to 40 (in Radcliffe) and 249 (in Bury), by far the highest numbers for the decade. Hints of these difficult times are found in the Bury parish burial records in the 1590s and early 1600s, with references to: 'several poore people or women'; 'two poore passengers'; 'a pore woman who died in a barne'; 'a poor boy'; 'the infant of a poore passenger'; 'a wanderer drowned'; 'a poore criple born of a barowe'; 'a poore child found dead on Burie more'; 'a poore child which was found about Nuttall'; and 'a child found dead aboute the Bentilee'.[17]

In short, poor administration, lawlessness, famine and illness stalked the land. But there was also another side to life in Lancashire during the late sixteenth and early seventeenth centuries. By the late sixteenth century, Manchester was beginning to produce linen rather than wool and, with the introduction of fustians (a mixture of linen and cotton), the town's manufacturers were already beginning to move into more specialised production.[18] As Manchester grew in size and importance, it began to depend increasingly on textile manufacturing, while in the outlying areas new opportunities presented themselves, including food production for the growing town, or making a little money other than in farming and labouring, perhaps in spinning yarn or weaving. By the early 1600s, people in villages such as Radcliffe and Bury were already working in their cottages and fields to feed the entrepreneurs of Manchester. Soon, some Manchester dealers were making plenty of money: two individuals, for example, left estates worth £1,500 and £2,344 in 1598 and 1609 respectively.*[19]

William Camden, antiquarian, historian and soldier (1551–1623) caught something of the vibrancy of the people of Lancashire in *Britannia*, which was published in 1586. Although he approached his visit to Lancashire 'somewhat against my will' due to the difficulty in tracing the origin of place-names (one of his main interests), he was determined not to neglect 'the harty good Lancashiremen'.[20] He praised the quality of the land, the 'plaine and champion'

---

* £1,500 in 1598 is equivalent in terms of 2010 prices to £227,000 (retail price index) or £4,050,000 (average earnings). £2,344 in 1609 is equivalent in terms of 2010 prices to £341,000 (retail price index) or £6,510,000 (average earnings). Officer's *Purchasing Power of British Pounds from 1264 to Present, 2011* (http://www.measuringworth.com) has been used to compare the value of pre-decimal sterling to its 2009 decimal value.

References to monetary values within the body of this text are cited in pre-decimal sterling (pounds, shillings and pence), in which: 12 old pence (styled as 12d.) = 1 shilling (1s.) = 5 new pence (5p); and 20 shillings (20s.) = £1. Thus £1 6s. 8d. = £1.34.

areas suitable for barley and wheat, the valleys for their oats, the 'moist places and unwholsome called Mosses' for the turf they provided for the fires and the 'mucke', or peat, that was used to enrich the soil. He commented that

> ... a man may judge of the goodnesse of the soile partly by the
> constitution and complexion of the inhabitants, who are to see to
> passing faire and beautifull, and in part, if you please, by the cattaile.
> For in their kine and oxen, which have goodly heads and faire spread
> hornes, and in body are well proportionate withall, you shall find in
> maner no one point wanting that Mago the Carthaginian doth require,
> as Columella specifieth out of him...

Although Camden never mentioned the village of Radcliffe by name, he would have passed through it on his travels. His journey from Rochdale to Manchester took him through Bury ('a mercate towne nothing inferiour to the other [Rochdale]'), Chat Moss (now part of Salford), Holcroft Moss and, probably, Wigan and Bolton – all places within a ten-mile radius of Manchester. He was full of praise for Manchester itself and lauded the ancient families of the North for their '... provident moderation with simplicity standing contented with their owne estate ...', and contrasted these virtues with the '... riotous expense and superfluity, usurious contracts, voluptuous and vicious life, together with indirect courses and crafty dealings ...' that had caused the downfall of the great families in the South. The north and south divide, it seems, was already firmly in place.

Church and society

Shortcomings in the administrative systems of the County Palatine meant that much of the responsibility for running local affairs fell to the often ill-equipped parish authorities. Between 1597 and 1601 parish officers became responsible for the care of the poor, including the provision of relief payments and burials. They often had a say in the licensing and running of alehouses, matters of bastardy, and fines for being absent from church (known as recusancy).[21] They also oversaw the repair of minor roads and bridges, a task that could lead to endless wrangles over who should do what, and who should pay the bills. In the mid-1500s, for example, the main road that ran between Manchester and Bolton via Prestwich and Radcliffe passed through no fewer than eleven townships, each of which was a separate highway jurisdiction.[22] Parish officials were often hard put to keep the local peace at a time when disputes over property and land were often settled in open conflict by armed men fighting on the mosses and moors around Manchester rather than in the local manorial or duchy courts.[23] In short, Lancashire's villages and hamlets had to be largely self-regulating, with much of the burden of upholding the law falling upon the shoulders of the petty constables or churchwardens.

However, the church in Lancashire was often no better suited to carrying out this task than was the civil administration. Its rural parishes extended over wide areas and were frequently in the charge of non-resident clergy who were usually notoriously poor as a result of general inflation and the practice of commuting their tithes of produce to money. Revenue from the larger parishes, moreover, was often siphoned off by laymen or well-connected absentee rectors, leaving the curates and chaplains to subsist on small fixed stipends and hand-outs from their congregations.

To add to all these difficulties, the newly reformed Church was still struggling to secure its hold upon the minds and purses of its local congregations. When Ralph and Dyna were married, it was little more than 50 years since the Act of Supremacy (1534) had been passed forcing the break with Rome. Resistance to the new ways of the reformed church was often strong, particularly in Lancashire where many Catholic families nominally embraced Protestantism, as the new laws demanded, but continued to practise the old faith by celebrating the Mass in secret. This reluctance to follow the new religion was compounded by indifference and superstition. Witchcraft continued to challenge the religious establishment and was said to be prevalent in the Radcliffe area.[24] Thirteen witches were tried and convicted in 1612 for the alleged murder of 13 people by witchcraft in and around the Forest of Pendle, just 25 miles from Radcliffe. '... The county was known in London for its religious backwardness – a place where the Catholics ... and the religiously uneducated or plain uninterested were believed to exist in dangerously large numbers ...'[25]

The newly reformed local churches had acquired a pivotal administrative task in 1538 with the requirement that they keep regular records of births, deaths and marriages and, in 1597, that they deposit a duplicate copy annually in the registry of the diocese. Fifty-nine parish registers in Lancashire survive from before 1600, including three (for Whalley, Whittington and Farnworth) that date back to the introduction of the new system in 1538.[26] This system of parish registration provided the state with a lucrative source of income as well as a means of controlling people's lives. The power to grant marriage licences now no longer rested with the Pope. Instead, local parsons, vicars and curates carried out the task as the local representatives of the Archbishop of Canterbury. The licence fees rose as the needs of government grew and soon justices of the peace, rather than church officers, were made responsible for their collection. Unsurprisingly, a market in illegal marriages continued to flourish. In 1597 Parliament debated the subject of these 'clandestine' marriages performed in 'Places peculiar' and carried out by '… vagrant, unlearned, dissolute, drunken and idle Stipendaries, Vicars and Curates: Who are placed in the Rooms of the rich Men; who have divers Livings; and are not Resident. And they receive the Profits …'[27]

When Ralph and Dyna Pendlebury married in 1594, there were still plenty of ways of having a union between two people recognised within a community other than through a church ceremony: hand-fasting, troth-plighting, ceremonies without banns, unions marked outside a church in a 'lawless' church or a prison, or ones sanctioned by Licensed Clandestinity.[28] Where money was in short supply and there was little likelihood of having substantial wealth to pass on to children, there was not much to be lost by avoiding the official church fees. A note in the Radcliffe parish register in 1702 shows that clandestine marriages were still practised in Radcliffe over a century later when '… Mary Rigley is also said to be clandestinely married to a young man by a Couple-Beggar, & removed or removing out of Radcliffe …'[29] A couple-beggar was a person who married poor people or beggars to each other.

The church of St Mary the Virgin in Radcliffe nevertheless dominated the local community and was the place where so many Pendleburys were baptised, married and buried. It was built on the site of a Saxon church, although nothing remained of that building by the time that Ralph and Dyna were married. Its baptism records survive from 1557, its burials from 1558 and its marriage records from 1560. The neighbouring village of Bury's records date a little later, to 1590, perhaps delayed by the construction of a new church building.[30] These records provide a treasure-trove of information about births, deaths and marriages, with occasional insights into local life that are tantalisingly brief. What, for example, led the Bury clerk in 1614 to describe Mr Henry Halstead at his burial as 'a painfulle [i.e. assiduous] p[re]acher at Bury'?

Wonderful though they are, these local parish records are far from complete. For example, there is no trace of any one by the name of Pendlebury before Ralph's marriage in 1594; and, of his eight children, only Isaac's name appears again after his baptism. There could be a number of explanations for these gaps. The system of recording was relatively new and it relied upon someone being available who could write. More significantly, perhaps, the parish record system was the means by which the new church order not only sought to impose itself on the local villagers but also to raise money for church and state. In times of hardship, many family events went unrecorded.

On the cusp of change

It seems, then, that Lancashire was set apart from much of the rest of England by its distance from Westminster, its poverty, lawlessness and sense of independence. But life in the county palatine also had its own kind of vibrancy. Resistance to the rules of church and state, and the growth of alehouses, testify to a resilience that resisted even the attempts made by the puritan non-conformists, later in the seventeenth century, to suppress most kinds of amusements in the shire.[31] The cotton trade was growing; the population was rising; and villages around Manchester were developing into small towns in response to the demands of that increasingly prosperous trading centre.

By the time the Pendleburys first appear in the records in 1594, the villagers of Radcliffe probably lived for the most part in small two-roomed wood and thatched cottages, clustered initially around the church but soon extending along routes leading to the neighbouring larger villages of Bury, Pilkington and Bolton. The village was no longer a place of sleepy rural tranquillity. It lay along the Bury main road that passed between Manchester and Blackburn. A rare glimpse of the amount of traffic passing through Radcliffe during this period is provided in a petition that has survived from 1632. In that year, officials from Blackburn appealed for help in maintaining a ford near Whalley (23 miles from Radcliffe) that lay on the main road from Clitheroe, Manchester, Bury and 'other markette townes'. The petitioners estimated that '... there is commonly 200 or 300 Loaden horses every daie passe over, besides great numbers of other passengers ...'[32]

Large numbers of travellers passing through meant that the beer flowed and the inns were full. It was to the Pendleburys' good fortune that they were alehouse and inn keepers and thus well placed to benefit from this trade, as the next chapter reveals.

CHAPTER TWO

The early Pendlebury innkeepers

A GAINST this backdrop of turbulence, hardship and change, the Pendleburys' history begins in the two villages of Bury and Radcliffe, in their two parish churches, both of which, coincidentally, were dedicated to St Mary the Virgin, and with two men of same name: Ralph Pendlebury.

Exactly in what way Ralph Pendlebury of Bury was related to Ralph Pendlebury of Radcliffe is uncertain. However, it seems that related they were, given that both their first and second names were extremely rare at the time and that they belonged to the congregations of two very closely associated churches. The churches of Bury and Radcliffe lay just over two miles apart, linked by a busy road bordered intermittently by clusters of cottages; and several families moved from one parish to the other in the course of their lifetime. *Redivalls*, for example, was a group of houses on the Radcliffe–Bury road which straddled the two parishes. Although most of the occupants of these dwellings appear in the registers for Bury, just a few are named in the Radcliffe records. Bury even records the burial of Richard Haslam 'from Redivalls buried at Radcliffe'. The Pendleburys later owned property here, and '*widow Haslam*' was a tenant of Nathan Pendlebury in 1794. The likelihood of the two Ralphs being related – and indeed of being father and son – is strengthened still further by the fact that they were both associated with selling beer at a time when occupations usually passed from father to son. Bury Ralph was a beer seller and so too was Radcliffe Ralph's grandson Nathan. In short, identical names, the proximity of their places of worship – along with a shared association with beer – point to Bury Ralph being related to Radcliffe Ralph; and the chronology suggests that their relationship was one of father and son.

Ralph and Susanna Pendlebury of Bury

Establishing a father–son relationship between Bury Ralph and Radcliffe Ralph allows some rich personal detail to be added to the early story of the Lancaster/London Pendleburys because two detailed probate inventories survive listing the belongings of Bury Ralph and his (probably second) wife Susanna.

Pendleburys of Radcliffe

Thomas Whytheade of Bury

Elizabeth

Unknown (1) = **Ralph of Bury** = (2) **Susanna Whythead** (–1608)
alehousekeeper
(–1608)

Jane (2) = **Ralph** = **(1) Dyna Allens**
(–1623)   (–1611)

Samvell (1594–) Abram (1596/97–) Ester (1598–) Renolld (1600–) Anne (1601–) Elizabeth (1603–) Edmund (1606–) Alis (1608–)

Rye (1602–) Ane (1604–) Isake = Sara Macone (1606–83) Susan = James Holt (1609/10–)

Nathan (1646–1725) innkeeper

Richard (1878–1831) innkeeper

Tom (1810–63)

Thomas (1859–1900) carman in London Docks

messenger, tobacconist, warehouseman

**The proposed early origins
of the Pendleburys, derived from
the parish registers of
Bury and Radcliffe**

The first document (1608) lists the goods and chattels of Ralph Pendlebury of Bury, and the second (also 1608) those of his wife Susanna Pendlebury of Bury. Ralph's inventory was drawn up and witnessed nine days after his burial in May 1608. A note on the reverse shows that he left everything to his wife Susanna, and, when she herself died five months later, his clothes, and some of the same items of furniture listed in his belongings, were still to be found listed among her belongings.

Ralph and Susanna's itemised belongings were extremely modest compared to most that survive from inventories of the period. However, they were not among the poorest of the villagers for at least they had sufficient furniture and clothing to justify the trouble of having a document drawn up by someone who could write and who was probably paid to do the task. All four witnesses were local men who had been married in Bury; the inventories were written in 'Secretary Hand', the style routinely used in official documents in Tudor and Stuart times. Illustration number 1 on page 20 shows the inventory of Raphe Pendlebury of Burie', May 1608.

The items Ralph left to his wife are the kinds of goods – clothes, bedding, furniture, pots and pans and household linen – that provided the essentials of a simple but comfortable style of living. Some of the terms are self-explanatory, but others are not. Several ('pewter', 'chistes', 'stoundes & barrele, 'kears' and 'boardes and treaste') are also listed in his wife Susanna's inventory and are explained below. A 'seck' may refer to a sack, a bed or a type of wine. The comparative value of the different items reveals that anything involving material (clothing and bedding) was most costly, followed closely by brass and pewter objects, and then bacon.

As an alehouse keeper, Ralph would have operated at the hub of Bury village life. The alehouse was where day-labourers and husbandmen would meet to gossip and hear news, where 'every man hath his penny to spend at a pinte in the one, and every man his eare open to receive the sound of the other'.[1] It was a popular meeting place for itinerant travellers and textile traders who would also be in a good position to spread news and gossip. Although brewers were regulated by parliament (the size of ale barrels, for example, was standardised in 1531, while in 1552 all alehouses had to be licensed by the Justices of the Peace), many alehouses remained unlicensed, particularly as ale-selling was a well-established by-employment of the poor.[2] Ralph's alehouse, however, was probably licensed as his occupation was mentioned in this legal inventory document.

Ralph's death was quickly followed by that of his wife Susanna. Susanna was buried in October 1608 and on the very same day an inventory of her goods

1　The goods and chattels of 'Raphe Pendlebury of Burie', May 1608.[3] A transcription is given below.

A true Inventorie of the goods of Raphe pendlebury late of Burie deceased Alhouse keeper prised by francis Barlow Gefferey Haslam John Pendleburie and Thomas Heward the xvi[th] day of maij Anno: Dom: 1608

		s.	d.
Imprimis	Apparell for his bodie	24	0
Item	in beddinge	46	8
Item	in brasse and pewter	20	0
Item	two chistes	5	0
Item	for stoundes & barrele & kears	15	0
Item	in boardes and tre[a]ste	5	0
Item	in cheare and stooles	2	0
Item	in iron wares	8	0
Item	in bacon	16	0
Item	in Napkins and towells	5	0
Item	in pottes and a seck	3	0

	£	s.	d.
Summa totalis	vii	ix	viii*

---

*　£7 9s. 8d. is equivalent in terms of 2010 prices to £1,110.00 (retail price index) or £19,000 (based on index of average earnings).

20

and chattels was drawn up and witnessed by three of the four people who had signed her husband's inventory five months earlier. The handwriting suggests that both lists were written by the same person.

The endorsement to Susanna's inventory is poorly written in abbreviated Latin. It records the appointment of her sister Elizabeth Whithead as her executrix and the bequest of her goods and chattels to her two daughters, Elizabeth and Alicia. These names provide some clues as to Ralph and Susanna's immediate family. Ralph's marriage to Susanna Whitehead probably took place before the surviving Bury registers begin in 1590. These registers show four

2 Inventory of the goods and chattels of Susanna Pendlebury, 1608.[4] A transcription is given overleaf.

A true Inventorie of all the goods of Susanna Pendlebury Late wyfe of Raphe pendlebury Deceased pryssed by francis Barlow Geffarey Haslam John Pendleburie Edmond Fenton Esq the vth of October Anno Domi: 1608

		s.	d.
Impri[mis]:	for apparell of hir Late husbande & hir owne	xliii	iiii
Item	for beddinge and bedstockes	xxxi	viii
Item	iii litle cheestes	vi	viii
Item	for Lininge yearne and tawe	vi	viii
Item	a fyre Iron a brendrethe & other Iron Stuffe	xii	——
Item	in Pewter and Brasse	xx	——
Item	a Litle counter trestes chears & formes & other bourde with quessions	x	——
Item	for stondes barrell kyres & other wooden vessell	xvii	iiii
Item	Napkins towel & a pillowbewre	vi	——
Item	in Butter & pottes and trenchers	vii	——
Item	a Secke & a wooden charger	iii	——
Item	a Lininge wheele cannell and turves and coles a paiere of woollen cardes	vii	vi
Item	in hennes	——	xx
Item	in mucke an olde barrel & a seack	ii	——
Item	in other Vesselment	——	xii
Item	in money	xix	ii
Summa totall		**ix£**	**xvs***

---

* £9 15s. is equivalent in terms of 2009 prices to £1220.00 (retail price index) or £19,300 (average earnings).

children born to them: Anne (baptised 1601), Elsabeth (1603), Edmund (1606) and Alis (1608). Only two of these children, it seems, were still alive at the time of Susanna's death: Elsabeth and Alis, one about five years old and the other a baby of only a few months (the Bury parish registers merely record the death of a 'Pendleburie, Child' in 1606). Susanna probably died from childbirth complications; she left her two very young children in the care of her sister.

Susanna's inventory provides a more detailed picture than her husband's of their lives as alehouse-keepers as it lists clothing, furniture and the kind of equipment they would have used to brew and sell beer. 'Bedstockes' were the front and back parts of a bedstead between which the cross bars were laid. 'Cheestes' were the chests in which items of clothing and other goods were commonly stored. 'Tawe' was the fibre of flax or hemp that was used in spinning and rope-making. A 'brendrethe' was either a wooden stand for a cask or a grate or gridiron for supporting cooking utensils above a fire. Given its association here with iron, it probably means the latter as the term also appears in the sixteenth-century inventory of Thurstan Tyldesley, from Tyldesley (seven miles from Radcliffe) where it is included among a list of cooking utensils: 'on great ponne ij; Lytell pons and vij skelletts xiiij; on brendreth and on ffriynge pone iij s'.[5] 'Pewter' was a reference to drinking vessels. A 'counter' was a container or abacus; 'trestes' were wooden stands used to support boards to make a table; and 'quessions' were cushions (the phrase 'In bordes treasles fformes and bedstokes' also appears in other early Lancashire inventories). A 'pillowbeare' was a pillowcase. A 'trencher' was either a knife or a platter or serving dish (probably the latter here). A charger was a large serving dish or plate. 'Cannell' was bituminous coal, 'turves' were slabs of peat and 'coles' was probably a type of glue or size. 'Cardes', used in pairs, were for 'carding', that is straightening the fibres of wool or flax etc. preparatory to spinning. 'Vesselment' probably referred to various containers and utensils.[6]

A picture emerges from these inventories of a comfortable home and alehouse. This, then, was perhaps the environment in which Radcliffe Ralph grew up. Susanna, however, was most unlikely to have been his mother, given the gap of 30 or so years between his birth and the births of her daughters in the early 1600s. Whether or not these inventories were once attached to a will that disposed of buildings or land is not known. Perhaps the alehouse passed down through the family because Radcliffe Ralph's grandson Nathan was later to become an innkeeper.

Ralph and Dyna Pendlebury of Radcliffe

Any doubts about the London Pendleburys' lineage disappear with the appearance of Ralph Pendlebury and Dyna Allens on the occasion of their marriage in Radcliffe parish church in June 1594. From their time onwards, a direct line of descent can be traced down to their sixth great-grandson Thomas Pendlebury who died in London in 1900. Dyna was the daughter of Myles and Alis and came from a large Radcliffe family. She was about 26 years old when she married.

Dyna was already in an advanced stage of pregnancy when she married Ralph as their first child, Samvell, was christened nine weeks later (although Samvel's father was not named, it is assumed that he was Rauffe and Dyna's first child as

3 The register of St Mary's Radcliffe, 1594.[7] An entry near the bottom of the right hand page reads: 'Item Raüfe pennellbery and Dyna Allens married the xxv …'

there were no other adult Pendleburys recorded in Radcliffe at the time). The medieval custom of handfasting, or trothplight, was still, it appears, practised in Radcliffe at this time. This was the practice whereby two people promised to marry each other, behaved as if they were married, and then ratified their union only when the bride became pregnant. This practice, widespread in the Middle Ages, survived longest in the more remote parts of northern England.[8]

Eight children born to Ralph were christened in Radcliffe church between 1594 and 1609. Only one of these, Isaac, appears again in the parish registers, a reminder that a significant number of births, deaths and, possibly, marriages went unrecorded in the first half of the seventeenth century. Isaac's details, however, are sufficient to enable the direct family line to be traced through him to the nineteenth-century London Pendleburys.

CHAPTER THREE

Civil war and religious upheaval: Isaac Pendlebury, 1606–1683

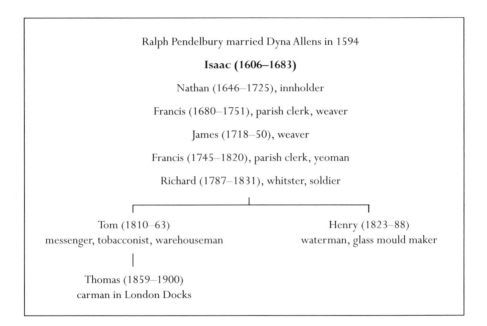

Ralph Pendelbury married Dyna Allens in 1594

Isaac (1606–1683)

Nathan (1646–1725), innholder

Francis (1680–1751), parish clerk, weaver

James (1718–50), weaver

Francis (1745–1820), parish clerk, yeoman

Richard (1787–1831), whitster, soldier

Tom (1810–63)
messenger, tobacconist, warehouseman

Henry (1823–88)
waterman, glass mould maker

Thomas (1859–1900)
carman in London Docks

RALPH and Dyna's son Isaac lived to the good age of 75 and witnessed the unrest and confusion caused by the violence of the English civil wars (1642–51) and their aftermath. He felt at first hand the impact of the religious changes that took place as the official religion swung between the established Protestant orthodoxy and a new puritan non-conformity. Gaps in the Radcliffe registers reflect this disruption, with no baptisms recorded in the years 1653–58 and 1673–80, no burials in 1641–50 and 1674–78 and only two marriages in 1653–60 with none in 1665–67. These are the very years in which Isaac would have been expected to marry and have any children baptised so his family record inevitably remains patchy.

Fortunately, however, at least some of the events of his life are recorded. We know that 'Isake s. of Raufe Pennelberi' was baptised in November 1606, the youngest recorded son of Ralphe and Dyna. He had a 'base' son Nathan in 1646 (from whom the London Pendleburys are directly descended). Thirteen years later, he married Sara Macone in a ceremony conducted by Mister Picke (a Presbyterian minister, see below, page 30). Isaac and Sara had one child, also named Isaac, who was buried just four days after his baptism in 1660. Sara died in 1674 at the age of 49, nine years before Isaac's death in 1683.

Radcliffe in the seventeenth century

Isaac's long life spanned a good part of the seventeenth century and he lived through extraordinary times. Although Radcliffe was a small, close-knit and interdependent village community, its location astride the busy trading route between Manchester and Bury ensured that its inhabitants knew about, and were affected by, events in the world beyond. The seventeenth century was a period of momentous social, political and economic change; and inns and alehouses, such as the one run by Isaac's son Nathan (and probably before that by Isaac himself), would have buzzed with news and gossip. It was a time of great scientific advances: William Harvey's discovery of the circulation of the blood; the foundation of the Royal Society; and Isaac Newton's publication of *Principia Mathematica*. Notable architects (Inigo Jones, Christopher Wren); thinkers (Thomas Hobbes); writers (John Bunyon, Samuel Pepys, John Milton); artists (Lely, Van Dyke) and playwrights (John Dryden, John Vanbrugh) flourished. It was also a time when England's trading, colonisation and conquest extended to India (the East India Company was founded in 1614); North America (the first permanent settlement was founded in Jamestown in Virginia in 1607, while the *Mayflower* sailed from Plymouth to New England in 1620); and the Caribbean (the English took over Jamaica in 1655). This expansion led to clashes with the French and the Portuguese and to three Anglo-Dutch wars between 1652 and 1674. It was also a time of great religious and political upheaval: the growth of godly or puritan non-conformists, in opposition to the adherents of a more high-church, ceremonial style of worship; the execution of an Archbishop (Laud, in 1645) and of King Charles I (in 1649); the overthrow of the monarchy, a bitter civil war, the establishment of a republic; the restoration of the monarchy (with Charles II); and the flight of another king (James II). The century culminated in a 'glorious bloodless revolution' during which the Bill of Rights was passed establishing England as a constitutional monarchy, with two Dutch royals (William and Mary) as joint monarchs.

No doubt many ordinary Lancastrians had little time or opportunity to take much interest in such grand affairs of state: they had enough to do to feed their families and to avoid becoming embroiled in the civil and religious disputes that erupted sporadically around and about. Lancashire was still a relatively poor county, from the gentry downwards, with 'regular economic setbacks and devastating epidemics' during at least the first half of the seventeenth century.[1] There was a major agricultural catastrophe in 1622–23, and the accompanying sharp rise in the death rate in both Radcliffe and Bury (see earlier) were followed by further food crises (in 1638, 1647–49, 1657–62 and 1674–75) when barley harvests failed (barley was the staple diet of the poor) and petitions for Poor Law relief peaked at the Lancashire Assizes.[2] Life could be particularly precarious for the woollen workers, especially when food shortages and high prices coincided with a shortage in cotton wool and hence no work. James Roylands of Westhoughton (just eight miles west of Radcliffe) complained (in 1653) that he had '... beene forced to sell both bed cloathes and back cloathes with other household goods towards the maintaineing of his children and soe it is that your petitioner [for Poor Relief] being a fustian Webster and now little to be begotten with it, and hee hath noe more goods to sell ...'[3]

Fortunately mass starvation on the 1622–23 scale was avoided, perhaps in part due to the redistribution of wealth from ratepayers to the vulnerable poor via the Poor Relief. In Prestwich (three miles south-east of Radcliffe), for example, relief costs doubled during the 1674–75 crisis. Nevertheless, periodic outbreaks of disease continued. In 1630, plague killed more than half the inhabitants of Bolton (just five miles from Radcliffe), leaving only 887 survivors in the town.[4]

To hunger, lack of work and pestilence was added from 1642 until 1651 the disruption brought about by the civil wars between Parliament and the King.[5] It was inevitable that both sides would fight fiercely for control of Lancashire because the county offered a potential route for any pro-royalist invasion from Ireland (where rebellion and the threat of an attack led Cromwell to invade that county in 1649) or Scotland (which crowned Charles Stuart – later to become Charles II – its king in 1651). The struggle in Lancashire was to be particularly bitter because local loyalties were divided, with Manchester and Bolton important parliamentary strongholds in an area mostly sympathetic to the royalists. Battles, sieges, skirmishes and hand-to-hand street fighting were regular occurrences in the area. A siege of Manchester by the Royalists in 1642 resulted in the death of over 100 men at the Battle of Salford Bridge. Battles also took place at Wigan, Preston, Warrington, Leigh and Whalley, all centres with royalist sympathies that lay within a 30-mile radius of Radcliffe. Lancaster was taken by parliamentarian forces in 1643 and retaken and plundered by the royalists in 1644 before being recaptured for Parliament; Liverpool was captured by the flamboyant royalist commander Prince Rupert in 1644 and re-taken by parliament a few months later. In July 1844 one of the most decisive battles of the civil wars took place 30 miles from Radcliffe, at Marston Moor just west of York. After two hours of fighting, Prince Rupert's forces were defeated, with several thousand men killed. In 1644 Bolton, just five miles up the road from Radcliffe, was besieged and captured for the King by Prince Rupert. The bitter street fighting that followed led to widespread destruction of property and a notorious massacre during which at least 1,000 townsmen and soldiers were killed.[6]

The year 1644, when Isaac Pendlebury was 36, was a particularly grim one for the people of both Radcliffe and Bury. Opposing armies for the King and Parliament marched down their streets as battles were fought for Bolton, Lancaster, Liverpool and the like. A fight on Bury Moor at the top of Black Lane, not far from Radcliffe Bridge, resulted in many deaths; the bodies of those killed were buried in a mass grave at Coggra Fold Farm.[7] Neighbouring Bury, with its mainly royalist sympathies (the Lord of Bury was the royalist Lord Derby[8]), must at times have resembled a garrison town.[9] A few days after the siege of Bolton, for example, Prince Rupert gathered his troops together in Bury where he was joined by 5,000 cavalry reinforcements before marching off, via Wigan, to besiege Liverpool. Hints of these struggles can be found in the burial records of Bury parish church: an entry in May 1644 records that '7 strange souldieres weare buried this weeke', followed in June by two burials of 'a strange souldior a cavalier'.[10]

Anyone living in Radcliffe during these years would have been deeply affected by the fighting and the hardship that accompanied it. Several harrowing reports were written during the period, which clearly indicate that agriculture and trade were disrupted, and that illness and death accompanied food shortages. Even after the restoration of the monarchy in 1660, neighbouring Bury was in sorry state. In 1664 nearly half the population of about 1,000 were living in poverty, with 80 per cent of the houses exempted from the newly imposed Hearth Tax because of poverty, or containing only one hearth. It is a sign of the dominance of the church within the local community that the rector numbered among the 18 wealthiest citizens, with a spacious house containing ten hearths.[11]

The part that Isaac Pendlebury played in the civil wars remains unknown. If he was drawn into the fighting, it would have been at the behest of the largest landowner in the area, because that is how local communities, often with little enthusiasm for either side, were expected to align themselves. Colonel Ralph Ashton of Middleton was the major landowner in the village and Isaac was almost certainly his tenant, as were the later Pendleburys: Francis Pendlebury, in his will of 1749, left to his son Robert, 'My Estate commonly caled or known by the Name of par Court with two Acres of Land thereunto belonging he paying the sum of forty shillings yearly unto Sir Ralph Ashton Barranite in lew of Lortsrent and also acquit the same from all such Loays and imposesions as shall be equivalent thereunto'. Robert, in turn, left (in 1762) his brother Nathan 'Som Estates or Cotages under Sir Ralph Ashton Baranight of Middlton'.

Ashton, one of Lancashire's five Members of Parliament, was firmly on the side of Parliament and therefore so was Radcliffe. He was a convinced puritan non-conformist who had attended the same Cambridge college as Oliver Cromwell.[12] He played a leading part in the siege of Manchester and the defeat of the royalists at Salford Bridge in 1642, and commanded forces at Preston, Wigan, Warrington and Lancaster. In 1645, when he was obliged as a Member of Parliament to give up direct military command, he became a member of the Lancashire committee set up by parliament to oversee the administration and conduct of military affairs.[13] He sponsored the Reverend Thomas Pike, an ardent puritan non-conformist, as minister of Radcliffe church (see below) and later became a lay member of one of Lancashire's Presbyterian classes.[14]

Something of the religious fervour of the times is captured in the Bury burial records. Geoffrey Lomas of Heap was described as 'a very zealous professor' (1643); Robert Broadly was 'a very godly man exiled from Halifax sojourning at Heywood' (1643); Mr William Rawstorn, a 'wrong priest', was buried in 1646; and phrases such as 'a very godly man' and 'a very pious woman' are used to describe individuals who died during 1646. Elsewhere, at Horwich (about 11 miles from Radcliffe), a preacher named Henry Pendlebury (no known relation) was described as a 'godlie Orthodox ... well qualified ... painfull [i.e. diligent or assiduous] godly preachinge minister'.[15]

Amid the turmoil, many parishes struggled to maintain their registers. A note in the register for Eccleston (17 miles from Radcliffe) provides one explanation for the many gaps in their records: '... there is many that is unregistered by reason of Prince Rupert coming into Lancashire and this booke being hid for fear of the enemie taking it ...'[16]

Radcliffe church appears to have continued functioning during these years, although its registers are patchy (see above). Its ministers bear testament to the volatile religious feelings of the times. During the period of the Commonwealth, for example, it had a parliamentarian minister, Thomas Pike, who had at least four children while he was at Radcliffe and was a member of the Bury Presbyterian Classis from its formation in 1647.[17] It was he who conducted the marriage of Isaac Pendlebury and Sara Macone in 1659. Three years later, as religious and political fashions changed, he was expelled from Radcliffe.[18] After his expulsion, he gathered together a puritan non-conformist congregation at Blackley, where he licensed a house of worship. On his death in 1672, he was reported as saying that the best preparations of the best of men are little enough when they come to die.[19]

Thomas Pike was a well-regarded churchman: *The Commonwealth Church Survey*, completed in 1650, described him as 'a godly preaching minister, well qualified in life and conversation'. It noted that his appointment was in the gift of Ralph Ashton of Middleton and that his income came from '... glebe lands belonging to the said Rectory thirty pounds per annum, and in rents thirty shillings per annum, and in tithes twenty eight pounds ten shillings per annum'. The survey provides an insight into the church and its congregation.

> ... And the said Church is distant from Cockey Chappell three myles or thereabouts, And from Bury Church three myles or thereabouts, And from Prestwich Church foure myles or thereabouts; And that there is not any neede of erecting a new Church or Chappell with in the same p[ar]ishe.
>
> And that there is wth in Pilkington in Prestwich p[ar]ishe theise famylies followinge that Resorte vsually to the said Church of Radcliffe; vidzt, John Davenports, Margarett Davenporte, k vidowe, the family And Occupants of RicJiard Kenions tefite, the family of Peter Walker, Roger Walkers, James Walkers, Thomas FletcJiers, Henry Siddalls, Mary Radcliffes, Richard Walkers self, Richard Walkers Jur, Lawrence Carters, John Blakelows, John Cromptons, Willm Barlowes, Richard Raivsthornes, James Scholefields; And in Little Leaver the familyes of Rauffe Sftarples, Richard Sharpies, John Sharpies, George Aynsworth, John Leadbeater, James Rothwell, John Mason, Thomas Mason, John Heywood; all these are nearest adiacent and wth in two statute myles vnto the said Church of Radcliffe, and fitt to bee vnyted to the said p[ar]ishe ...[20]

Pike was succeeded as minister by a very different kind of man. Charles Beswick was perhaps something of an opportunist, as he appears to have changed his religious allegiance on more than one occasion during his lifetime. He is thought to have begun his career as a zealous persecutor of puritan non-conformists on behalf of the established church: he sought to have Oliver Heywood, a great Yorkshire non-conformist preacher, arrested; and in 1665 he made 'bitter complaints' to the justices about 'conventicles' (unlawful meetings of five or more people held outside the auspices of the Church of England). Soon after, however, he fell out with the church authorities. In 1671 he was suspended by his bishop and described not only as 'a scholar and no mean poet' but also as 'a dissipated and immoral man'. He was again in trouble in 1685 when a sentence of deprivation was pronounced.[21] By 1689 he was described as being 'conformable' (i.e. by implication not a follower of the Anglican Church). The Radcliffe registers record him as having two daughters and two sons, one of whom was 'buried at Manchester on south side of Quire in the Ally over against little doore leading to Earl of Darbys Chappell'.[22] Beswick himself was buried in Radcliffe in December 1697.

Isaac Pendlebury's goods and chattels, 1683

Given the vicissitudes of life in Radcliffe in the mid seventeenth century, Isaac Pendlebury did well to survive into his mid-seventies. If he ran a beer-house (like Ralph Pendlebury of Bury before him and his son Nathan after him) during the 1640s and 1650s, his livelihood might well have been precarious. Many puritan non-conformists regarded alcohol as little short of the work of the devil. When Manchester born Charles Worsley, for example, was appointed by parliament to the office of major-general of Lancashire, Cheshire and Staffordshire in 1655, he enthusiastically set about closing down alehouses, collecting taxes, persecuting Quakers, and cracking down on vagrants. He claimed to have shut down 200 alehouses.[23] Other puritans, however, were more tolerant and, given that many townships were more or less self-regulating, Isaac's fate as an ale-housekeeper, if such he was, would have very much depended on the attitude of the Radcliffe landowner Ralph Ashton and the minister Thomas Pike. Given that the latter is known to have been particularly zealous in his beliefs, Isaac would have best avoided any association with the beer trade until well after the restoration of the monarchy in 1660.

A letter of administration and an inventory of Isaac's goods have survived from the year of his death in 1683. The scribe wrote in a beautifully ornate hand, and the first paragraph of this administration is written in Latin, using the standard wording of the time. The document is interesting because it describes his son Nathan as an innkeeper and as the 'natural and lawful Son and administrator' of all his father's goods, chattels and produce. Nathan would have expected to inherit his father's estate under the law of primogeniture but, given that Isaac died intestate, the use of this wording reinforced his right to do so despite being a 'base' son. An inventory accompanies the letter of administration.

4 Letter of Administration, Isaac Pendlebury, 1683.[24]

5   Inventory, Isaac Pendlebury, 1683[25] A transcription is given below:

May 2nd 1683

A True and the perfect Inventory of all the Goods and Chattalls of Isaack Pendlebury late of Rattcliffe deceased as followeth.

		£	s.	d.
Imprimis	in Bedstocks and bedding	01	06	08
Itm	In two little chests and one Box	00	07	00
Itm	One p[ai]r of Loomes and one Wheele	00	10	00
Itm	In Debts	00	10	00
Itm	In ready Money	03	08	00
Itm	In App[ar]ell	00	16	00
	In all	06	17	08

Prised and Inventoried by Us
   Roger Walker
   Richard Walker de Crosse
   Roger Lomax

Isaac owned very little at the time of his death. The total value of his goods and chattels was only £6 17s. 8d., considerably less than the value of the goods that Susanna Pendlebury of Bury (his possible step-grandmother) had left in 1608 (£9 15s.).* The paucity of goods listed suggests that Isaac (assuming he too was an innkeeper) had, by the time of his death, already passed on most of his responsibilities to his son together with all the usual furniture, household utensils and brewing equipment associated with running an inn. Aged nearly 80, he would have spent his last days doing a little spinning and weaving on his wheel and loom to help pay for his keep while his son Nathan ran the inn and sold beer. This would explain why Isaac's goods were so modest: a bed and bedding, a little chest, clothing and a loom and spinning wheel. His small sum of money accounted for over half the estimated value of his other goods.

Isaac Pendlebury lived a long life through eventful times in country and church alike. Plague had been reported in Manchester in the year before he was born. He was only fourteen years old when the harvests failed and famine hit Radcliffe and Bury. In his early thirties, civil war broke out between the King and Parliament; and his only known surviving son, Nathan, was born just one year before the severe food crisis of 1647 and two years after the storming of nearby Bolton by the royalists. He was married by a fervent puritan non-conformist preacher and buried by a priest who had been accused of depravity. He did well to live to such a ripe old age, and it is good to think of him in his later years sitting by the fire spinning his yarn and over a tankard of beer telling his many stories to the villagers and travelling tradesmen who gathered round him to listen.

His innkeeper son, Nathan, inherited his father's good health and resilience along with his goods and chattels. It is to him that this account turns next.

---

* £6 17s. 8d. in 1683 is equivalent in terms of 2010 prices to £859 (retail price index) or £12,900 (average earnings).

CHAPTER FOUR

From humble beginnings: Nathan Pendlebury, 1646–1725

Ralph Pendelbury married Dyna Allens in 1594

Isaac (1606–1683)

Nathan (1646–1725), innholder

Francis (1680–1751), parish clerk, weaver

James (1718–50), weaver

Francis (1745–1820), parish clerk, yeoman

Richard (1787–1831), whitster, soldier

Tom (1810–63)
messenger, tobacconist, warehouseman

Henry (1823–88)
waterman, glass mould maker

Thomas (1859–1900)
carman in London Docks

Base son of Isaac

Nathan was illegitimate, at least in the eyes of the church. He was described as Isaac's 'base' son when his baptism was registered in 1646. Illegitimacy was not uncommon, as the often very precise wording of the Radcliffe parish entries reveals.

... John a base sonne of Marie Dosine, purposed to bee begoten by John Livsey, Bury (1656); Thomas base child of Mary Diggles by Abraham Allen since pretendedly marryed (1680); James base son of

Anne Brooke Bury p: but then servant in Radcliffe and James Smith then of Bury but now fled into Yorkshire (1689); Nathan reputed son of Nathan Walker and son of Mary Walker basely begotten (1690); Margret d. of Mary Brey servant to James Gaskell Cat Hole, Middleton p: basely begotten by John Romsbottom, Gigg Bury p: (1692); Anne Basterd child of Mary Lomax who declares herself an inhabitant of Radcliffe: which in her extremity she fathered upon James Key of Prestwich p ...[1]

Nathan was 37 years old when his father died in 1683. He already had at least two children: a three-year-old son Francis (the third great-grandfather of Thomas Pendlebury of London) and a two-year-old daughter Elizabeth. He may also have had a third child who later became known as 'Nathan jn-r' and who married Esther Rothel in 1702, had nine children and died in 1728 (Nathan jn-r's parentage is unfortunately unrecorded as his baptism would have fallen during the gap in the Radcliffe records, 1673–80). Two more children followed in quick succession: Ann, baptised in 1683, and Amy, baptised in 1684. Four or five children in as many years took their toll on his wife Amy, and she died either in childbirth or soon after because her burial in February 1684 was followed only four weeks later by that of her young baby.

So, in 1684 Nathan found himself a widower with three or four young children under the age of four. At some stage he began a relationship with a widow, Anne Crompton, who also came from a family of innkeepers (three of them are recorded as such in the parish registers). Together they had an illegitimate child in 1691, also christened Nathan, who died a few weeks later. The baptisms of three more of his children (Cornelius, Alice and John) were recorded between 1694 and 1702. He may have married Anne Crompton at some stage because a person called 'Ann w. of Nethen Pendlebury' was buried in May 1725, three months before his own death in August 1725.

Nathan was described as an 'innkeeper' rather than an 'alehouse-keeper' when his father's Letter of Administration was drawn up in 1683. This suggests that he had some wealth and social standing within the village. Inns, unlike alehouses, usually provided accommodation as well as food and drink and during the seventeenth century were regarded as rather superior to the more lowly beerhouses.[2] They were places where people met and did business. In Lancaster, for example, some of the most prosperous innkeepers ran large and well-established inns and were among the leading citizens of their day, unlike the less fortunate owners of smaller inns or alehouses who often needed to supplement their incomes with other work.[3] A village such as Radcliffe, strategically placed on the busy road between Manchester, Bury, Bolton and Lancaster, would have been an excellent place to locate an inn, and there is a good chance that Nathan and his family enjoyed a reasonable standard of living.

In normal circumstances, when Nathan's first wife died and left him with several young children to bring up, he would have turned to his immediate family to help him. For, with death such a frequent occurrence, close relatives were used to helping out in situations such as this. However, it appears from the records that there were no other adult Pendleburys around at the time in Radcliffe who might have looked after his children. Instead, he probably turned for help to members of his wife's family, the Walkers.

The Walkers of Radcliffe

Nathan's wife Amy came from the prominent Radcliffe family whose name first appears in the parish marriage records in 1560. Her father and at least two other Walkers were butchers. By the time Nathan and Amy married, a large number of people with the surname Walker lived in Radcliffe: 27 adult male Walker burials were recorded in the 100 or so years between 1657 and 1758, plus others in the marriage and baptism records. The occupations of the Walker men, noted at their burials, provide a vivid insight into Radcliffe society between about 1660–1760. Their number included: a besom maker (a maker of brooms); a bricklayer; two butchers; two tradesmen; a whitster (a bleacher of cloth), two hatters and seven weavers; a cooper (someone who made or repaired vessels made of wooden staves and hoops, such as casks, barrels, tubs, etc.); a labourer; a forester (a man who looked after woods, normally on a gentleman's estate); a wheelwright; four husbandmen (tenant farmers, often keeping animals); a farmer; a landlord; a yeoman (a farmer who owned his own land and who qualified to serve on juries and vote for shire representatives). A Nathan Walker (a farmer) lived at Radcliffe Hall (once the impressive home of the Radcliffe family but now split into smallholdings[4]) in 1703 alongside Roger Walker, a landowner with a smallholding.

Although Nathan was unable to sign his name at the bottom of the Letter of Administration in 1683, his son Francis became sufficiently literate to become parish clerk. This supports the argument that Francis was brought up by members of the Walker family after his own mother died. It may have been through them that he learned to read and write; and that it was with their support that he began his prosperous career as a cotton weaver. Under their guidance, too, he may have become involved in church affairs because the

Walkers were active in the parish: three of them – Peter, James and Richard – served as church wardens during the 30 or so years that Francis was to be a churchwarden and parish clerk.

CHAPTER FIVE

Weaving, parish affairs and velvet breeches: Francis Pendlebury, 1680–1751

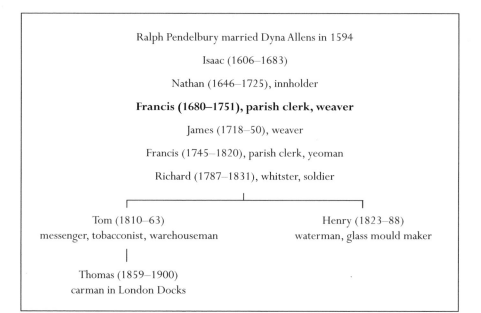

Ralph Pendelbury married Dyna Allens in 1594

Isaac (1606–1683)

Nathan (1646–1725), innholder

Francis (1680–1751), parish clerk, weaver

James (1718–50), weaver

Francis (1745–1820), parish clerk, yeoman

Richard (1787–1831), whitster, soldier

Tom (1810–63)
messenger, tobacconist, warehouseman

Henry (1823–88)
waterman, glass mould maker

Thomas (1859–1900)
carman in London Docks

F RANCIS, son of Nathan the Innkeeper, presided over a remarkable upturn in the family fortunes. By the age of 34, he had become parish clerk of Radcliffe, a position he was to hold for 33 years. He fathered 11 children and, when he died, at the age of 71, he left land and property to his heirs. After his death, his youngest son, Nathan (1722–96), succeeded him as parish clerk and built up the family fortunes still further.

Francis was 23 when he married Anne Bury in April 1703. Anne was pregnant at the time of their marriage, and their first child was baptised five months after their wedding. Francis inherited his father's longevity, as did many of his children. Anne lived to 71 and all but three of their children (Joseph, Emy and Thomas) survived into adulthood, with four living into their sixties or seventies (Elizabeth, Richard, Anne and Nathan). They enjoyed a comfortable existence at the heart of village society, thriving on the prosperity brought them by the burgeoning textile industry. Francis began life as a 'wollen weaver'; two of his daughters married weavers; four sons became weavers; and one son (Richard) was a felt-maker and hatter. His life was defined by family, textiles and parish affairs. That so many of his family lived to such a good age is a measure of the quality of life that they all enjoyed.

Textiles and prosperity

From this point in our story the fortunes of the Pendleburys in Radcliffe are inextricably linked to the prosperity of the Lancashire textile industry. As that industry flourished, so did the Pendleburys, so much so that several of them accumulated sufficient property to justify the expense of making a will (Francis in 1749, his son Nathan in 1794, Nathan's wife Ann in 1799, and grandson Francis in 1815). Francis, Nathan and Francis junior became parish clerks, described themselves as yeomen, and lived to a good age (71, 72 and 75 years respectively). They were fortunate to live in a period before competition from the large factories had begun to crush small-scale businesses.

Francis's working life began at a time when there was a dramatic increase in the demand for Lancashire cotton. Until about 1700, England had produced woollen and linen, but not cotton, goods, the latter being imported from India. In 1700 a government ban on imported cotton goods allowed a home-based cotton industry to develop using raw materials imported from the colonies. Since much of this cotton came from the English colonies in America, ports on the west coast of Britain, such as Liverpool, Bristol and Glasgow, became important in determining the sites of the new cotton industry. Despite opposition from the wool and linen manufacturers, the production of cotton prospered and, with it, Lancashire. The county palatine was well placed to lead the cotton industry: it was close to Liverpool; it had a damp climate which was good for spinning the yarn; and it was already a centre of wool production which meant that the fustian wool or linen that was needed to strengthen the warp for weaving was ready to hand.[1]

The two processes of cotton production, spinning and weaving, were initially very much home-based 'cottage' industries, but the discovery of new and more efficient ways to spin and weave raw cotton during Francis's lifetime led to the use of machines by groups of people working together in specialist premises instead of individually in their own cottages.[2] The parish records reveal that the introduction of machinery had come early to Radcliffe. The baptism of a son of 'Rodger Walker the dutch loom weaver' in 1683 is a reference to the engine loom that represented an important first step on the road to full industrialisation. These looms were worked by groups of weavers gathered together in special sheds owned by the wealthier weavers who employed them. By the 1760s, nearly all commercial weaving was probably being done this way.[3]

When Francis began working, weaving was still a generally slow, laborious process whereby the width of a piece of cloth was limited to the stretch of a man's arms. With John Kay's invention of the flying shuttle, however, it became possible to weave wider pieces far more quickly. Kay, who patented his invention in 1733, lived in Bury, just a couple of miles down the road from Radcliffe, and the Radcliffe weavers no doubt were among the first to benefit from his innovation. Faster weaving meant that more thread was required to keep the weavers busy and this prompted a search for better ways of spinning. A number of near-simultaneous solutions were developed in the 1760s and 1770s, primarily the spinning jenny, invented by James Hargreaves in the 1760s, the water frame patented by Richard Arkwright, and the spinning mule which was invented by Samuel Crompton. The flying shuttle and the new spinning machines were still small enough to be worked at home in a large room dedicated to the purpose and so enabled men with a small amount of capital to flourish, although Richard Arkwright and his imitators were to pioneer a new factory-based approach to spinning at Cromford and later around Manchester.

During Francis's lifetime, the Pendlebury weavers worked together in large rooms dedicated to handloom weaving. As the industry developed, so these rooms were increasingly supplemented by loomshops, which were usually set up in special buildings to allow a larger number of weavers to produce higher quality cloth more efficiently. Only the more prosperous weavers could afford to construct them and to employ non-family members to work in them. Nathan (1722–96) probably and Francis (1745–1820) certainly owned and ran these small-scale precursors of the industrial revolution. One provision in Francis Pendlebury's will in 1820, for example, was that John Radford (one of his many tenants), '... by an Agreement between us is not to pay above Five pounds any year until May 1822 because he build a Loomshop in the year of our Lord 1810 at his own expence and Thomas Baron is Witness to the same ...'[4]

Churchwarden and parish clerk

Status for Francis and the later Pendlebury men came not only from their thriving business, but also from their ability to read and write and play a role in local affairs. From at least 1714 onwards, one or other of the Pendleburys – Francis, his son Nathan, his half-brother Isaac and his grandson Francis – were closely associated with the affairs of the church either as churchwardens or, more significantly, as parish clerks. As such, they occupied a respected place in Radcliffe society.

Churchwardens operated at the very heart of village life, present at baptisms, marriages and funerals. By the early 1700s, their role had become temporal rather than religious; they were normally appointed by the parishioners rather than the church and could usually only be removed from office by resolution of an extraordinary meeting of the parishioners. They were primarily church treasurers, responsible for holding parish stock on behalf of the parishioners and for accounting to an annual parish meeting for the goods and funds in their care. They had to report to the Ordinary on his Visitation about the state of the church buildings, ornaments and equipment, and could be compelled to raise a church rate or to spend parish funds if money was needed for the fabric of the church or for its services. They were also required to maintain order and decency in the church, particularly during services and, under the direction of the Ordinary, to allocate church seating. In short, their work was crucial to the routine operation of local affairs, in much the same way as that of modern-day local councillors.[5]

The parish clerk was an even more influential local figure than the churchwarden. Parishioners likewise had the common law right to appoint (and remove) an individual from the office. By Francis's time, parish clerks were usually laymen rather than minor clergy, but they nevertheless remained closely involved with the religious side of the church. The clerk often played a leading part in the conduct of services as well as the choice and quality of the hymns sung and the music played; and during divine service it was usually his duty to lead the singing and the responses of the congregation. He had overall responsibility for the accuracy of the parish registers and, from the mid seventeenth century onwards, may even have taught the village boys to read and write. An account of education in Devon during this period describes how large numbers of endowed parish schools for the education of the village poor were opened under the supervision of the parish vestry or trustee. The parish clerk or a husbandman holding land usually acted as the village schoolteacher.[6]

Francis became parish clerk in Radcliffe in about 1711 and was still described as such at his burial in 1751 (in January 1711, at his son Joseph's baptism, he was described as a 'wollen weaver', but by the time of Joseph's burial a year later as 'Parish Clerk').

The legacy of Francis Pendlebury

As Francis neared the end of his life, the people of Radcliffe were shaken by an event reminiscent of the civil wars that had devastated the area a century earlier. Between September and December 1745, the area was awash with soldiers of King George and of the Jacobite pretender to his throne, Charles Stuart. There would have been no escaping them as Jacobites marched from Scotland to Derby via Manchester and back again, pursued by an army of at least 10,000 of the king's men. An account by Richard Kay, who worked in Bury, describes how people gathered at Hulton Lane, on the western outskirts of Radcliffe, to watch the rebels pass on their way from Manchester to Wigan.[7]

Francis drew up his will in 1749. He was already in poor health, '*being Sick in Body but of perfect Memory and Understanding*'. It was probably sickness that forced him to relinquish his position as parish clerk, because in April 1750 he signed off the annual parish record as one of the 'Church Wardings' instead of parish clerk.

In his will, which extends over two large sheets of paper, Francis felt able to describe himself as a 'yeoman'. He left a total of five houses with land: one dwelling and personal estate to his wife Anne; one house with two acres of land to his son Robert; another with a shippon (cow house), adjacent orchard and fields to his son Nathan; a dwelling house and garden to his son James; and a house to his son Stephen. He gave a sum of money to all three of his daughters and to his grandson, and an annual allowance during their lifetime to two of his sons. He owned a fine set of clothing, including 'one hoas coat and one pair of breeches which are of Cotton Velvet', which he left to Nathan. He thus left something to each one of his living children, and made Nathan joint executor with his wife Anne. Perhaps he was particularly close to his youngest son Nathan: it was Nathan who succeeded him as parish clerk and who managed to build up the family fortunes still further.

It is good to imagine Francis teaching the local children to read and write; or to picture him, dressed in his best house coat and velvet breeches and surrounded by his family, singing lustily as he led the congregation of St Mary's each week at Sunday worship.

6   Francis Pendlebury's will: last part, signature and seal, 1749.[8]

A hint of scandal: James, 1718–1750

Francis Pendlebury was a deeply respectable man: a successful cotton manufacturer and the literate clerk of the parish. However, in 1737, his son James caused a bit of a scandal in the village. James, aged just nineteen, ran away with his sweetheart Alice Smethurst. They were married ('James Pendlebury and Alice Smethers') in the Peak Forest Chapel in Derbyshire, where the minister had the power to grant marriage licences outside the jurisdiction of the bishop (a service similar to that offered at Gretna Green). The fact that they had to run away to get married suggests that Francis disapproved of the match and withheld his consent. Perhaps he was worried by the fact that both James and Alice were under-age or dismayed that Alice came from a family of innkeepers. In any event, father and son were later reconciled because Francis left James a cottage and a garden in his will. James, however, did not live long enough to enjoy his inheritance because he died, aged only 32, just a few months before his father.

   Three of James's sons survived into adulthood and prospered: Richard (1739–1826) had no fewer than 13 children and died aged 87 (see later); and James (1747/48–1820) became a relatively wealthy farmer. When the latter died in 1820, his estate included an income of £335 from mortgages and a clock, couch chair and oak chest. James feared that his three sons (James, Cornelius and William) might quarrel over his will and added a codicil: 'And if any disputes or litigation arise among the Legatees in my Will named respecting the disposal of my Property otherwise than is in my Will directed, I order in such case, that the cause or causes of such disputes or litigation have no more than one shilling severally, and his or their respective shares to be divided equally among my peaceable legatees.' [9]

The middle son, Francis (1745–1820), forms the direct link between the sixteenth-century Radcliffe of Ralph and Dyna Pendlebury and the early nineteenth-century London of Richard Pendlebury. He had 12 children and became parish clerk; his fortunes are described in Chapter 7. Before that, however, the story turns to James's youngest brother Nathan, who was both parish clerk and a successful man of property.

CHAPTER SIX

Parish clerk and man of property: Nathan Pendlebury, 1722–1796

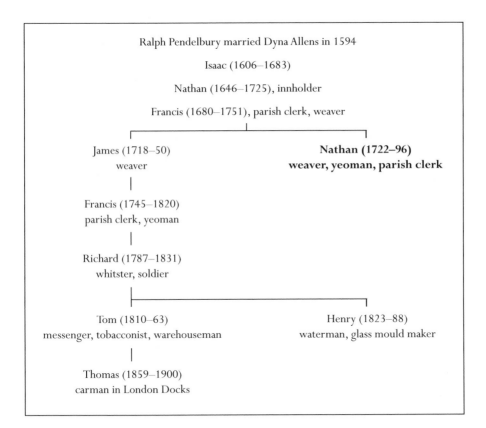

Ralph Pendelbury married Dyna Allens in 1594

Isaac (1606–1683)

Nathan (1646–1725), innholder

Francis (1680–1751), parish clerk, weaver

James (1718–50)
weaver

Francis (1745–1820)
parish clerk, yeoman

Richard (1787–1831)
whitster, soldier

Tom (1810–63)
messenger, tobacconist, warehouseman

Thomas (1859–1900)
carman in London Docks

Nathan (1722–96)
weaver, yeoman, parish clerk

Henry (1823–88)
waterman, glass mould maker

NATHAN was a weaver, like his father Francis. With the property he inherited, and no doubt helped by a shrewd business sense, he was well placed to take advantage of the opportunities that the Lancashire cotton industry now offered to those with some capital. When he was 23, he married Ann Woods, who may already have owned property in her own right.[1] Six years later, he inherited a house, orchard, fields and a pair of cotton velvet breeches from his father. In 1762 he accumulated more property when his childless older brother Robert left him a third share of 'Som Estates or Cotages under Sir Ralph Ashton Baranight of Middlton'.[2] He died a wealthy man at the age of 74.

Nathan and Ann were married for over 50 years. Although there is no record of them having had any children, the couple 'adopted' a young baby girl called Ann Smethurst. (Adoption as such had no legal status in England until the Adoption of Children Act, 1926; before that, private arrangements were sometimes established via a solicitor.) Baby Ann was Ann Pendlebury's grandniece, the daughter of her brother Benjamin Woods' child Margrit Woods. Margrit married Thomas Smethurst in 1776 and their first daughter, Betty, was born two years later. Sometime during 1779 Margrit became pregnant for a second time but died either giving birth or soon after because baby Ann was baptised in Radcliffe on the same day (9 February 1780) that her mother was buried. The little girl assumed the Pendlebury name and became known as Ann Pendlebury Smethurst; and when she became pregnant at the age of 16 and gave birth to an illegitimate daughter, she christened her Margaret Pendlebury Smethurst. Ann Pendlebury Smethurst was left considerable property by Nathan, and his wife Ann appointed her as one of her executors and left property in trust for baby Margaret (see below).

Parish clerk and local dignitary

Nathan's name appears frequently in the church registers as 'clark' over a period of nearly 40 years between 1754 and 1793. He was a leading local dignitary. In 1787, for example, he witnessed the deed for the consecration of a new burial ground in Radcliffe along with other worthies: Richard Assheton (Warden of Manchester); Thomas Pearce MA (Prebendary of Chester); James Lipon MA (Rector of Prestwich); Thomas Foxley MA (Rector of Radcliffe); John Ashworth, Thomas Deakin and John Yates (Church wardens); and William Nicholls (Notary, Public Secretary to the Lord Bishop of Chester).[3]

Parish officials could be rather pompous individuals. William Radcliffe, the diarist, paints an amusing picture of a Sunday service in Mellor, a village about 20 miles north-west of Radcliffe. There, in 1794, two years before the first Sunday School is thought to have opened in Radcliffe,[4] an elderly clergyman gave a long sermon preaching against the sins of machinery-breaking '... whereupon his church warden, a respectable yeoman, rose in his seat opposite the pulpit and told the preacher that it would become him better to follow his text than to ramble away about such temporal affairs ...'[5] It is not difficult to imagine Nathan Pendlebury taking it upon himself on occasion to reprimand the vicar at St Mary's. However, his attention to his many relatives suggests that he was a kindly and generous man with a strong sense of family (as indeed was his wife, Ann).

Nathan's legacy

As a Lancashire weaver, Nathan benefited from the high earnings that were associated with the closing years of the eighteenth century. These were the days when a handloom weaver could expect to receive four guineas for weaving a piece of fabric 24 yards long.[6] With property and a good income from rents, he would have cut a striking figure.

> … The [weaving] trade was that of a gentleman. They brought home their work in top boots and ruffled shirts, carried a cane, and in some instances took a coach … many weavers at that time used to walk about the streets with a five pound Bank of England note spread out under their hat-bands, they would smoke none but long 'churchwarden' pipes, and objected to the intrusion of any other handicraftsmen into their particular rooms in the public houses which they frequented …[7]

Nathan drew up his will two years before he died, leaving property, possessions and money to his wife, Ann, with the instruction that they were to be passed, on her death or remarriage, to his brothers' children or grandchildren, and to his wife's brother's grandchild (Ann Pendlebury Smethurst) and to her sister (Betty Smethurst) should she die childless. If his wife should remarry, she was to receive only one pound and one shilling (i.e. one guinea) plus a mahogany chest (which she probably brought with her when she married), the marriage bed and its bedding. This was a commonplace practice. A man was able entirely to control what happened to his estate after his death by ensuring that his wife lost everything if she chose to remarry.

Nathan's will was a lengthy one, taking up two full large sheets of paper. In it he described himself as a 'yeoman' and he signed with a firm hand. The total value of the estate was valued at less than £600 at probate.* The will in all its details demonstrates how far the Pendleburys had now advanced, at least in terms of wealth, from their days as innkeepers who could neither read nor write.

---

* £600 in 1796 is equivalent in terms of 2010 prices to £46,000 (retail price index) or £665,000 (average earnings).

Summary of the terms of Nathan Pendlebury's will, 1796[8]

Alice Heap [niece]	A tenth share of Nathan's Principal Money after Ann's death.
Robert Heap [nephew]	Tenement + 3 cottages and shed in Rushy Meadow + A tenth share of Nathan's Principal Money after Ann's death.
Sarah Heap [niece]	A tenth share of Nathan's Principal Money after Ann's death.
William Heap [nephew]	In occupation of cottage in the Old Bull's Head which now passes to Betty Smethurst + A tenth share of Nathan's Principal Money after Ann's death.
Ann Pendlebury (née Woods) [wife]	All property until her death so long as she does not marry again, including other household goods, furniture, printed curtains; + during her lifetime the interest from money invested from sale of surplus goods, stock of cattle + interest on all Nathan's Principal Money (Bonds and securities); if she remarried, a mahogany chest of drawers, bed and bedding, and one guinea.
Anne Pendlebury [niece]	A tenth share of Nathan's Principal Money after Ann's death.
Francis Pendlebury [nephew]	All the cottages in Swinton.
John Pendlebury [grandnephew]	Parkhill Tenement in Redivals + cottage, garden & premises he occupies in Old Peters + half share in wearing apparel.
Nathan Pendlebury [grandnephew]	All of Old Peters (four tenancies including his own) except for two cottages.
Peter Pendlebury [grandnephew]	Parkhill Tenement in Redivals after death of John.
Richard Pendlebury [nephew]	A tenth share of Nathan's Principal Money after Ann's death.
Richard Pendlebury [grandnephew]	Parkhill Tenement in Redivals after death of John + cottage, garden & premises he occupies at Old Peters.
Ann Pendlebury Smethurst [grandniece of Nathan's wife Ann]	Messuage & tenement + building at Bull's Head except for cottage occupied by William Heap.
Betty Smethurst [grandniece of Nathan's wife Ann]	If sister Ann dies without children, Messuage & tenement + building at Bull's Head except for cottage occupied by William Heap .
James Woods [wife's nephew]	A tenth share of Nathan's Principal Money after Ann's death.

By the time Nathan came to make his will, he had outlived all ten of his brothers and sisters. He therefore divided his property and money between their surviving children (i.e. his nephews and nieces) and his wife's two grandnieces. He owned at least 15 cottages and three tenements (lodging houses) and it was his income from rents that enabled him to accumulate his bonds and securities. It was a considerable achievement for a man who had inherited from his father a 'Dwelling house … with the Shippon orchard and the Croft and Bottom' and a third of his brother Robert's property.

By local standards Nathan and his wife no doubt lived in a rather grand style. Ann, too, owned additional property in her own right, including '…three Houses with the appurtenances situate in higher lane in the manor of Pilkington

7   Mow Crop Brow, Radcliffe, in the 1870s. Nathan Pendlebury's wife Ann (1728–99) left a 'messuage or Dwellinghouse with the garden and premises belonging situate at Mough brow in Radcliffe' to Ann Pendlebury Smethurst. (Bury Archive Service B07849)

…' She left two of these houses to Ann Pendlebury Smethurst, one of them to be held in her trust until her 'natural child' Margaret Pendlebury Smethurst (then aged two) reached the age of 18. Ann Pendlebury Smethurst also inherited '… [a] messuage or Dwellinghouse with the garden and premises belonging situate at Mough brow in Radcliffe …', together with 'household furniture Plate Linen and … wearing apparel', and baby Margaret and the prized mahogany chest.[9] However, despite her independent wealth and her 50 years of marriage to such a notable local figure as Nathan, Ann was unable to sign her name, a reminder of the very different position that women then occupied in their society.

Nathan left a substantial legacy to his nephews and nieces but in so doing unwittingly sowed the seeds of a bitter family dispute. His nephew Francis later left the five Swinton cottages he had inherited from Uncle Nathan to his four sons Thomas, Nathan, James and Richard. Their quarrel about who was entitled to the rental income was a bitter one that later came to dominate the nineteenth-century letters between the Pendleburys in London and Lancashire.

CHAPTER SEVEN

The changing face of Radcliffe: Francis Pendlebury, 1745–1820

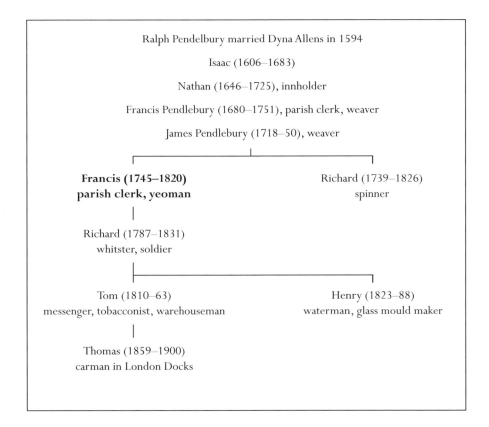

Ralph Pendelbury married Dyna Allens in 1594

Isaac (1606–1683)

Nathan (1646–1725), innholder

Francis Pendlebury (1680–1751), parish clerk, weaver

James Pendlebury (1718–50), weaver

Francis (1745–1820)
parish clerk, yeoman

Richard (1739–1826)
spinner

Richard (1787–1831)
whitster, soldier

Tom (1810–63)
messenger, tobacconist, warehouseman

Henry (1823–88)
waterman, glass mould maker

Thomas (1859–1900)
carman in London Docks

F R A N C I S was five years old when his father James died. His mother, Alice, who had eloped at such a young age to marry his father, was left to bring up five young children on her own in the house and garden left to her husband by his father Francis (senior). Francis junior, like his father, became a weaver. He married Anne Pollett in 1765 and they had 12 children, eight of whom survived into adulthood.

Big families were a mixed blessing, at least in economic terms. A large number of children provided a ready cohort of spinners to supply the weavers but it also meant that there were many mouths to feed. In 1784, with seven children to support, six of whom were under the age of 12, Francis was supplementing his weaver's income with a turn at grave digging. An entry in the Radcliffe parish register[1] for that year records: 'Settelled with Francis Pendlebury for making graves and paid him of and he gettes to make 3s. 11d.'*

Wealthy Uncle Nathan seems to have kept a fatherly eye on young Francis. It was almost certainly through him that Francis learned to read and write; and when Nathan became ill in 1793 it was Francis who succeeded him as parish clerk. When Nathan drew up his will, he left Francis '… all my freehold Cottages or Dwelling houses and premises situate in Swinton in the Parish of Eccles in the said County to hold to him the said Francis Pendlebury his Heirs and Assign for ever …'[2] By the time Francis took full possession of these five cottages (in 1799 after Nathan's wife Ann's death), many of the cotton weavers of Radcliffe were beginning to struggle as the competition from the big new factories grew steadily stronger.

The rise of the large cotton mills

Uncle Nathan had lived at a time when handloom workshops were still flourishing and when those who owned even a small amount of property had a distinct edge over those who did not. Not only could they draw an income from rents instead of having to pay rent to someone else, but also, at least as importantly, they owned buildings that could be used to house handlooms. At a stroke they could become small-scale employers rather than hired workers and so take full advantage of the demand for cotton. Nathan was just such a man. By the time he died, he had managed to accumulate a considerable amount of property, including tenanted cottages and at least three tenement houses. There is a hint that Francis was also an employer of weavers, though on a more modest scale than Nathan, because he specifically stated in his will that one of his tenants, John Radford, was to pay less rent because of the loom-shop he had built at his own expense.

By the time Francis died in 1820, however, the loomshops upon which the prosperity of the Pendleburys was founded were being outpaced by bigger and faster machines. As the relentless search for more efficient ways of spinning

---

* Three shillings and 11d. in 1784 is equivalent in terms of 2010 prices to £17.90 (retail price index) or £252 (average earnings).

sufficient yarn to feed the weaving machines gathered momentum, so the work-base began to shift away from homes and loomshops to the new large factories. A key invention in this process was Richard Arkwright's water frame (1769) which improved the quality of the thread; its early dependence on fast-flowing water to provide its power had seen the first generation of water-powered cotton spinning mills being located in the Derwent Valley of Derbyshire, from Cromford to Belper, but early in the nineteenth century the geographical advantages of lowland Lancashire – inexpensive coal, better transport networks and a long tradition of hand-based cotton production – resulted in Lancashire and the Manchester area in particular becoming the unchallenged centre for the mill-based cotton industry. In 1779, Samuel Crompton's spinning mule combined the principles of the spinning jenny and the water frame to make an even tougher and finer cotton thread. Then, in 1785, Edmund Cartwright patented the power loom. Driven initially by water and then by power from a steam engine (Boulton & Watt's pioneering steam engines with separate condensers, which were the first to be able to provide rotative power for direct use by machinery, were introduced from 1781), this loom revolutionised the weaving process. By the last decade of the eighteenth century, cotton mills were being constructed across Lancashire to use the latest technology. Spinning mules provided the fine, but strong, thread that could be used by the weavers on their power looms. By the 1820s both spinning and weaving were being mechanised on a wider and wider scale; and, with a large textile manufacturing base and also a central role in the merchanting and marketing of cotton, Manchester was well on the way to earning its name of 'Cottonopolis'.

Such immense and rapid change had a profound effect on the lives of Francis Pendlebury and his many children, and on the people in Radcliffe and Bury generally. In the space of less than a generation, the need for skilled highly paid workers had been overtaken by the demand for young untrained people to work the fast powerlooms for relatively low wages. The handloom weavers found themselves less and less able to earn a living wage, particularly as wages were driven down still further by an influx of Irish factory workers. The construction of more and bigger factories coincided with an expensive and prolonged war against France, crop failures, famine and political unrest. In 1808, 6,000 weavers gathered on St George's Fields in Manchester to call for a 33 per cent wage increase, the average pay for an 84-hour week having now fallen to about eight shillings.* On the following day, 15,000 protestors

---

*   Equivalent in 2010 prices to £24.30 (retail price index) or £308 (average earnings).

gathered on the same spot, the dragoons were called in and opened fire, and one man was killed. Protestors, known as Luddites, smashed machinery and damaged factories wherever they could.[3] In 1817, handloom weavers planned the 'Blanketeers March' to London, and a year later another demonstration of cotton workers and miners led to one man being killed. In 1819, the infamous Peterloo Massacre took place: troops attacked a peaceful reform meeting in St Peter's Fields, Manchester, killing around 17 and wounding many more.[4] At about this time, eight people were executed at Lancaster, four for mill-burning, three for breaking into a house to steal food, and one for stealing potatoes, while at Middleton four were killed during rioting. Later in the same year, 35 calico producers backed the call for a minimum weavers' wage and one of them, James Hutchinson, came from the village of Elton, only three miles from Radcliffe.

The changing face of Radcliffe

Radcliffe, then, lay right at the heart of this social and political unrest. It can have little resembled the small seventeenth-century village that Ralph and Dyna Pendlebury and their children had once known. The huge impact that the growth of the cotton trade had had upon village life can be traced in the changing profile of employment. The parish registers include details of male occupations in the burial records during three blocks of years (1653–97, 1708–50 and 1751–83) and a comparison reveals the full extent of the revolution that was taking place. In the earliest period, back in the time of Nathan, the innkeeper, roughly similar numbers of people were working in the weaving industry as on the land (35 per cent and 29 per cent of all recorded occupations respectively). By the latest period (1751–83), however, when Uncle Nathan was busy consolidating his fortune, the cotton industry had become predominant, with over half the men working at spinning, bleaching, weaving or felting.

The village had also grown in size since the time of Ralph and Dyna and, as it grew, was attracting an ever more diverse set of skills to service the needs of its inhabitants. In the 1660s, for example, there was only an innkeeper, a butcher and a stonemason listed in the burial records alongside the cotton and land workers. Nearly a hundred years later, the occupations were far more varied. Now the cotton and land workers lived alongside a blacksmith, a bricklayer, a butcher, a carpenter, a cobbler, miners, a cooper, the curate, a miller, innkeepers, a nailer, a papermaker, the parish clerk, a plasterer, a shoemaker, a skinner, a soldier, a tradesman and a wheelwright. In the course of just over a century, Radcliffe had moved from being a small village where many people still worked on the land to a small town with many service industries catering for an expanding number of predominantly cotton workers.[5]

William Radcliffe has left a detailed picture of the life of the cottage-based cotton worker who formed the bedrock of Radcliffe society in his description of a small village (Mellor) 20 miles to the north-west of Radcliffe, in the year 1770. His account pre-dates the full effects of industrialisation and describes cotton workers at a time when they were still relatively prosperous.[6]

> ... Cottage rents at that time, with convenient loom shop and a small garden attached, were from one and a half to two guineas per annum. The father of a family would earn from eight shillings to half a guinea at his loom, and his sons, if he had one, two or three alongside of him, six or eight shillings per week; but the great sheet anchor of all cottages and small farms was the labour attached to the hand wheel; and when it is considered that it required six or eight hands to prepare and spin yarn ... sufficient for the consumption of one weaver, this shows clearly the inexhaustible source there was for labour for every person, from the age of seven to eighty years (who retained their sight and could move their hands) to earn their bread – say, from one to three shillings per week, – without going to the parish ...

This was not an idle society. Everyone who could work, worked. And large families such as Francis Pendlebury's enjoyed an economic advantage over smaller ones, providing that everyone stayed healthy enough to keep working.

However, not even the largest family could compete against the new entrepreneurs who had the know-how and the capital to build the factories that changed the nature of the cotton industry for ever. Robert Peel, a yeoman from Blackburn (and father of Sir Robert Peel of later Corn Laws fame) was particularly active in the Bury and Radcliffe areas from about 1770.[7] His factory at Bury was built several hundred yards upstream from Radcliffe Bridge and was one of the first mills to use the spinning jenny. His fortune grew when he introduced a scheme for importing paupers wholesale from London poorhouses to tend the machines. His factories had an evil reputation, with the one at Radcliffe Bridge considered particularly bad. The children employed there slept on an upper floor of the building and were bound to work there until they reached the age of 21. They were unpaid and were kept locked up each night. Shifts were typically ten hours in length, and children returning from a day shift would sleep in the same bed as children leaving for a night shift. In 1784 there was a bad outbreak of typhoid at the mill. Doctors called in to assess the situation recommended leaving the windows open at night, fumigating rooms with tobacco, cleaning rooms and toilets regularly, and bathing children occasionally. The report forced magistrates to abandon the practice of binding parish apprentices to any mill not adhering to these conditions and prompted Robert Peel to introduce a bill into Parliament to improve factory hygiene, which later became the Factory Act of 1802. Over time, conditions at the mill improved and by the mid-1790s John Aikin praised the working conditions there. During an inspection in 1823, local magistrates reported that the factory at Radcliffe, unlike many others, was adhering to all requirements of the Factory Acts.

A dwindling legacy

Although Francis died a yeoman with property, he was never as wealthy as Nathan. Unlike his grandfather Francis and Uncle Nathan, he failed during his lifetime to increase the amount of property he had inherited. He probably suffered from very poor health in his final years: although he did not die until 1820, the last reference to him as parish clerk was in 1814 and he made his will in 1815. By the time he died in 1820, he had only the five tenanted cottages in Swinton that he had inherited from his uncle to leave to his wife and his children. His will stated

> ... Then I give devise and bequeath unto my loving Wife Ann
> Pendlebury all my Freehold Cottages or dwelling Houses situate
> in Swinton in the Parish of Eccles in the said County now in the
> occupation of Widow Longworth and her son, Widow Walton, Richard
> Johnson, James Walton, and John Radford (and the said John Radford
> by an Agreement between us is not to pay above Five pounds any year
> until May 1822 because he build a Loomshop in the year of our Lord
> 1810 at his own expence and Thomas Baron is Witness to the same) for
> and during the time and Term of her natural life if she continues my
> Widow...[8]

In his will Francis made no mention of the house where he and his wife Ann lived. Perhaps by the time he made his will they were already staying with his second oldest son James. James probably succeeded him as parish clerk sometime after 1815 because there is a note in the parish register that reads 'James Pendlebury resigns the Office of Clerk to Robert Barlow September 1st 1822'.[9] Francis certainly seems to have been close to James because he appointed him as one of his executors. He can have had little idea when he made his will of the bitter in-fighting that his legacy would bring to his family.

Difficult times

Francis had two brothers, Richard and James. Between them they fathered at least 28 children and all lived to a good age. Richard, however, was no stranger to poverty. In 1794, he was dependent on parish relief when magistrates ordered the overseers of the poor of the parish of Radcliffe to evict him, with his wife Esther and their five children (Nancy, James, Thomas, Martha and Peter), from Radcliffe to neighbouring Elton.[10] Fortunes improved for him in 1799 when he inherited a tenth share of Nathan Pendlebury's 'Principal Money' after the death of Nathan's wife Ann. He and his wife had 12 children; Esther lived to the age of 74 and Richard to the age of 87.

All four of Francis and Anne's sons started their working lives in cotton: James was a calico printer and Thomas, Nathan and Richard were whitsters (bleachers). Only James stayed working within the industry; he remained a traditional block-printer until his death in 1864, despite the bitter disputes against industrialisation that were led by the Block-makers Union.[11] The others sought their fortunes elsewhere: Thomas joined the navy, Nathan became a carter, and his youngest son Richard enlisted in the army. By the time Francis died, his Richard had lost his arm at the Battle of Corunna and was living in London. With him, a new chapter in the history of the Pendleburys was about to begin.

Wealth and poverty in 1826 Radcliffe

A church rate book for St Mary the Virgin Radcliffe for the year 1826 reveals that many of the households were living on very modest incomes. The majority are listed as paying less than three shillings for the year of a tax levied at the rate of one shilling and three pence in the pound.[12] However, a number of individuals paid considerably more: Samuel Key, a butcher (£2 4s. 8d.); the 'Proprietor of Canal and Reservoir' (£4 3s. 3d.); Robert Hampson (£5 1s. 6d.); and William Hampson, a manufacturer (£4 13s. and £35 19s. 2d.). The inequalities of wealth are self-evident.

Six Pendleburys are listed in this rate book: William (Meadow & Hall, 3s. 9d.); Nathan (Withings, 14s. 1d.); Thomas (Carter, 3s. 5d.); Thomas (Steel House, 1s. 10½d.) and Betty (Trustys, 3s. 9d.); Cornelius Pendlebury (pays William Booth over Bulls Head 1s. 10½d.). Several of these people were related to Francis. Cornelius (a calico printer) and William (a farmer) were his nephews, and Nathan and one of the two Thomas's were his children and named in his contentious will. Siblings of Richard, and uncles and an aunt to the London Tom Pendlebury (1810–63), they formed a tightly knit, if quarrelsome, group of people. Only one, Nathan, had earnings well above the average and, in his own eyes at least, he seems to have been a figure of some importance, as later references in the Pendlebury letters show.

Even as late as 1841, Radcliffe was a relatively small centre in a relatively rural setting.[13] But long after Francis's son Richard had joined the army and his grandson Tom had settled in London, it had become a truly industrial landscape. A traveller's account from 1897 describes the approach to Radcliffe Bridge.

> ... You will have sight again, between high shelving banks of fields and hedgerow fences, of wooded cloughs and colliery shafts, of old stone houses and modern mills; and at Radcliffe Bridge, you will find yourself passing through a manufacturing community, which, with its cotton spinning, weaving, bleaching, calico printing, machine making, and other works, has gathered itself together into a township estimated to contain upwards of twenty thousand persons ...[14]

CHAPTER EIGHT

Wounded at Corunna:
Richard Pendlebury, 1787–1831

Ralph Pendelbury married Dyna Allens in 1594

Isaac (1606–1683)

Nathan (1646–1725), innholder

Francis Pendlebury (1680–1751), parish clerk, weaver

James Pendlebury (1718–50), weaver

Francis (1745–1820), parish clerk, yeoman

Richard (1787–1831), whitster, soldier

Tom (1810–63)
messenger, tobacconist, warehouseman

Henry (1823–88)
waterman, glass mould maker

Thomas (1859–1900)
carman in London Docks

R ICHARD's fortunes differed greatly from those of his father. Francis had been a literate parish clerk who had worked all his life as a handloom weaver in Radcliffe. Richard, however, was unable even to sign his name; he left home at a young age in search of a very different life. And, with him, one branch of the Pendlebury family moved from Lancashire to London.

In 1805, Richard had just turned 17 and was facing the somewhat daunting prospect of life as a whitster (bleacher) in the increasingly industrialised manufacture of Lancashire cotton. He had probably already been working as a bleacher for several years because children were usually put to work at a very young age. Nothing about making cotton cloth was particularly easy or pleasant: dust, fumes, heat, noise and dim lighting, together with long hours of monotonous work for low wages, often produced chronic ill-health in the workers. But bleaching was an exceptionally nasty process. It involved dipping and stirring woven cotton cloth into liquid bleach, working in rooms that were hot and filled with steam, and using sulphuric acid, chloride of lime and soda. It probably came as little surprise to his family when Richard enlisted in the army, attracted by the guarantee of food and clothing, the promise of adventure, and the offer of 16 guineas.*

Enlistment

When Richard enlisted in 1805, the drive to recruit men into the army to fight Napoleonic France was at its height; he was probably attracted by one of the many recruiting parties that toured the country putting on a good show with plenty of drink and entertainment to attract recruits. Others close to Richard also served in the armed forces: James and Matthew Wolstenholme from Radcliffe (his future wife's relatives) had been soldiers and his uncle Thomas (Old Tommy) was in the navy for a period. The enlistment bounty, of course, was an enormous inducement in itself, even though part of it had to be spent immediately on essential equipment. By the time Richard was recruited, the bounty had risen to 16 guineas, half of which was paid immediately upon taking the oath.[1] This must have seemed like a fortune to young Richard.

The bounty was a large amount of money for any weaver, particularly at a time when the textile trade was in difficulties. A depression in that trade usually led to the recruitment of an above average number of weavers, particularly in areas such as Lancashire and the West Riding of Yorkshire where a well-developed industry had led to a concentration of young men with little or no work or very low wages. It was easy enough to tempt the weavers by contrasting their damp and monotonous existence with the delights of an open-air life somewhat misleadingly proclaimed by the recruiting sergeant. Comparative recruitment figures at the time for the different counties show that Yorkshire (1,315 recruits) and Lancashire (978 recruits) far outstripped the other counties; Norfolk supplied the next highest number (483), but most counties provided fewer than 100.[2]

Richard was not the only young man from Radcliffe to join the army at this time. John Heap attested three days before him and Richard Kay, who

---

* Sixteen guineas in 1805 is equivalent in terms of 2010 prices to £1,060.00 using the retail price index and £13,800.00 using average earnings.

was the same age as Richard and also fought at Corunna, joined three weeks later.[3] John may have been a distant cousin and was almost certainly a close friend: two Pendleburys had married into the Heap family (John Heap married Elizabeth Pendlebury in 1734 and their four surviving children received legacies from Nathan Pendlebury in 1796). A generation later, in 1774, Richard's Uncle James married Alice Heap. Encouraged by war fever, the promise of a bounty and no doubt egged on by his friends, Richard was enlisted into the 1st Foot Guards of the Duke of York's Regiment in Manchester on 25 January 1805. He declared on oath that he was a whitster by trade and born in Radcliffe Bridge. His age was recorded as 16, his height five foot five inches, his complexion 'fresh', his eyes 'grey' and his hair 'light'.[4] He was in fact older than the age recorded (17½, not 16 years of age). Perhaps he looked unusually frail and young for his age.

Richard in Sicily and at Corunna

Richard's period of service in the Foot Guards started about five months after his enlistment, in July 1805. He fought in two campaigns, in Sicily in 1806–07 and in Spain in 1808–09. On both occasions, he was in the 8th Company of the 3rd Battalion under the command of Lt. Col. Moreton.[5] During these years, his battalion trained and campaigned alongside the 1st Battalion in which a foot soldier called John Collett, an agricultural labourer from Kent, served. Using information already collected about Collett's campaign it is possible to reconstruct in some detail what happened to Richard during these years.[6]

Richard saw very little real fighting until the battle of Corunna itself in early 1809. For the first 18 months or so after he enrolled, he was in Kent where most of the army was kept busy training and building defences. He was first stationed at Deal barracks and then at Chatham, drilling and marching for many tedious months before being sent to Plymouth. In December 1806, after many delays and false starts due to the stormy weather, he set sail for Sicily. He spent nearly a year on the island, saw nothing of the enemy, and was troubled by the heat and by sickness. In late October 1807 his company set sail from Sicily for Gibraltar and thence for England, arriving back in Portsmouth exhausted from sickness and a dreadful sea voyage. He then marched, at times knee-deep in mud, back to his barracks in Kent.

For much of 1808, Richard remained in Kent. On 13 March, he was back in Radcliffe for his wedding to Rebecca Wolstenholme, daughter of James, a weaver. The copy of their marriage certificate is the earliest document to survive in the nineteenth-century Pendlebury material. Within seven months of his marriage, Richard was sent to Spain. His company, under the overall command of Sir David Baird, landed in Corunna and, after being cooped up in their ships for two weeks, marched south for several days towards Salamanca, via Santiago and Lugo, with the intention of defending Madrid against the French.[7] Madrid, however, surrendered, and Baird's men were ordered just before Christmas to turn back to Corunna via Valencia while Sir John Moore, the overall commander of British forces in Spain, took a slightly different more southerly route via Benavente.

Thus began Moore's legendary 'March of Death'. Rain, snow, uphill marching with a shortage of footwear, semi-starvation and forced marches all took their toll. With them marched over 1,000 soldiers' wives and children who had ignored Moore's orders and accompanied the army into Spain. The men were regularly marching 11 hours a day, carrying heavy loads through thick mud and snow. News of the full horrors of the retreat took time to reach England. Not surprisingly, the discipline of many of the British regiments of foot disintegrated and the troops ravaged the countryside and villages through which they passed. With the French still some distance behind, Moore's army finally reached Corunna on 11 January 1809 in a state of total exhaustion.

Richard and his fellow soldiers were fortunate to have marched with Baird rather than with Moore on the 'March of Death'; they were better equipped, better fed and less fatigued having only recently arrived from England. Nevertheless, his journey was still an arduous one. A private, who was also marching with Baird, wrote

> ... I shudder as I reflect on the groaning of the dying and the curses of the living ... the army was in a wretched condition, from the want of provisions, shoes, and blankets ... When we got upon the mountainous roads we found them covered with deep snow ... When we halted ... the earth was our bed, the sky our covering, and the loud winds sang us to sleep ...[8]

The British neared Corunna and, with the French fast approaching, watched anxiously for the boats to arrive to take them back to England. By 14 January, 250 ships were anchored off-shore and the sick, the wounded and the cavalry were quickly loaded on board. The transport ships intended to carry the bulk of the army back to England did not, however, reach Corunna from Vigo until 15 January. With the French closing in, the waiting men were said to be in a state of cheery defiance, relieved at the prospect of going into battle after so many weeks spent in miserable retreat. Richard's company formed part of

Baird's division, stationed on a ridge overlooking the village of Elvina, to the south-east of Corunna.

The day of 16 January began misty and cold, with both sides waiting and watching. At about 2 p.m. the French attacked. Baird's men above Elvina, Richard among them, were almost immediately bombarded by fierce cannon fire from the French. When Baird was wounded, Sir John Moore took his place, watching and directing the battle from Elvina; and it was there that he was fatally hit. The fierce fighting continued, focusing on the village, with the French approaching from the south and the east. Richard and his fellow soldiers were ordered forward to assist the regiments in Elvina itself and, after a grim battle fought with bitter fury on the slippery gorse- and rock-covered ridges, succeeded in driving back the French.[9] For many of the soldiers, including Richard, it was their first taste of real battle. The noise was deafening, casualties were high and the ammunition ran low; and it was not until nightfall that the French finally retired. Richard's left arm was severed just below his elbow. Wounded and no doubt in great pain, it is to be hoped that he was on one of the first boats to leave Corunna bound for England on 17 January.

The voyage back to England after the defeat was a horrible experience, particularly for men (and the women and children with them) who were hungry, exhausted, wounded or dying. Driven by a ferocious south-westerly gale, the journey was rough and fast. The sea storms were so violent and persistent that the increasingly sickly soldiers were unable to disembark for several days. When they finally did, a soldier named Benjamin Harris wrote that they looked 'more like the rakings of hell than the fragments of an army'.[10] Reports from *The Times* paint a vivid picture of the scenes at Plymouth as the sick, wounded and dying arrived.

> ... Now indeed, we have the miseries of war brought home to our own
> doors ... occasioned by the arrival of so many transports with troops
> ... wounds of some of whom have never been dressed, while others
> are dying from want ... upwards of £500 have been subscribed for
> the relief of the sufferers ... and every woman, of every description,
> who had a second garment, has given it to the sufferers. Every house
> has become a hospital; for every family receives a sick or wounded
> person, giving food, and necessaries of all kinds ... great numbers are
> dying every day ... Ladies in person attend the sick and wounded,
> dressing the wounds of the soldiers themselves; thus supplying the
> want of sufficient numbers of medical men, at the same time that
> many of the wounds, from not having been examined, were in a putrid

and most offensive state ... Every female in Plymouth is employed in
making shirts, petticoats, caps, gowns, and necessary clothing for the
women ...[11]

Where was Richard Pendlebury during these dark and difficult days? His arm
may already have been amputated as it was increasingly the practice to carry out
amputations swiftly on the battlefield to reduce the danger of death by gangrene;
alternatively, it may have been amputated aboard a heaving and tossing ship on
the voyage back to Plymouth, as was the arm of his commander Baird.[12] Richard
was barely 21 years old. No doubt bewildered and in great discomfort, he was at
some stage taken to London, hopefully by boat rather than coach for a journey
overland would have lasted many hours along jolting roads in the winter months.
It would have been agony for a man whose arm had been so recently amputated.

An indication of the seriousness of Richard's wound and of his suffering is
to be found in the fact that his official discharge from the army was delayed
by some months. Temporarily assigned to General Clinton's company, he was
officially discharged from the army on 3 July and three weeks later admitted to
the Royal Hospital Chelsea. His discharge papers read

> Richard Pendlebury private in M. Genl Clinton's Company in the
> Regiment aforesaid: born in the Parish of Ratcliff near the Town of
> Manchester in the County of Lancaster was enlisted at the Age of
> 17 Years; & 9 months and hath served in the said Regiment for the
> Space of three Years and two hundred & ninety four Days, as well as
> in other Corps, after the Age of Eighteen, according to the following
> Statement, but in consequence of Loss of the Left Arm is rendered
> unfit for further Service, and is hereby discharged ... the following
> is a Description of the said Richard Pendlebury. He is about 21 Years
> of Age, is 5 Feet 6½ Inches in height, with brown Hair grey Eyes fair
> Complexion, by Trade a Bleacher.
>
> STATEMENT OF SERVICE
> 1st Foot Guards from 3 Oct. 1805 to 3 July 1809
> Total Service as Private 3 Years 274 Days

An additional note added in the margin of the document read: '1 Foot Guards
Duke of York Richd Pendlebury Aged – 21 Served 3 nine-twelfths years Lost
his left arm Ratcliffe Lancashire a Bleacher 9d'.[13]

Life after the army: Richard, Rebecca, Tom and Henry in London

Richard was required to have a medical examination before he could be admitted to hospital, and a record of his examination has survived, along with those of 159 other wounded soldiers seen on the same day. Entries were brief. Richard's read simply 'Richd Pendlebury 39/12 service; 21; lost his left arm; Radcliffe; Bleacher; 5' 6½" Brown [hair] Grey [eyes] Fair [complexion]'.[14]

A few individuals listed in the register have campaigns noted alongside their names. The details bear witness to the scale of the struggle between two great empires: the battles of Vimeira, Pondicherry, Calcavelos, Corunna, Buenos Ayris, Protaia; and campaigns in South America, Portugal, Flanders, and Egypt. The hospital must have been overflowing with the wounded and sick. Richard would have taken his place alongside the 26 people who were listed on the same page as him. Their injuries make sad reading: one blind, one nearly blind and one deaf; two consumptive; two 'ruptured'; four 'worn out' (one with a bad leg and the other rheumatic) and one sickly and debilitated; two with loss of limbs (one right leg, one left arm), fractures (thigh, limb), a disabled leg and a 'swelled' leg from the kick of a horse; one 'deranged' and two with epileptic fits; one with 'ill health' and one with 'infirmity'; one with 'incontinence of urine and debility'; and one who was 'scropholous' and one 'paralytic'.

The pension of 9d. per week that Richard was awarded seems to have been the going rate for the loss of a limb. Four other men listed as wounded at Corunna received similar pensions:

Age	Injury	Pension
36	Lost arm	9d.
24	Lost arm near shoulder, contused breast wound	1s.
28	Lost right hand	9d.
35	Contracted arm and wounded	9d.

The lowest pension, of just 5d. a week, was given to a 59-year-old whose sight had been injured. The highest awards appear to have been granted to older men or to the very sick and incurable:

Age	Injury	Pension	
60	Worn out	2s.	½d.
51	Worn out	2s.	2½d.

67

44	Chronic rheumatism	2s.	1d.
52	Pulmonic affection and worn out	2s.	
30	Disability from syphilis	2s.	½d.

What is striking about this register is the number of men who are described as 'worn out'. It is a reminder of their relentless and troubled passage across northern Spain. Marching featured heavily in any soldier's life. Richard himself had spent more than two years marching backwards and forwards across Kent and Sussex before his far more gruelling trek over the Galician mountains in Spain. In the aftermath of Corunna, people were outraged to hear that so many of the soldiers had marched across mud and snow almost shoeless. When Sir Marc Isambard Brunel, of engineering fame, asked to see a sample of the footwear worn by the soldiers, he discovered that a layer of clay had been inserted, presumably for cushioning, between the inner and outer soles. As soon as this clay became damp, the shoes disintegrated. Brunel quickly set about inventing a machine to make shoes that were sturdy and that differentiated between left and right feet, and these he sold to the British army, which issued them to the soldiers from 1812 onwards.[15]

Richard' pension was increased in 1814 (from 9d. to 1s.), and he continued to be classified as an in-patient until 1819. A note in his records reads 'Chelsea College, 26th Dec. 1819 Outpatient from this date. Signed William Noy [rest illegible] Admitted 27 July 1809 House 31 July 1819 Chelsea.'[16] Even as an in-patient, he and his wife Rebecca spent some time together (in either Lancashire or London), and their first two children, Tom and Ann, were born and baptised in St Mary the Virgin, Radcliffe, in 1810 and 1812 respectively, and baby Ann was buried there in 1813. By 1815, however, he and Rebecca had settled in London, in Strutton Ground, close by the Chelsea barracks and hospital. Here their third child (Ann Pollett Pendlebury, named after Richard's mother Ann née Pollett) was born in early 1815; it was to No. 12 Strutton Ground that Richard's pension was directed in 1820; and it was very near here, at Queen Square, that their fourth child, Henry, was born in the spring of 1823. His birth record gives Richard's occupation as 'Pensioner of 1st Ft Guards'.[17] Nothing further is known of Richard's whereabouts between 1823 and his death in Radcliffe in 1831; and no record has been found of either his wife Rebecca or his daughter Ann Pollett.

Queen Square was a focus of military activity. It contained a barracks where a number of 1st Foot Guards are known to have enlisted.[18] There was a concentration of military buildings nearby. The Square was situated right next to Petty France where in both 1821 and 1822 the Poor Law Rate books list an 'Infirmary 2nd Regiment Footguards'. Henry may have been born there (it closed in May 1823) or in a similar infirmary.[19] The infirmary lay just a few 100 yards to the north of Strutton Ground where Richard was living in 1820.

The same Poor Rate records suggest that the area around Queen Square and Strutton Ground was one of poor lodging houses, almshouses and hospitals. The entries for Strutton Ground, for example, contain references to households 'excused at Petty Sessions' from paying rates, particularly in 'Perkins Rents', with three people who 'will not pay'. Nearby could be found: Westminster Hospital, with 39 males and 40 females; Emmanuel Hospital, with 21 males and 26 females; the prison, with 70 men and 39 women; Palmers Almshouses, with 10 men and 14 women; and several houses with between 30 and 40 occupants. There was also St Margaret's and St John's Workhouse with a staggering 447 inmates.

Although very little is known about what happened to Richard and Rebecca between the time of Richard's discharge from the army and his death in Radcliffe in 1831, it seems highly likely that their lives centred around the Queen Square area and the military presence there. It is tempting to think of them both working in the kitchens of the barracks under the supervision of a certain cook called William Barnard. William had a daughter Gussy who lived in Greycoat Street in 1815 and in South James Street in 1829, only a short distance from Strutton Ground.[20] At some stage, Richard and Rebecca's son Tom met and fell in love with Gussy. By 1834 he was writing her a love letter from St Paul's Churchyard (see below, page 71).

Richard died in 1831, presumably in Radcliffe, as it was there that he was buried. Richard's final years may have been eased by the small amount of the Swinton rent money he was entitled to under the terms of his father's will. If so, it can have been only in his very last years as he would not have received his quarter share of the rents until after the death of his mother Ann, and after a total of £80 had been distributed to his four sisters Betty, Nancy, Alice and Ann.

Richard left two young sons, Tom (aged 21) and Henry (aged 8). Henry was taken into the care of his Aunt Ann and her husband Joseph Barron and set down roots in Yorkshire, although he remained close to his brother and always showed a fondness for London life. Radcliffe-born Tom was raised in London, married a Londoner and lived and died a Londoner. With him, this story now moves from the outskirts of Manchester to Bermondsey, the Thames and the great warehouses of St Paul's.

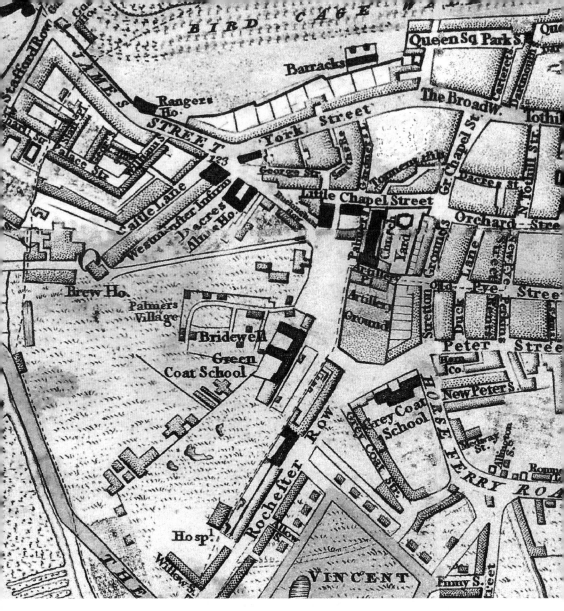

8 Addresses in Westminster, 1815–34.[21]

Greycoat Street (to left of Greycoat School) Tom's future father-in-law William Barnard lived at No. 13, 1815.

Strutton Ground (to right of artillery ground) Richard living at No. 12, 1821 and 1823

Queen Square (top, just to right of the barracks) Henry Pendlebury born here, 1823.

Emmy Street (bottom right) Tom's future mother-in-law Caroline. Barnard lived here, 1832

Charles Street (top left, off Stafford Row) Tom's future wife Gussy lived here with mother, 1834 onwards.

The Royal Hospital Chelsea is situated just outside the bottom left corner of this map.

CHAPTER NINE

'I niver throw dirty warter in any man's face': Tom and Gussy, 1836–1837

T HOMAS PENDLEBURY, son of Richard and Rebecca Pendlebury, was baptised on 15 July 1810 in the church of St Mary the Virgin, Radcliffe, on the outskirts of Manchester, almost nine months after his father had been discharged from the army after losing part of his left arm at the battle of Corunna. 'Tom', as he was called by his friends, spent much of his childhood in Westminster. By his early twenties, he had settled permanently in London and was working in the St Paul's area with many of the people who feature later in this story – Joseph Barron, the Milners, and Robert Jaques.

In 1834 Tom was in love. He wrote a long love letter to Gussy Barnard:

St Pauls Churchyard, Private

My Ever Dear Augusta,
I feel my self verry unhappy conserning matters which you are acuainted with, but i hope it is for the better that you are thinking of changeing your sittuation of life.

My Dear girl i wish you well with all my hart, and never shall i forget you for your love and kindnis to me so long as i live my Deares girl you may rest your peaseful mind about what you mentioned to me on sunday last, belive me, Thomas is not one of that kind, i niver throw dirty warter in any man's face so my Dear you need not fear that.

I pondered all the sunday afternoon with reading your letters which you sent me in our loving days, but when i look back i cannot help sieghing. My Dear Gussey, you may think light of this but it is no jest.

I thought nothing would of parted us but Death do not think me to rash with you but my Dear i am sorry to say i have found a greate alteration in you lately not but what you would do any thing for me that lays in your power, but i cannot concive that you have that Love for me that you had once or else it is emagination, i cannot tell.

But my Dear girl, if you will in plain terms tell me if you have that love for me as you had once, and love no other, then i shall be satisfied and i shall be at rest and know what to do, my Dreams has been verry strange, moore so on saturday night. I know there is a party that is triing verry hard to set you against me but i do not give a dam for them…are all Born, but not all Buried i may be able to give them a turn some day.

My Dearest Girl, these few lines comes with my kind love to you if it will be accepted if not, i cannot help it.

I am going to islington every day til Wedensday and shall not be home before nine aclock but if you will please to answere this by post i shall be more satisfied than waiting to see you on wedensday, and it will please me better.

Believe me to be your ever afectionate Tom till life remains when you have writen answere please to Burn it as i wish no one to see it but yourself

Thos Pendlebury …

Tom was literate, unlike his father. He wrote easily and his spelling and handwriting were good. Although he used little or no punctuation, this was not uncommon at the time. Even quite literate people avoided using full stops and capital letters in their domestic correspondence. He certainly wrote better than his younger brother Henry who was brought up by Ann and Joseph Barron in Yorkshire. He may have learned his skills under the auspices of his grandfather Francis or great-granduncle Nathan, both parish clerks of Radcliffe.

Gussy Barnard and her family

Tom's sweetheart Augusta (Gussy) was a Londoner through and through. Like Tom, she had grown up in the streets around Queen Square barracks, and her parents are likely to have known his. Her father, William Barnard, described variously as a 'King's Cook', a 'Cook', a 'Gentleman' and a 'Domestic Servant Cook' was more affluent than Tom's because he was able to leave sufficient money to be put into a trust for his daughters. A few details of William's life – and a nice image of him storing his important papers in a red morocco leather box – have survived in a legal document drawn up four years after his death

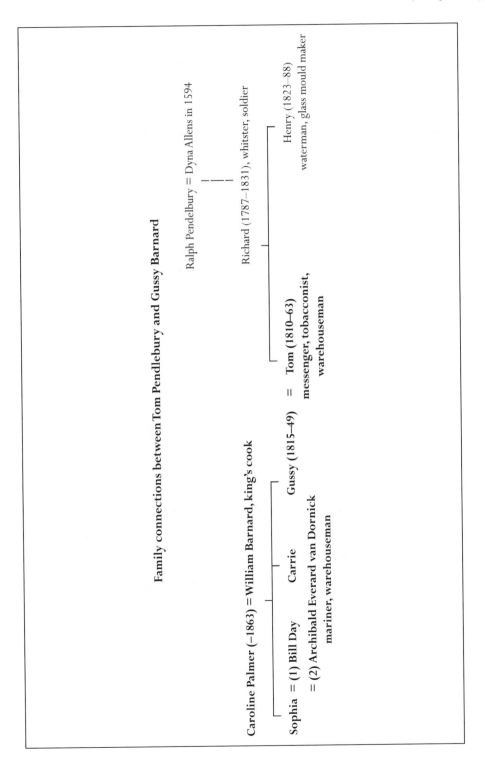

Family connections between Tom Pendlebury and Gussy Barnard

Ralph Pendelbury = Dyna Allens in 1594

Richard (1787–1831), whitster, soldier

Henry (1823–88)
waterman, glass mould maker

Tom (1810–63)
messenger, tobacconist,
warehouseman

=

Gussy (1815–49)

Caroline Palmer (–1863) = William Barnard, king's cook

Carrie

Sophia = (1) Bill Day
= (2) Archibald Everard van Dornick
mariner, warehouseman

My Dearest girl, these few lines comes
with my kind love to you if it will bee
accepted if not i cannot help it
I am going to islington every day til
wedensday and shall not be home
before nine oclock but if you will
please to answare this by post i shall
be moore satisfied than marching to see
you on wedensday and it will please
me better

belive me to be your ever
afectinate Tom till life
remains when you have written
answare please to Burn it
as i wish no one to see it
but yourself

T.W. Pendlebury
7 St Pauls Church
Yard

9 The final page of Tom Pendlebury's letter to Gussy Barnard, 8 June 1834.

when his widow Caroline went to court to swear an affidavit about his will in order to access her legacy. Caroline Barnard, her sister Mary and his daughter Caroline (Gussy's older sister) appeared before the magistrates, and their voices still echo through the rather dry legal language.

The affidavit records that Caroline Barnard, her sister Mary Painter and her daughter Caroline, all living at 13 Frederick Street Regent Street Vauxhall Road, appeared in court to swear that Caroline (senior) was the widow of William who had lived at 5 South James Street and died in September 1829.[1] Caroline explained that William had worked as a cook in the late King George III's kitchen and drawn up his will just before being sent out to France in 1815 'on the occasion of King Louis' (probably a reference to the restoration of Louis XVIII in 1814). He had left this will in the safekeeping of his wife during his six weeks absence and, when he returned, Caroline '... saw the same and read it and that shortly after the death of the said deceased found the same in a red morocco case or dressing case which the said deceased kept constantly by him amongst receipt for money and other papers of importance belonging to the said deceased ...'

Caroline declared that the document had remained in her possession until its disappearance a year or so after she found work as a housekeeper. Her daughter also testified to the fact that she had seen her father's will on several occasions in his red morocco case and, together with her aunt, swore that her mother was the only named legatee. They all agreed that the will had not been seen for over a year, that it left everything to Caroline, and '... that they verily believe that the same has been accidentally burnt or destroyed and they verily believe that there is not ... or copy of the said will ...'

It can have been no coincidence that Caroline Barnard appeared in court on the very day of her oldest daughter Sophia's marriage to a young man called William Day. No doubt Caroline wanted to release some of the trust money to pay for the wedding or to give her daughter as a dowry. She would no doubt have done the same when her other daughter, Gussy, married Tom three years later.

The Barnards remained an intimate part of Tom's world. Charles Street, where Gussy lived with her mother and two sisters at the time the Pendlebury letters begin, was next to Queen Square where Tom's brother Henry had been born in 1823. Gussy's older sister Sophia, with her first husband William Day and, after his death, her second husband Archibald Everard Van Dornick, regularly joined Tom and his brother Henry in their jaunts around town: they were the 'Bill and Sophie' and the 'Archie and Sophie' mentioned in Henry's letters to Tom. Gussy had two other sisters: Caroline (who appeared in court with her mother and who was probably the 'Carrie' or 'Carrey' mentioned in several early letters); and Maria, who was living at the Charles Street address in 1841.*

Gussy's mother remained close to all four of her daughters. Carrie and Maria and, later, her grandson William, lived with her at times; and, towards the very end of her life, she moved in with her daughter Sophia van Dornick at 4 Bear Lane. It was here that she died in 1863, at the age of 81, from 'General Debility'.

Robert Jaques, the *Java*, India and an enduring love

At the time that Tom was writing love letters to Gussy, he was working periodically for Robert Jaques. Jaques was a master mariner and merchant who had worked for the East India Company and still travelled on occasion to India. In 1836 he took Tom with him. Tom needed the work, but the timing could not have been worse. He was actively wooing Gussy and very much in love with her but was not yet assured that she would become his wife. There are hints in his letters to her that their courtship was not entirely without its difficulties and he had still not succeeded in marrying her over two years after his first known love letter written from St Paul's Churchyard.

Tom sailed to India aboard the *Java*. When he boarded her towards the end of June 1836, she had just returned from a voyage to Bombay (*The Times* reported her leaving Amsterdam bound for London on 17 June). He had to wait around on board for several weeks until the ship was finally ready to sail. This was standard practice as these great trading ships were often delayed until they were nearly full before setting sail: half-empty ships meant a loss of profits so vessels were often forced to wait while aggressive advertising was used to attract cargo and passengers. Three notices appeared in *The Times* a few weeks after Tom's return that show how the system worked.[2]

December 2nd	FOR BOMBAY, the fine, first-class, British-built ship JAVA, 560 tons register, JOHN TODD, Commander. She has an airy poop and excellent accommodations for passengers. Lying in the London Docks. For freight or passage apply to Messrs. Lyall, Brothers, and Co., Great St. Hellen's; or to Henry and Calvart Toulmin, 8, George-yard, Lombard street.

---

* This information is taken from the 1841 Census. Basic facts about names, ages and addresses that are linked to census years (1841, 1851, 1861, 1871, 1881, 1891 and 1911) are taken from the website http://www.ancestry.co.uk where they are produced in partnership with the National Archives. Individual source references have been omitted.

December 14th   FIRST SHIP direct for BOMBAY, the fine fast sailing British-built ship JAVA, A1, burden 560 tons, coppered and copper fastened ...

December 21st   FOR BOMBAY DIRECT, – NOTICE TO SHIPPERS. – The JAVA, AI, burden 560 tons, JOHN TODD, Commander; lying in the London Docks, now completing her loading. Shippers are respectfully requested to have goods alongside and cleared on Saturday morning, 23 inst. Early application to be made to Henry and Calvert Toulmin, 8, George-yard, Lombard street. N.H. The fine AI ship Indus will succeed the above vessel, and will sail positively on the 15th January, 1838

Tom was in Gravesend by 27 June, but it was not until five weeks later (3 August) that *The Times* reported that the *Java*, bound for Bombay, was 'entered

10   The *Queen* East Indiaman, 1842.[3] The *Java* in which Tom sailed would have been similar to this ship.

outwards for loading' at the Custom-House. Three letters have survived from this period of waiting, and they all show Tom's high state of anxiety not only about leaving behind the girl he loved but also about the long, difficult and dangerous voyage that lay ahead in a ship that was already well past its prime.

Gravesend June 27th 1836

My Dearest Augusta,

I write this to wish you goodbye for twelve months, I hope this letter will find you in good health as it leaves me at present. I hope you will be a good girl till I return. My dear girl I spent a very unhappy day on Sunday but I am in better spirits now we are getting under way to sail on Tuesday evening, and I have good hopes to be home within the time stated. God bless you my dearest girl give my best love to mother and Carrey and not forgetting...and all other enquiring friends.

Believe me my dearest Gussey to be yours while life remains,
Thomas Pendlebury

A shortage of ship's hands caused further delay. Poor Tom! His next letter (undated) sounded even more anxious.

My Dearest Augusta

I should like to hear from you to know how you are getting on. I am sorry to say we cannot go for the want of hands. My dear girl you must write as soon as possible and direct to Thos. Pendlebury on board the Java Gravesend with speed with the general post.

Yours very fondly Thos.
Write immediately
Charles I think is going with us

Gussy did reply quickly to Tom's great satisfaction, as his next letter (dated 'Sunday') to her shows.

My Ever Dear A ...

Your Letter to me was so proudly received that i could not refrain from shedding a tear i am sorry to say that there is not time for you to come down on monday as we sail at 4 in the morning gold would i give to see you if possible my Dearest sorry am i to hear of you being unwell but i hope and trust you will be soon better for my sake for you i live and happy will be the day when i return my Dear make things ready for my return you know what. my Dear I am sorry i left London not but i am well hearted for every boddy is very kind to me but unhappy on acount of leaving you my Dearest. You speak of Charles being with me on Sunday it true he was and i should of sent a note by him only i expected to come to London i hope you are not angry –

i am happy to say that i have got my friend Charles with me witch makes me much more comfortable and we mess together. Charles es sister will call upon you in course of the week please to give my kind love to Bill and Sophia ... all other inquiring friends you may not ... afternoon till i return but do not ... i am twelve months gone as our ship sails Home good for ever bless you my Dear girl

belive me to be your constant and true lover Thos. Pendlebury

'Carrey' was Gussy's older sister Caroline who later worked as a servant in Cornwall Terrace. The 'Bill and Sophia' mentioned in this letter were Gussy's husband-in-law and sister; 'Charles' was probably Charles Milner, brother of Robert Milner. Tom's unhappiness at being parted from Gussy is clear. They were now as good as betrothed, and Tom had Gussy's 'little ring' (see the letter below) to comfort him on his long journey.

Little did Tom know that the ship on which he travelled was later to become infamous for her ill-fated voyage to Australia two years later. 'That horrid ship, the *Java*' had been built in the Calcutta Dockyards in 1811 during the Napoleonic Wars.[4] She was a large merchant ship, constructed of teak and used for some years by the East India Company. She regularly sailed to North America, the West Indies, South Africa and New Zealand as well as to ports closer to England. After Tom's return in August 1837, for example, she made another short voyage before setting sail for India again in early 1838.

Tom's voyage was a difficult one: the seas were rough, the mast broke, food ran short and his employer Jaques was 'as unhappy as he could be'. This long letter written aboard ship and posted in Mauritius is, sadly, the only letter that survives from Tom's journey. It was postmarked 6 February 1837.

Maurouses [Mauritius] 18th October 1836

My Ever Dear and long lost Augusta,

It is with pleasure i write to you hoping this letter may find you and your Mother and Carrey and all friends well i am happy to say that I am enjoying a good state of health but i cannot boast of being happy for moor reasons than one the first my love is on your account for leaving you behind my Dear girl i am sorry to say the ship is the most uncomfortableest i ever was in the only comfort i have is to read your letter when i can get in a quiet corner i am sorry to say that my friend Charles is not much company for me for he has been so verry ill all the voayge he is a mear skeliton but he seems to be getting better every day but to make amens he has scalded his foot wich has made him keep his bed a fortnight longer i beg of you my Dear to give his kind love to his sister but not to tell her any thing to make her uncomfortable My Dear girl whe have had some verry seveuir weather two gales of wind one of them carryed away the missen mast but no one lost but near losing the ship and all hands i am much pleased with the passage for i am getting as stout and jolly as a sand boy but cannot boust of being happy and for reasons you may easly ges

I hope nothing has happened since my departure conserning what we talked of at our last parting for it as troubled me a great deal but my Dearest girl i hope at my arival home i shall find you and all things comfortable i shall wish you to write to me when you hear of the arrival of the ship wich will be before whe get to gravesend for i have a reason for your not coming on Board you must direct it as before to be left but should you ascertain the day and you come down i will come on shoore to meet you i hope my love you have been a good girl and you will find me the same to you my life please not to forget the Box that is you know whare we calculate about being home about the latter end of May should nothing happen us i am sorry to say that Mr Jaques is as unhappy as he can be but my other master that is companion is a mad but a jolly good fellow and he cheers us up at times.

My Dearest girl i shall spend my Christmas in Calcutta and i hope you will drink my health altho i am absent and far a way and i shall do the same i am sorry i cannot give you any account of any places for i have not seen land since i left Portsmouth, but i shall be able to spin you a good yarn when I return of my travels which will amuse you many a hour. my Dear girl I wish I was with you now, it should take some trouble to part us but i hope the time will soon come when we shall meet again your little ring is a great treasure to me as well as a pleasure for when i look at it i think of you and cannot help seighing which relives the heart for a time.

Whe are now about one month sail from Calcutta, the place whare this letter come from is the ile of France whare we are obliged to run in for Bisquits and water so verry short of provisions, my Dear Augusta i should like to heare from you if you can spare time to

write a long letter with all the particuloor news. Mr Jaques will have
letters forwarded to him at Santlena but you need not go to St Pauls to
enquire but go by these directions and I shall be shoore to receive it.

Address To Thomas Pendlebury Ship "Java" St Helena
Care of Horatio Hardy Jerusalem Coffee House Cornhill, London
write by the end of February 1837 & send it to Cornhill post paid
My Dear girl please not to fail writing if you have time for news
from you will be as good as gold to me my love.

Belive me to be your true and affectionate lover Thos. Pendlebury

Ile de France was the eighteenth-century name for Mauritius, and the
Jerusalem Coffee-House was one of the oldest of the city news-rooms, frequented
by merchants and captains connected with the trade with China, India and
Australia. Mauritius and India, and a Christmas spent in Calcutta, must have
been exotic experiences for young Tom.

Back in London, Gussy continued to live with her mother and one or more
of her sisters at 19 Charles Street. Two short letters belong to this period, both
sent to her by 'E. Heath'. In the first, the writer asked her to visit her and in
the second gave instructions for some material she wanted. The letters are dated
18 July and 1 February.

My Dear Miss Barnard
    Will you have the goodness to come up to me today if Possible you
can if you think it worth your wiel
    Your very affectionate
    Sert E Heath

and

My Dear
    Don't bay me a blond vale for my bonnet I think I shall like it better
with out an you may bay me a verry neat little flaure for my bonnet cap
if you please.
    Mind it is very neat and Prettey
    Truly E Heath
    We forgot Sulk linen for my Cape you must get it for me if you pl

Gussy, it appears, was doing some dressmaking for Elizabeth Heath, a spinster in
her early fifties and the oldest of seven female and four male servants working for

Sir John and Lady Beckett in Shalford Place, Marylebone. As the senior servant, Elizabeth had some status; hence she wrote to Gussy more or less as an equal and, in her second letter, very affectionately. Shalford Place was a 'smart' address in 1841: next door to the Becketts lived a barrister and two doors away George Hayter (a 'painter of history') who was a notable English painter (Queen Victoria appointed him as her Principal Painter in Ordinary and knighted him in 1841).

In July 1837, after eleven months on the high seas, the *Java* with Tom aboard was safely back in home waters. An announcement in *The Times* gives a flavour of society on board these great sailing ships.

> July 14th 1837 Java, off Portland:
> From Bengal, Madras, and St. Helena, the East India ship Java, Captain R. Jobling (Hon. Company's Service), sailed from Sandheads [sandbanks just to the east of Ceylon], February 15, from Madras Roads [Bay of Bengal] March 5, and from St. Helena May 29. The following is a list of passengers embarked on board the Java:-
> From Madras, his Excellency the Right Hon. Lieutenant-General Sir Frederich Adam, K.C.B. and G.C.M.G., late Governor of the Madras Presidency; Lieutenant James Talbot Airey, Her Majesty's 3rd Regiment or Buffs, Aide-de-Camp to his Excellency.
> From Calcutta, Mrs. Smoult, Mrs. Parish, Mrs. Strange, and Mrs. Hemming; W.H.Smoult, Esq., Barrister and late Registrar of the Supreme Court of Calcutta; the Rev. Dr. Parish, D.C.L.; Captain Strange, Her Majesty's 26th Regiment or Cameronians; Captain Bracebridge Hemming, ditto (died on board at Madras, February 25); Lieutenant J. Shum, ditto, Commanding Her Majesty's Invalids on board; Ensign Robson, ditto (died at sea, April 5th); Lieutenant Moulrie, 57th Regiment Bengal Native infantry; Dr. Thompson, Bengal Medical Establishment; Masters Alexander and Thomas Strange, Miss Elizabeth Hemming, and 43 invalids; 3 women and 7 children from Her Majesty's regiments in India; William Cook, European, servant to W.H.Smoult, Esq.; and 1 native Ayah, servant to Mrs. Smoult.

The following passengers also embarked from the *Java* at Madras:

> from Calcutta:– The Rev. Mr. Anderson, missionary; G.S.Morris, Esq., Bengal Civil service; Captain Cooper, Her Majesty's 45th Regiment; Captain Shell, 12th Regiment Madras Native Infantry; Lieutenant Baynes, Bombay Artillery; Lieutenant Kaye, Bengal Artillery; Ensign

11 Tom and Gussy's marriage certificate, 1837.

Moorcroft, Madras Native Infantry; Mar Hallowell, R.N.; John Peters, Esq., Madras Civil service; Miss Blenkinsop and 4 native servants.

The likes of Tom and his master Robert Jaques received no mention. *The Times* concluded its notice with the words '... Ships spoken with, The Prince Regent yacht, Captain Cogan (Indian Navy), all well, on the 5th of March, entering Madras Roads, with the Right Hon. Lord Elphinstone, the present Governor of the Madras Presidency, on board ...' Thus was news spread about the whereabouts and safety of vessels and the noteworthy people aboard them.

On his return, Tom lost no time in tying the knot. Little more than a month later, on 29 August 1837, he married Gussy in her local parish church of St Margaret, Westminster. He gave his profession as 'messenger', and his brother-in-law William Day acted as one of the witnesses, with Gussy's sister Caroline being the other. Within two years, Tom and Gussy had moved from her mother's address to their own lodgings in Jane Street Broad Wall Lambeth.

Postscript on the *Java*[5]

The *Java* had time to make one other long voyage before she set sail from London to Portsmouth in 1839 on the start of what became a notorious voyage to Adelaide in southern Australia. It was just two years after Tom had sailed in her and she was overloaded with emigrants. The newspapers described her as 'a large ship which left St Katherine's Dock [London] ... with upwards of 300 emigrants on board for South Australia, the sides of which were so rotten and decayed that the carpenters who were engaged in fitting her out declared that the planks would not retain a screw or nail.' Her master for this particular ill-fated voyage was a man called Driver who knew her well: he had sailed her between London and Calcutta in 1825 and between London and India in 1833. On this voyage, however, it was the attitude of the crew, and of the Surgeon-Superintendent, rather than the poor state of the ship, that brought the passengers so much misery. By the time she docked in Holdfast Bay (Adelaide), 30 of her passengers had died from disease, malnutrition and starvation. The *Java* ended her life as a coal hulk off Gibraltar before being broken up in 1939.

CHAPTER TEN

'Murky' but the best place to live:
Tom Pendlebury's London, 1833–1863

The Leviathan metropolis

It was impossible to tell where the monster city began or ended, for the buildings stretched, not only to the horizon on either side, but far away into the distance, where, owing to the coming shades of evening and the dense fumes from the million chimneys, the town seemed to blend into the sky, so that there was no distinguishing earth from heaven.[1]

M AYHEW's words, written a year before Tom died, described a London that had grown beyond recognition during the 30 years that Tom had lived there. Between 1833 and his death in 1863, Tom, first with Gussy and then, after her death in 1849, with his second wife Jane, lived in the area around present-day Waterloo East Station. He rented accommodation in Catherine St, Jane St, John Street, Curtiss Hatch, Roupell St and Brad St, all within a few minutes' walk of each other and less than half a mile from the river. It was an unhealthy, overcrowded, noisy and dirty place to live, even before the chaos caused by the arrival of the railways.

Lambeth Marsh

The streets where Tom lived were all built upon what was loosely termed Lambeth Marsh in the eighteenth century when most of the northern part of Lambeth was marshland intersected by numerous ditches. The construction of Westminster Bridge Road and Kennington Road in about 1750 led to the development of some houses and then a road (now Upper Marsh and Lower Marsh) built across the marshes towards Westminster Bridge. Tom's patch was known as 'Wild Marsh' because it was low-lying swampland open to the

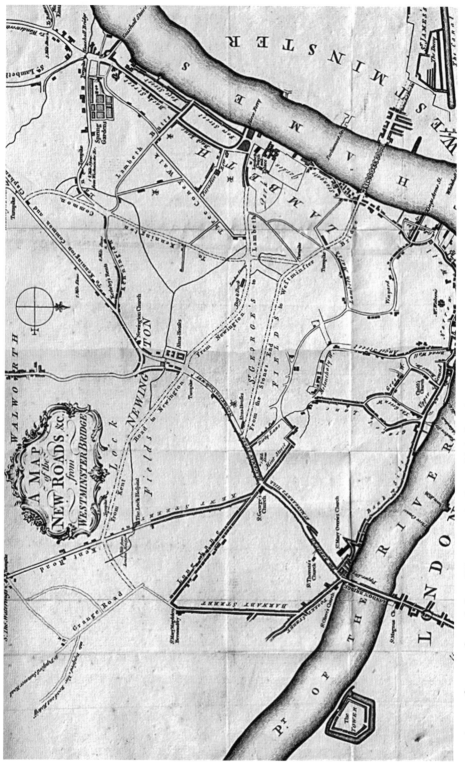

12   A map of new roads south from Westminster bridge, published in the Gentleman's Magazine, 1753. (South is at the top of the map.)

tidal waters of the Thames. It was for this reason that a leading botanist called William Curtis (1746–99) had earlier chosen to establish his Lambeth Botanic Garden here.[2] The area around these streets was not a good place to live, even for bog plants. William Curtis had chosen this location as the site of his garden because 'the situation being low, renders it peculiarly favourable to the growth of aquatic and bog plants'. However, he decided to move the garden to Brompton in 1789 because

> ... I had long observed with ... regret, that I had an enemy to contend with in Lambeth Marsh, which neither time, nor ingenuity, nor industry, could vanquish; and ... the smoke of London, which, except when the wind blew from the South, constantly enveloped my plants ... In addition to this grand obstacle, I had to contend with many smaller ones ... such as the ... effluvia of surrounding ditches, at times highly offensive ...[3]

The 'Hatch' in Curtiss Hatch (the small street where Tom and Gussy lived between 1843 and 1849) referred to a 'halfpenny hatch', a gate at which people paid halfpenny tolls to use short cuts across private land. 'Curtiss Hatch' was probably a gateway that allowed people to cross Curtis's land to visit his garden. When Curtis died, his estate was sold to John Roupell, a wealthy 'gold refiner', and redevelopment began to cater for the people who were flooding into London during the boom years that followed the final defeat of Napoleon in 1815. Lambeth Marsh was slowly drained as the newly formed Surrey and Kent Sewer Commission began to construct cesspits.[4] Waterloo Bridge, opened in 1817, stimulated further building in Lambeth Marsh and Prince's Meadows. Roupell began to construct houses in the Curtiss Hatch and Roupell Street area in about 1820.

At the time that the 1841 Census was taken, when Tom was still living in Catherine Street, Curtiss Hatch's small collection of buildings was home to 10 households, the heads of which were, for the most part, small artisans and traders. The census of that year lists: a bootmaker; two carpenters; a tailor; a housepainter; a copperplate smith; a bedstead maker; a shopman; and a laundress. There were a number of young children and young working adults who still lived at home with their parents. This latter group included a 'birther', a lawyer's clerk, an errand boy, a hat maker, a hat trimmer and a hat boy. Tom and Gussy's house at 2 Curtiss Hatch was relatively new but probably of fairly poor quality.[5] It was a pity that it was built on reclaimed marsh land. People who lived in such low-lying areas were particularly vulnerable to water-borne illnesses such as cholera: indeed, it was here that Gussy died of cholera, in 1849.

When Gussy died, Tom stayed at several temporary addresses before his second marriage to Jane Harding in 1850. Tom and his new bride quickly moved back to lodge with Mrs Skirving at 1 John Street. It was here that their first four children were born: Rebecca Jane (1851), Ann (1853), Thomas (1858) and Thomas William (1859). It was here, too, that baby Thomas fell ill with whooping cough which turned to pneumonia three weeks later and led to his death in August 1858. In the spring of 1861 they moved to 10 Brad Street where their youngest child, Emily Augusta, was born on Christmas Day 1862. Her birth was followed less than three months later (on 10 March 1863) by Tom's death, of lead poisoning.

Mrs Skirving

Mary Ann Skirving, Tom and Gussy's John Street landlady, lived with her husband James at 1 John Street and was still living there in 1861. James, a warehouseman and, later, a glassware-houseman, was only five years older than Tom. They had two children and never took in more than two people as lodgers, which suggests that Tom and Jane moved out of their house only when they needed more room after the birth of their third child.

Mrs Skirving is mentioned three times in Tom's correspondence and was clearly as much a family friend as a landlady. The first occasion is in a letter from Joseph Barron (Tom's aunt's husband) in Mexborough, sent in September 1834 after his visit to London for Tom and Gussy's wedding.

> ... According to your request we have sent a small ham 12½ lbs weight at 8d per lb 8 shillings we sent it by Capn. Elsworth on the ship Hopewell he delivers his cargo at Brooks Warf or thereabouts Operthems St London he set sail from Mexbro on the 6th of Septr instant if you settle with Mr Elsworth all will be right.
>
> I sapose the ham is for Mr and Mrs Scorving and give our kind respects to them bauth and tell them I think I shall never forget Blackfriars Bridge and Paternoster Row

The second reference to her comes in a postscript from Robert Milner in Yorkshire to Tom in London. 'Make my best regards to your very worthy friend Mrs Scriven.'[6] The third reference is found in a letter from Joseph and Ann Barron written to Tom after their visit to the Great Exhibition in London in

1851: '... Please give our respects to Mr and Mrs Skirving for their kindness to us during our stay with them. Excuse my lateness in writing.'

Joseph Barron, almost like a father to Tom, was building up a successful glassworks in Mexborough. 'Capn. Elsworth' was Edward Vinicombe Elsworthy, the captain of a packet ship registered in Falmouth; he lived near Regent's Park and was 62 years old at the time. Joseph's reference to Edward Elsworthy, Brook's Wharf and Upper Thames Street reveals his close friendship with another Yorkshire glassmaker, John Kilner, who was a couple of years younger than him and also born in Hunslet. John Kilner moved to Thornhill Lees in 1844, set up the Providence Glass Works, and began to build boats suitable for transporting finished bottles from Yorkshire to his London warehouse in Brick Hill Lane via Brook's Wharf (near St Paul's Churchyard). The Kilner Brothers later transferred their warehouse from Brick Hill Lane to Brook's Wharf and then to Horse Shoe Wharf. In about 1869, a much larger warehouse was opened at the Great Northern Railway Goods Station at King's Cross.[7] Both Joseph Barron and Tom's brother Henry worked for the Kilner brothers (see below, page 116).

Paternoster Row was well known as a street of booksellers; it ran along one side of St Paul's cathedral, with St Paul's Churchyard (where Tom worked) on the other.[8] The Barrons would have walked from Upper Thames Street and across Blackfriars Bridge to the John Street/Roupell Street area where Tom lived and Joseph and Ann stayed.

No doubt everyone knew everyone else in the small roads around Roupell Street, sandwiched in between the busy thoroughfares of Waterloo Bridge Road, the New Cut and Great Surrey Street (now Blackfriars Road). But calm and peaceful it was not. During much of the time that Tom and Gussy, and then Tom and Jane, lived here the area was blighted by the construction of the railways.

The coming of the railways

From 1844 onwards, the London and South West Railways were busy extending a railway line from Nine Elms Bridge to a new station, Waterloo Bridge. Curtiss Hatch and John Street were about four minutes' walk from the new station and the new railway track ran along the back of Tom and Jane's house in Brad Street. The dust and noise must have been unbearable as the ambitious construction required a series of arches to be built to carry the railway line above the marshy land around Waterloo Road. The building work just went on and on. Waterloo Bridge Station was still unfinished when it opened in 1848 and, after a series of alterations, had to be rebuilt in 1853. However, this was not the end of the disruption that Tom and his family faced. In 1854, for example, the

13 Over London by rail, by Doré, 1872.⁹ The location of this image is unknown; it is probably near the rail link between Vauxhall and Cannon Street; it recalls the cluster of crowded terraces dissected by intrusive railway arches to be found in the Waterloo East area where Tom lived.

London Necropolis and National Mausoleum built the Necropolis Station near the present-day Waterloo Station to carry coffins (with bodies) to Brookwood Cemetery in Woking (Surrey). Finally, after Tom's death but still during the lives of his second wife and children, a junction was constructed right by the Brad Street/Waterloo Road junction to allow trains to swing northwards across the river to the new Charing Cross Station. A new station, Waterloo East, was opened in 1869 to try to rationalise the chaotic development of new platforms and 'stations within stations' that characterised the area and to separate the trains that terminated at Waterloo and Charing Cross.

A report from the *Illustrated London News* (1 July 1848) describes the scale of the undertaking to extend the railway from Nine Elms and refers to the animal pens and detritus littering the area around Tom and Gussy's home.

... This new line was laid out in 1844 ... The site ... for the Waterloo terminus was then vacant ground, to a great extent occupied as hay-stalls and cow-yards, and by dung-heaps, and similar nuisances. This area will eventually comprise eleven acres and here will be distinct termini, in addition to that to be used immediately; and the principal facade and entrances, in the York-road, will present a frontage 600 feet in length. The length of the extension from Nine Elms to Waterloo Bridge Road is two miles, and about 50 yards; and the whole ... is upon a viaduct, at an average height of 20 feet above the level of the ground. The main bridges are six in number ...

Throughout the 1840s and 1850s, therefore, Tom and his family were living on what amounted to nothing less than a busy building site: '... A rapid deterioration followed the coming of the railways to Lambeth: streets were cut up and buildings torn down or dismembered, while the series of dark, damp arches under the lines encouraged the more disreputable element of the population to the district ...'[10] Then, once the trains were running, the area was dominated by the noise and smoke erupting from their engines and by the congestion their passengers caused. Dickens famously described the coming of the railways to Camden Town: '... Night and day the conquering engines rumbled at their distant work, or ... stood bubbling and trembling there, making the walls quake, as if they were dilating with the secret knowledge of great powers yet unsuspected in them, and strong purposes not yet achieved ...'[11] This was one of the prices that Tom had to pay for living at the industrial and commercial heart of Victorian London.

Industry along the Thames

Railways were not Tom's only problem. Within half a mile of where he lived, an 1872 map shows warehouses and factories crowding the banks of Lambeth and Southwark: an iron foundry; numerous wood yards and sawmills; wharves (pottery, cement, stone, copper, iron); the Lion Brewery; several lead works and a tall tower in which lead shot was made; store yards and cranes; and the Phoenix Gasworks.[12] By now Southwark and Bermondsey had become a centre for iron founding, leather tanning and working, wire and glass making, ship building and breaking, anchor smithing and many other kinds of industry. When refrigerated storage arrived in 1861, Hay's Wharf was rebuilt, and perishable goods from around the world began to pour in to the manufacturers who set up processing plants to receive them: Peak Frean Biscuits, Jacob's Crackers, Sarsen's

14 A City thoroughfare, 1872.[13] This image of Pickle-Herring Street (which ran alongside the Thames near London Bridge, in the heart of Bermondsey's leather market district) shows jostling crowds and merchandise of all shapes and sizes fighting their way down the narrow street towards the bridge.

Vinegar, Courage Beer, Cross & Blackwell Soups, Hartley's Jam, Pearce Duff Custard Powder and Spiller's Dog Biscuits. At the end of Tom's street was a kamptulicon factory which spewed out noxious fumes as it turned india-rubber into an elastic floor cloth that served as an early form of linoleum. And nearby stood another brewery, a lead works, a prison, a workhouse, an asylum, a disused grave yard, stables and a cab stand.

Victorian cities experienced high mortality rates and occasional epidemics such as cholera; believing that such outbreaks were caused by foul air, medical men and commentators discussed at length what they described as the 'stinking miasma' of the poor areas of the inner city. Indeed, Tom's neighbourhood would not have smelt pleasant. Apart from all the industrial pollution from nearby factories, there was the smell from animals and their detritus, from the horses that pulled the carriages, and from the cattle, sheep and pigs that were driven through the busy streets or kept and slaughtered in local yards. A traffic count in Cheapside and London Bridge in 1850 showed 1,000 horse-drawn vehicles an hour passing through these areas during the day.[14] A huge amount of manure was created and it had to be removed from the streets: in wet weather straw was scattered in walkways and storefronts to try to soak up the mud and the wet filth. As the population of London grew, so did the number of horses, from an estimated 11,000 in the early part of the nineteenth century to more than double that by the 1850s and to at least 200,000 by the end of the century.[15]

The smell of animals and rotting meat was overpowering. Butchers preferred to collect their animals live from Smithfield and to drive them home to their private slaughter-houses because it was difficult to keep dead meat fresh for long in the days before refrigeration. In 1842, Chadwick's Sanitary Report noted that slaughter-houses were found in the most populous areas and that they contributed offal and manure to the street sweepings and privy excrement that formed dunghills nearby.[16] Many butchers kept a couple of animals in their backyard before slaughtering them for processing and sale; an estimated 13,000 cows were kept in London in 1850.[17] Charles Pascoe, the brother-in-law of Tom's second wife Jane, worked as a butcher in Mitre Street, just south of the New Cut and there were plenty of other butchers in the area. To add the final touch to the disgusting brew of smells wafting around this area was the obnoxious-smelling Bermondsey Leather Market and tanning area (before the development of chemical treatments, urine and dog faeces were commonly used for tanning leather, and the effluent from what was England's largest concentration of tanning works was allowed simply to flow out into the Thames on the tide). It was less than half a mile from where Tom lived, and the prevailing breezes would have ensured that the stench reached him.

The Thames and travel by water

Tom can never have forgotten that he lived less than half a mile from the river Thames. He must often have walked or taken a horse-drawn cab along Great Surrey Street, across Blackfriars Bridge and along Bridge Street and Ludgate Hill to St Paul's Churchyard where his employers owned shops and warehouses for many years. The roads were crammed with people and the river teeming with boats because the years after Napoleon's defeat in 1815 had brought to London a boom in trade, industry, construction and people. Its population had doubled between 1801 and 1841, when it reached 2.3 million.[18] London was twice the size of Paris, four times that of Vienna and six times that of Berlin.[19]

The port of London – both the riverfront itself, which was crammed with wharves, and the many large new enclosed docks that were built downstream of the Pool of London from the late eighteenth century onwards – was the commercial heart of Victorian London. The river carried goods to and from the Americas, India and the Far East, Australia and New Zealand, Amsterdam and elsewhere. It was also used as the principal route for transporting textiles, iron, coal and tobacco in large quantities from other parts of England and abroad to the factories that grew up along its banks. London was by far Britain's busiest and most important port, and all the traffic to it had to use the river. By the 1850s, up to 600 ships could be moored at any one time alongside the quays of the port. The river also teemed with the 100 or so steam tugs ready to pull great ships into place and with the steamers who daily transported hundreds of passengers. In addition, watermen rowed passengers across and along the Thames, while lightermen 'swept' their unpowered river flats up and down the river, riding the tide and the flow of the river to transport goods to and from larger ships. It was unbelievably congested, and incoming ships could be greatly delayed waiting for a berth. Customs and Excise duty was worth almost an annual £38 million compared with the £10 million collected from property and income.[20] In 1845 Frederick Engels described the great docks of London with '... the masses of buildings, the wharves on both sides ... the countless ships along both shores, crowding ever closer together, until, at last, only a narrow passage remains in the middle of the river, a passage through which hundreds of steamers shoot by one another; all this is so vast, so impressive that a man cannot collect himself ...'[21]

The best place to live

There was, of course, another side to London: it was a place that offered plenty of entertainment and excitement. When Tom wrote in 1844 to his cousin James Wolstenholme in Radcliffe that London was a 'murky place' and that he wished he could be out of it, his cousin replied '… and I wish I was in it'. There was always fun to be had. Five minutes' walk from his home was the Royal Victoria Hall (now the Old Vic Theatre), built in 1816 on marshy ground just to the west side of a large ancient ditch dug to drain the marshes. In its heyday Edmund Kean and Grimaldi appeared there, but by 1834 only the crudest melodramas were being performed and its income came mainly from the sale of drink. It was said that the gallery audience would tie handkerchiefs together to form a rope that could be used to haul up large stone bottles of beer from the pit. In 1850 Charles Kingsley described its audience as '…the beggary and rascality of London … pouring in to their low amusement, from the neighbouring gin-palaces and thieves' cellars …' [22]

Other nearby attractions included the Canterbury Music Hall, opened in Upper Marsh in 1849, and the Bower Saloon near the junction of Upper Marsh and Stangate Street where rumbustious variety was on offer. Then, of course, there was the famous Astley's Amphitheatre, just by the south end of Westminster Bridge, which staged incredible spectacles, including Shakespeare on horseback. After the amphitheatre had been burned down for the third time, Astley's New Royal Amphitheatre of Arts opened in 1843 [23] and in 1849 the great horseback legend Andrew Ducrow starred in the 'New Grand Equestrian Military Spectacle'. [24] Tom, Gussy and Jane are unlikely to have missed out on Astleys, given its proximity and the crowds that were attracted by its magical performances.

The Pendlebury letters make no mention of any of these entertainments but they do reveal that Tom went to pubs and was certainly no stranger to gambling. Tom was generally regarded by his Lancashire relatives, and particularly by his brother Henry, as being something of a 'sport'. From his vantage point in London, Tom sent his relatives newspapers, fish, cigars and tobacco. In 1844 his Uncle and Aunt Joseph and Ann Barron thanked him for sending a newspaper, and his cousin James Wolstenholme wrote from Radcliffe '… We are much obliged to you for the favour of reading the newspaper as it was quite a new thing altogether for we had never seen one …' As a tobacconist, moreover, he was able to provide top-quality tobacco and cigars for his Lancashire relatives. In 1848 his cousin James Wolstenholme wrote

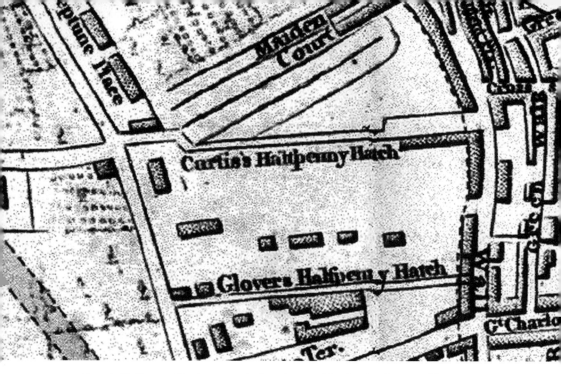

15   Curtis's Halfpenny Hatch in 1818 before the marshland redevelopment.[25] The railway line cut through the back gardens of Brad Street. The homes of Tom and Gussy, and then Tom and Jane, were all close by:

1839	Jane Street	1841	Catherine Street (tobacconist)
1843–1849	2 Curtiss Hatch	1849–1860	1 John Street
1860–1863	10 Brad Street		

16   The same area in 1872.[26]

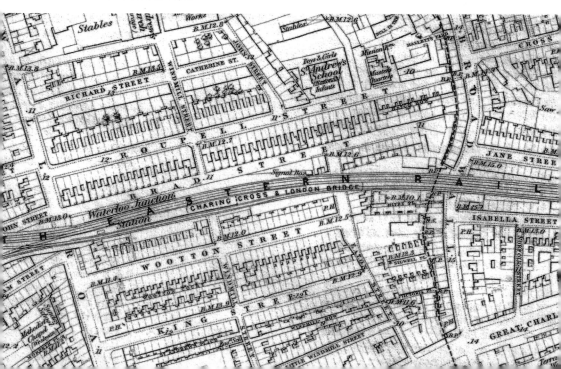

17   Jane Street, *c.*1930.[27] The small terraced houses were typical of the streets around Waterloo. The corner shop in the bottom right of the picture was a tobacconist ('Player's Weights Cigarettes' can still be seen advertised above one of its window and 'Ogdens St Julien Tobacco' on the wall beneath). This may have been Tom and Gussy's tobacconist shop in 1839 (before they moved to nearby Catherine Street). By 1841 another tobacconist had moved into Jane Street and, in 1851, a cigar maker.

> … Your esteemed favour has duly reached its destination and is much
> approved of, and all that remains on my part is to thank you for it. I
> am sure you have shown great respects but I sincerely hope the time
> is not far distant when we shall have an opportunity of returning
> gratitude for gratitude. my father approved of the tobacco very much,
> and is much obliged to you for it, for he says he never smoked milder
> tobacco in all his life …

Tom certainly knew his way around London. When Joseph Barron wanted to come to London with his son Joseph in 1851, he asked Tom to help.

> … This is to inform you that I and my son Joseph intend going to
> London to see the sights and shall be much oblige[d] to you to get us

97

a Bed – I intend to start on Sunday night by the Mail train on the
10th and if all be well shall be in London on Monday morning obout
5 o'clock and if you will have the goodness to meet us at the uston
Station it would be convenient as we are thouth strangers...

The changes that took place to Tom's immediate neighbourhood during
his lifetime are vividly demonstrated in a comparison of two maps from 1818
and 1872. Curtiss Hatch no longer exists, but its ten houses at the east end of
Roupell Street just beside Broadwall are clearly shown on an 1872 map of the
area (see page 96).

CHAPTER ELEVEN

Fun, 'flearups', and brother Henry

T o m always knew how to enjoy himself, even when times were hard. He liked to drink and to gamble and he could be good company. Thomas Perry (his brother-in-law), for example, wrote that he would like Tom to drop by to have a pipe with him. Letters from the Wolstenholmes, the Barrons and Robert Milner reveal that Tom kept in regular touch with a wide range of people, both by letter and in person, and that there were many friends and acquaintances who regularly asked after him. However, it is through his brother Henry's letters that Tom's conviviality truly comes alive.

Henry

Henry Pendlebury was born in Queen Square, Westminster, in 1823 and was 13 years younger than his brother Tom. His father died when he was eight years old (the date of his mother's death is unknown), and he went to live with his father's sister Ann and her husband Joseph Barron who already had several children of their own. Henry's letters and the comments other people made about him reveal a warm-hearted person whose adventures and sense of fun sometimes set him at odds with his rather god-fearing Uncle and Aunt Barron. His letters are filled with enthusiasm and erratic spelling, and he clearly enjoyed writing them.

Henry Pendlebury joined the glassworks business as soon as he was old enough, which pleased Joseph Barron enormously. The first reference to him in the Pendlebury documents comes in a letter from Joseph to Tom (July 1839). '... your brother Henry is well and getting pretty well on with his business ...' In 1841 Henry was in Castleford with the Barrons and working as a smith with his uncle. One year later, however, he had become restless and rebellious, much to Joseph Barron's disappointment. 'Mere idle theory' was not something that was encouraged in the Barron family.[1] Joseph wrote to Tom '... your brother Henry was very unruly for some time and was turned out of imploy with me he has been on the water about 6 Months and went to lodgings since that time there has been a way made for him to come back and he has now been working with me near 3 weeks and seems to be more attentive to his business ...'

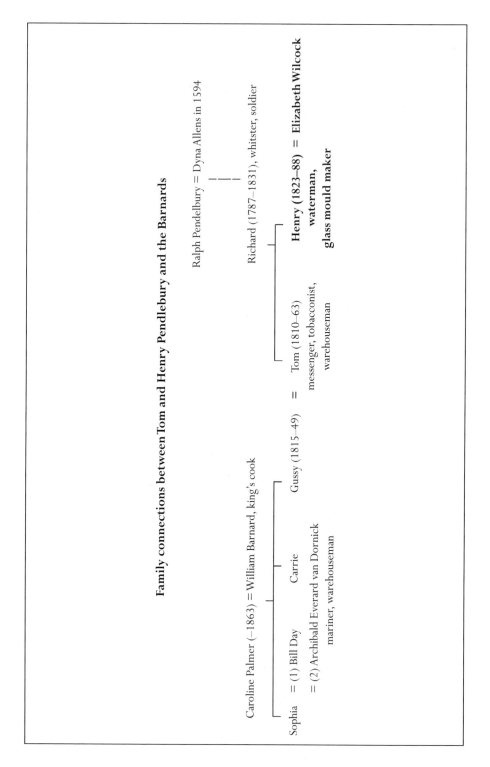

Family connections between Tom and Henry Pendlebury and the Barnards

Ralph Pendelbury = Dyna Allens in 1594

Richard (1787–1831), whitster, soldier

Caroline Palmer (–1863) = William Barnard, king's cook

Carrie

Gussy (1815–49) = Tom (1810–63) messenger, tobacconist, warehouseman

Henry (1823–88) = **Elizabeth Wilcock** **waterman,** **glass mould maker**

Sophia = (1) Bill Day
= (2) Archibald Everard van Dornick mariner, warehouseman

'On the water' is probably a reference to Henry's work on the boats. Glass-making was not the pleasantest of occupations, and Henry was probably pleased to escape it. Men worked in dusty, noisy and hot premises, handling sand, limestone, various chemicals and metals including lead, and mixing and heating these products to great temperatures. Glass blowers had to stand right near the open furnaces, their occupation '… only suitable to robust men with good chests …'[2] Henry's work making glass moulds from metal was probably little easier.

18   Letter from Joseph and Ann Barron to Tom and Gussy, 1841.

A couple of months after this (April 1843), Henry was in a more sober mood and wrote a serious letter to Tom advising how he might claim his due share of the Swinton cottage rents.

Brother Thomas Pendlebury

I wright these few lines to you oping that they will find you all in good elth as it leaves me at present I have recevied a leter from my unkil Thomas Hampson from Radcliff Bridge and they say in there leta that my unkil teld them that you might come at the time and you might have your shere with the others so if you will come down at the time to wher they draw at Black Bull in Swinton you will get yor shere with out they will, and if you cannot come your self you must send me but you must give me authority and sine your hand to it but it would be the bist for you to come down the first time your self, and the tim when they Draw is on the first Tusday in May and the first tusday in November so they send there Best respect to you and your wife also my unkil and sends there Best respect to you and my sister and my coussons sends ther kind love to you both please to wright as quick as psabil and tell us when you will come Down give my best respect to all inquring friends and my sister Pendlebury so no more from your afecened Brother Henry Pendlebury

god Bless

'Unkil Thomas Hampson' was married to Tom and Henry's father's sister Nancy. Both Hampsons became involved in the Swinton rent dispute, as a later chapter shows.

Henry could not resist adding a more personal footnote to this letter: '... Bake and dip freely ...' These words recall, perhaps, a Lancashire expression 'dip-an-bore' which referred to the practice of sharing a large dish of mashed potato with a hole in the centre filled with butter or a dish of porridge with treacle.[3] More probably, it refers to snuff-making: 'dipping snuff' was an expression used to describe the act of rubbing the substance on the gums and teeth, and 'bake' was a part of the process of preparing snuff. The manufacture of snuff formed an important part of Tom's work as a tobacconist, as a later chapter describes.

Henry loved London and often came to stay with Tom and Gussy. Joseph and Ann Barron were not always entirely happy about this. In December 1843 they wrote to Tom

> ... You say your brother Henry is stopping with you but you do not say
> what he is doing.
>
> Mr Relph called at cousin Hannah and he had 11 shillings that was
> due to Henry, he wanted to know if he might leave the money with
> her, she shed no tears over his passage to London. Look out for him,
> Hannah has got Henry four shirts according to order ...

'Mr Relph' was William Relph, a waterman, who lived in Castleford in 1841;
six years later, Henry was also working as a waterman. Hannah was Uncle James
Pendlebury's daughter, aged 20 at the time.

The Barrons were worried about Henry. He was, after all, barely 20 years old
and footloose in London. He may have stayed with Tom for some time on this
occasion because James Wolstenholme (Tom and Henry's cousin) asked Tom to
pass on his good wishes to Henry a few months later. Joseph Barron continued
to fret: Henry was on the move, though exactly where and for what purpose is
unclear. Joseph to Tom, July 1844

> ... We should have sent you an answer sooner but expecting your
> brother Henry coming sooner but they having to stop longer than they
> expected we delayed writing and he was not sure where they should
> go when they left us but he told us he would write and we recived no
> word from him yet, so we could not send you what we promised ...

A letter written by James Wolstenholme to Tom a month later reveals that
Henry went on a long sea voyage at about this time.

> ... I am sorry to hear that you have heard nothing of your brother for
> so long a period. I think something must have happened to the vessel
> which he was on, but I sincerely hope it is not the case, and I hope by
> this reaches you he will be arrived also ... I delivered the messuage of
> love from you to all the family and the same from us all in return to
> you and your highly esteemed wife, and the same to your brother if
> ever you may chance to see him again ...

Nothing is known about this voyage, but Henry may have been working,
like Tom, for Robert Jaques or one of his associates. Jaques, for example,
made several long voyages at around this time, including one in August 1842
when he commanded a large ship, the *Mary Ann*, which sailed from London
to Madras and Calcutta. In any event, it seems that Henry returned safely, as

no mention was made of him being missing in James Wolstenholme's letter in October 1844.

In May 1847 Henry married Elizabeth Wilcock at Leeds parish church. His occupation is described on his marriage certificate as a 'waterman', so it seems that he was 'on the water' for at least six years. Watermen usually carried passengers along and across rivers and canals. They often led rough and dangerous lives, but that may have been part of the appeal to young Henry. He clearly regarded Tom as something of a hero; and Tom worked for merchants and mariners, travelled around Britain and abroad by sea, and knew watermen. Henry often stayed with him in London, close by the Thames. The idea of working on the boats would have appealed to him, and it was an excellent way for him to assert his independence from the Barrons.

At his marriage in Leeds, Henry named his father as 'Joseph Pendlebury', a 'Smith'. The name was a combination of his father Richard's surname and Joseph Barron's first name; the occupation was Joseph's, and its use suggests that Henry looked upon Joseph very much as his father.

Two years after Henry's marriage, Tom's beloved Gussy contracted cholera. When she died in London in August 1849, Henry wrote immediately to Tom.

> Dear Brither
>
> I wright these few lines oping that they will find you all well as it leaves us all at present I have to inform you that your Ant Betty at Rattliffe was taking with a stroke on they 8 of this month and she nevr spoke more she was Bured on friday Last i am very sory to hear of your Wife being cut of so suding but it is they det that whe all mus Pay for they Lord givth the Lord taketh away Blessed bee they Name of they Lord but Dear Brother you must not let your self Drown with Grif you must Keep your spret up as well as you can.
>
> our rellithens is all well at present i mus conclude at present sonomer at present
>
> from Yours and seter
> Henry S Pendlebury
> Please to wright by Return of Post

'Ant Betty at Rattliffe' was another of Tom and Henry's father's sisters. Baptised Elizabeth, she married Thomas Gee and died in Water Lane Radcliffe, in August 1849, at the age of 83 of 'Old Age'.

Three weeks later, Henry sent Tom another letter.

Dear brother,

I wright few lines to you oping they will find you in good elth as it leaves us all at present Dear Brother i recivd your kind leterer Dated monday september 17th i am very sory to hear of your beeing so very low in sperits Dear Brother you hurt my filings to hear of it but i wold advize you to keep up your spirits as will as you can for if you dont you will thraw your self down ten to one and that will be worse than all Deer Brother dow take my ad vice and Dear Brother i should like you to com down if you could make it con viniat and sop with us at month or so and then whe cahd talk all maters over i think. Bil Pirs as been very sharp about they shop But i wish i had been ther I wold have let him know somthing that he was not awere of all to gether i think he might have litten you get settled before he had started upon that cornsorn but never mind if i am not with you, my hart is with you alwse But i wish whe was so that whe was to gether i shall bee hoping.

Please to let me know How you are coming on and dond not Delay.

Dear Brother i must hav childen sonomore at present from your Dutleful Brother and set you

Henry S Pendlebury

God Bless You so feur well at Present

'Bil Pirs' was William Pears, who lived near Tom in Bermondsey and was a 'tobacco master' for whom Tom presumably worked. Henry was none too pleased about the way he was treating his brother.

Tom sent Henry a locket of Gussy's hair and, three months later, Henry wrote to thank him.

Dear Brother,

I wright these few lines to you oping that they will find you in good ilth as it leaves us at present. i received your parsel containg they Pin and they Broach and they Lock of Hear of your Dear Agusta, wich i shall put it in a fraim in leter it Gussy 1849 fror they remberince of them that as gone to they appy relmys abuve where whe all shall meet in unety i hope and nevir to Part no more

i had Henry Charlesworth at our house on monday last and he told me that you was very well and whe had a better chat to gether about old times but he did not stop long about ½ houer as he had a nother frend with him and they had to go to see another frend at Bathey Car, so they only had a glas of ale and a Rosttaty i had pervided for them

19 Thornhill Lees Hall in the West Riding of Yorkshire. This timber-framed house was built by the Nettleton family in the early sixteenth century. The photograph shows how this fine building had declined over the centuries through age and neglect, but it gives an idea of the architecture of the period and place.

But they would not have eny you nevir named they over cakes in your leter How you like them

Please to let me know when when your coming Down so that i may know to make redy for you your unkil and Ant sends there Best respect to you and Your coserns all so Please to Give my Best respect to all inquiring frends and exept they same youre self sonomore at present from your Duteful Brother and Sister

Henry and Elizabeth Pendlebury

Please to come if you can make it convenient

Batley Carr is roughly half-way between Dewsbury and Batley and not far from Thornhill Lees. 'Rosttaty' (a 'roast tatie', 'rost tater' or 'roster') was a local expression for a jacket potato.[4] Henry Charlesworth was part of the tobacco chain that linked Yorkshire and London through the business of Charles Milner and Robert Jaques. He was born in Leeds but moved down to London where he worked, like Tom, as a tobacconist. He lived and worked in Spitalfields, not far from St Paul's Churchyard and Cannon Street, where Tom worked and the Milners had their warehouse; he was probably related to another Charlesworth, William, who was also born in Leeds and moved to London to work as a tobacconist in Union Street Southwark, only a few streets from where Tom had his shop. Henry would have liked entertaining Henry Charlesworth who was only four years younger than him and would have had plenty of London stories to spin. Not that Henry ever needed an excuse to share the food and drink he so obviously enjoyed; he loved company and there are references to cakes, meat and meals in all his letters.

Eleven months after Gussy's death, Tom married again. His new wife, Jane Harding, was 20 years younger than him, and it seems to have been a relatively quick courtship because Henry did not seem to know anything about her. Three months after the wedding, Henry wrote to Tom '... you never tould me who she was or wether i new er or not ...'

'Flearups' in Lambeth Marsh

Henry and Elizabeth soon began to have children of their own, but marriage did not mean that Henry had to stop enjoying life. It was Henry who used the phrase 'flearup' in a letter written to Tom and Jane in October 1850. The term 'flare-up' is a Lancashire slang word meaning a quarrel or drinking bout.[5] Henry's anticipation of fun shines through every line of this letter, even though the meaning of some of his words is now obscure.

Dear Brother and Sister
    I wright these few lines to you oping that they will find you bouth
in good elth as it leaves us all at present i have long expekted you
wrighting before now i thort that some thing was a mis for i wrote 2
Letters to you and i never recived no ancer back but you must excuse
me for not writing to you Dear Brother i am very sorry to hear of you
Being out of imployment But i Hope you will get in again before this
reaches you you say that you could like to see me and so could i like to
see you very much wen whe do meet whe will Have a flearup wich whe
shall meet abut may if all is well for i am comming to they exibiton
but more to see you then enithing and your Wife but you never tould
me who she was or wether i new er or not but you must give my Best
respects to archey and sofey and tell er that when i com to London
whe will go to they Play to gether archey and me will Have a Bloout

of dogs Boddy again and whe will go to Grenwich again and have some porther and whe will go to they Plough inn and beet they Poney up and Down they yard and by in they stabel again and come home in a cab i sent my Best respect to you by Mr Kinler [sic] But he never saw you for he cald at they ware house and they told him that you did not work there and he left word at they warehouse for you to meet him there on they Sataday at 5 a clock but you did not i am very sorry to hear of my faverite vick beeing kiled in Cannen Street i have to inform you that your unkil and Ant is doing very will but i hav not seen them thes 6 weakes My wife sends her Best respect to to your and your Wife and she sais that she thinks that your Wife will brueak you of being porley Please to give my Best respect to all inquring frends and recive they same your self and Wife sonomo at present from your Dear Brother and sister

Henery and Elizibeth Pendlebury

i have like to hav forgot to tel you that i Have not hard enithing of eny of them at Manchester

Please to wright By Return of Post at they Rum and Shovel or they Black Boy

The 'archey and sofey' whom Henry wanted to join his flearup were Archibald van Dornick and his wife Sophia, who was the sister of Tom's first wife Gussy. Archie described himself as the son of a 'Dutch Baron' and as a 'retired mariner' when he died in 1881, but he also worked, somewhat less glamorously, as a labourer, a warehouseman in a white lead works, and a watchman. Sophia and Archie lived for most of their married life at 4 Bear Lane, Southwark, about five minutes' walk from Curtiss Hatch and Brad Street, and it was here that Gussy's mother Caroline Barnard died in 1863. Sophia lived on to the grand age of 92. Neither the 'Rum and Shovel' nor the 'Black Boy' has been traced, though there was a 'Black Boy' public house in Bury.[6] Tom, however, clearly knew both the pubs well.

To come home in a cab, presumably after a night of heavy drinking, was to give the 'flearup' Henry's ultimate seal of approval. 'Dogs boddy' in the letter probably referred to a big meal; the term was sailors' slang for a staple naval food of peas boiled in a bag.[7] Public houses featured prominently in Henry's idea of a good time, and the references to 'Poney' and 'stabel' probably refer to the illegal betting that took place in many of them. The 'Plough Inn' was the Plough in Bermondsey Street, just round the corner from Nelson Street where Henry was to rent a house 15 years later when he and

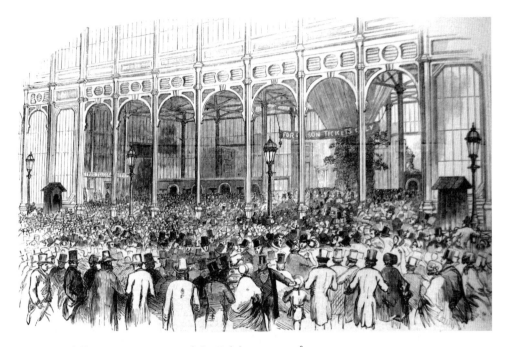

20 The Shilling Day – exterior of the Exhibition, 1851.[8]

his family came to live in London. Come what may, Henry was determined to cheer up his 'porley' brother Tom.

Henry's 'unkil and Ant' Joseph and Ann Barron's disappointment in his behaviour surfaced again in 1851 over the matter of the Great Exhibition. Henry failed to come to London to see the show despite (or perhaps because of) the fact that everyone seemed to think it would do him good. The 'Great Exhibition of the Works of Industry of all Nations or Great Exhibition' was an international exhibition held in the 'Crystal Palace' in Hyde Park from 1 May to 15 October 1851. An estimated six million people – equivalent to a third of the entire population of Britain at the time – visited. The 'shilling days' on which the entry fee was reduced were particularly popular.

The Barrons expected that Henry would want to come with them to the exhibition. But Henry was in one of his rebellious phases, having left his work at Kilner's glass factory without consulting Joseph. So, Joseph and Ann had to come down without him, hoping in vain that he would join them. In August 1851, Joseph wrote to Henry from Tom's house in London:

Dear Nephew,
   ... I know take up my pen to write to you hoping this will find

you & all the family well but feel much surprisd you have not made your case known to me sice you left Mr Kilner's I have seen the greate Exhibition and many other marvelous things in London too tadious for me to mentchon with pen your Ant is hear with me to conclude I feel disirous you whould come to London to see the Wonder of the World please give my respects to Mr Blun and I think he will let you come to the exhibition which will do you much good J Barron

Contrast the style in this letter 'Dear Nephew ... J Barron' with Joseph's letter to Tom two weeks earlier ('Dear Tom ... Believe me you affectionte uncle Joseph Barren'), and Joseph's disapproval of Henry's actions becomes clear. The wording of the last sentence of this letter suggests that Henry was now working for Mr Blunn, one of the two leading families in the local glassworks that dominated Catcliffe which had a population of only 273 in 1851.[9] Samuel Blunn employed 76 men, William was a manager and Charles and Joseph a warehouseman and apprentice glass-blower.

Tom likewise thought that Henry should have come to London to see the exhibition, but the note he added to his brother at the bottom of Joseph's letter was much warmer in tone.

Dear Henry,

Hoping you and your Wife and famely are quite well my Uncle and ant left London Last night for yorkshire hoping they arived quite safe I fully expected you up to see the Exerbition acording to promise you ought of come with your uncle and aunt for whe have had some reare sport in London i will thank you to drop me a Line by return of post.

Your afectionate Brother Thos. Pendlebury

Henry may never have received this letter, as it was found with an unaddressed envelope among Tom's papers in London.

Henry soon, however, made amends to the Barrons on their return to Yorkshire by visiting them and spending the whole day hearing about their London adventures. He wrote an exuberant letter to Tom and Jane a couple of weeks later.

Dear Brother and sister,

I wright these few lines to you oping that they will find you all in good elth as it leaves us all at Present i arived at Wakefield at 9 o'clock on sataday Morning all well and i arrived at my unkelis at 6 a clock at Night, and they are all well and i stopt all Day with them on they Sunday talking abought they Waunderful sights thy ad seen in London and about Bonepart and brasting is Chops with er cog att art ta Boney and abought Malby Muping Dope in the Dope Dish Dear Brother you Must send my Wife on Thursday Next in they Morning if you can for they Trains are so bad and so very hevey and you Must tell er that she will have to Change carriges at Knatnilinger station and arsk for they Wakefield train. Give my Best respect archey and Sofey and all inquering friend and except same your self sonomore at present from your efectnet Brother Henery Stapels [H] Pendlebury

give my bes respect to My Wife

Some of the references in this letter defy explanation, but Napoleon was clearly the butt of a number of popular displays at the exhibition. 'Brasting is Chops' may be a version of 'bursting his jaws', an old Lancashire expression.[10] 'Dope' may refer to opium. 'Knatnilinger' was Knottingley: the Knottingley to Burton Salmon line had opened only the previous year to allow trains to run from London to York via Knottingley where it was possible to change to the Leeds City Line that stopped at Wakefield. Wakefield was about five miles from

21 Wakefield (Westgate) railway station. In the background can be seen part of the ¾-mile long, curving viaduct that carried the line over the river Calder.

22 Henry's use of 'Stapels', 1851.

Thornhill Lees, where Henry and Elizabeth lived. Once again, Henry's wife Elizabeth was staying in London with Tom and Jane, showing not only how close the two brothers' families were but also how relaxed Henry was about allowing his wife to stay in London without him. He was happy for her to travel back to Yorkshire by train on her own. Not all men at the time would have tolerated such independence in a wife.

Henry signed himself as 'Henery Stapels Pendlebury', perhaps as a tribute to Edward Stables who had fought alongside his father at the Battle of Corunna before being mortally wounded at the Battle of Waterloo.[11]

By 1851 the first two of Henry's 11 children had been born, and he was living in Thornhill Lees, working once again for Mr Kilner at the glassworks there. He remained restless, however, to Joseph Barron's dismay. In July 1851, Joseph wrote to Tom, without comment, '... your Brother Henery as left Mr Kilner and is Living at a place cald Catcliff, about 8 miles from us ...'

The next letter from Henry to Tom and Jane was written in February 1853.

Dear Brother and sister

I wright they few lines to you oping that they will find you all well as it leaves us all at present. I recived your Letter and i am very sorrey to hear that your are so very uncomforterbul But i will see if i can get you a sitwaton if i can eney way But as for you going to australia my opinen i think you ad Beter stop in Eigland, for what are you going to Do when get theare i think they are as Bad of as som in this Cuntery i take no notice of they newerpaters for they Put enigthing in for to Peswade Pipel for to go and if you was for to go you whould Have to Do 6 penceworth of work for 6 pence so what is they youse of going so best yours selfves content Wile you hear from me again i shall wright or go to unkil Barran and see what i can Do for you i think he will give you a Plase of work my unkil was over at our Plasee a few weakes ago and he whants me for to go to work for him But i have not yet satled about it yet i have to inform you that whe hav got another Dorter on they first of September Last and they other too are as fat as a Yorkshire Pig they Glass Trade is verry Brisk at Present

i hav to infor you that that your unkil and ant is very porley they other Day Mr Kilner Cald and Told me for He ad Been there and seen them Please to Give our best Respects to Archey and Sofey and tel Him that i am Being well me and my Wife send our Best Respects to you bouth sono mere at Present from your efectnat Brother

Henery Pendlebury

i have a Beauteful Spaniel and i coal it name Vick But whe have no Pease Puding But whe have Plenty of Bones o they Black Boay My Porter.

In this letter 'Mr Kilner' was either John Kilner (who died in 1857) or one of his sons, perhaps John Kilner junior who was married to Joseph and Ann

Barron's daughter Ann. 'Archey and Sofey' were, of course, Tom's and Henry's good friends Archie and Sophia van Dornick. Henry regularly used the 'Black Boy' as a forwarding address and was known to like his porter. Henry's choice of 'Vick', the name of Tom's dog killed in Cannon Street in 1850, shows once again how close these two brothers were. The reference to 'Pease Puding' may be a private joke; Henry had shown his great fondness for this food ('dog's body') in an earlier letter. His 'dorter' was his third child, Emma.

Henry was in high spirit – and his daughters were 'as fat as a Yorkshire pig' – but he was still reluctant to work for Joseph Barron. And he was sceptical about all the extravagant claims being made in the newspapers about the wonders of a new life in Australia. Tom was struggling to find work at this time and had close friends who had just emigrated (George and Elizabeth Little, described later). It is not surprising that he was tempted to follow them. But Henry's advice was sound and sensible – life would be no easier on the other side of the world.

23 Bermondsey was the centre of the English leather-tanning industry. In Leathermarket Street may be found the Leather Exchange, upon which a number of roundels depict the hard and noxious work of the tanners.

Sadly, this is the last letter from Henry to survive. After 1851 the Pendlebury documents are spread more thinly and consist mainly of correspondence about Tom's second wife Jane and her family. It seems unlikely, however, that Henry and Tom's letters to each other stopped at this point. The two brothers were very close, as were their wives, and they had plenty in common. Each had a young family. Tom and Jane had four children between 1851 and 1862 (one of whom died at the age of six months), and Henry and Elizabeth had six. They often visited each other in Yorkshire and London.

After Tom's death in 1863, Henry managed a much longer stay in London. By 1866, he had become a 'blacksmith journeyman' and was living with Elizabeth and their nine children in the heart of the smelly and poor Leather Market district of Bermondsey, in Bear Lane, next door to the house that had once been rented by his 'flearup' friends Archie and Sophia van Dornick. Henry and Elizabeth later moved a few streets away to Crucifix Lane where their eleventh

24 The Kilners' London warehouse, Great Northern Railway Goods Station, c.1869–94. 'There is every conceivable kind of bottle, jar, and vial ... the smallest bottle made is the quarter dram flint vial; the largest is the fourteen gallon carboy.'[12]

child (and second son) was born in 1868. They named him Thomas in honour of Tom who had died five years earlier. They moved at least once more during their time in London, to Nelson Street (since renamed Kipling Street) where Henry went back to his work as a 'glass bottle mould maker', perhaps employed by William Kilner in his London warehouse in Horse Shoe Wharf or Kings Cross.[13] William was the son of John Kilner (close friend of Joseph Barron and founder of the Kilner jar business) and his brother had married Joseph and Ann's daughter Ann. In the close-knit community of glass producers, the Kilners would have seemed almost like 'family' to Henry, which may not necessarily, of course, have recommended them to him.

Apart from his brief period as a waterman, Henry stayed within the glass industry and always worked with metal, as his listed occupations show: smith, blacksmith at glass works, glassbottle mould maker, engineer, glass bottle mould maker, fitter, engineer, glass bottle mould fitter, blacksmith journeyman and

25 Mitchell's Terrace, Wombwell, c.1910.[14] Henry and his family lived here in his final years. Mitchell's colliery can be seen in the distance, to the left of the bridge over the Dearne and Dove canal.

116

26 Henry's son Thomas outside his fish and chip shop in Wombwell, *c.*1920.[15] Thomas's wife is on his left. It is just possible to made out the name T. PEN...RY above the shop.

mould maker.[16] These were highly skilled jobs and Henry would have been paid well.

Henry and Elizabeth no doubt remained in close contact with Tom's widow Jane when she was left with four young children, one a baby less than three months old, to support. Soon after Tom's death in 1863, Jane moved from Brad Street to New Street, which was only a mile or so from the Leather Market area in which Henry and his family settled in about 1865. It is easy to imagine Tom and Jane's children – Rebecca Jane, Ann, Thomas and Emily – racing through the streets of London to play with Henry and Elizabeth's children – Elizabeth, Mary, Martha, Henry, Matilda, Sarah, Sophia and baby Thomas (their three eldest having already left home).

By 1881 Henry was once again back in Yorkshire, working as a glass bottle mould maker in Wombwell. It was there that he died on 19 March 1888, aged 65, of chronic Bright's disease, a form of kidney failure. His wife Elizabeth survived him by three years and died, aged 63, in 1891.

Henry's son Thomas, born in London and named after Henry's beloved brother Tom, became a coal miner for a time before starting a fish and chip shop in Wombwell in 1897. He did the frying and his wife Elizabeth served the customers.[17]

117

CHAPTER TWELVE

'Bull baiting scum' at Swinton, relatives, and rent disputes, 1839 to the 1860s

H ENRY's letters to Tom, with their various references to relatives living in the Radcliffe area, are a reminder that they both shared common roots in Lancashire. Until at least the early 1850s, the Pendlebury documents are dominated by letters written to Tom by Ann and Joseph Barron and James (senior and junior) Wolstenholme. Many of these letters, it seems, have only survived because they contain references to the Swinton rent dispute. This dispute is a sorry but entertaining tale of inefficiency, cunning, drunkenness and deceit that left Tom cheated of his father Richard's legacy.

Francis Pendlebury's 1820 will

The inheritance dispute was all about five cottages in Swinton, a manufacturing centre on the outskirts of Manchester and about six miles south of Radcliffe. These cottages had been in the Pendleburys' possession for many years. Nathan (Tom's great-granduncle, 1722–96) had stipulated '... I Give and devise unto Francis Pendlebury Son of James Pendlebury all my freehold Cottages or Dwelling houses and premises situate in Swinton in the Parish of Eccles ...' When Francis, yeoman and parish clerk, died in 1820, he in turn left these five cottages to his four sons Thomas, Nathan, James and Richard (Tom's father). The clause that caused all the trouble was his instruction that, after his wife's death, and after his four daughters had received a fixed sum each from the rents of the five cottages, he would

> ... devise and bequeath to ... [my] ... four Sons Viz. Thomas, James, Nathan and Richard Pendlebury to have and to hold the said Freehold Cottages and premises and appurtenances belonging thereto unto the said Thomas James Nathan and Richard Pendlebury their

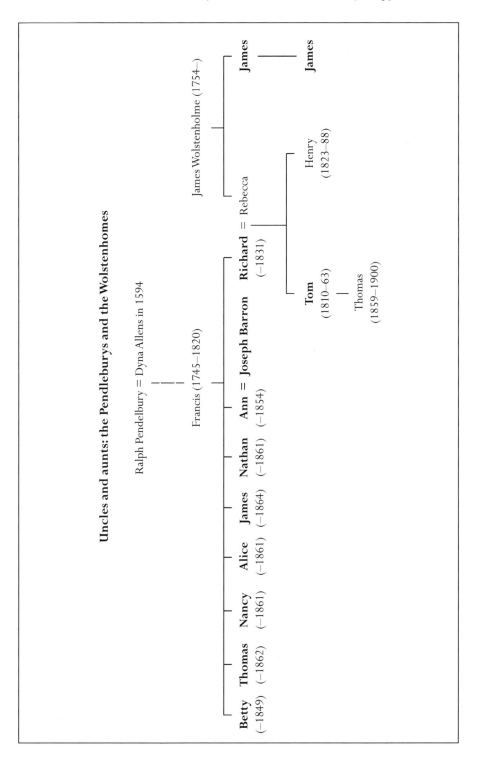

Uncles and aunts: the Pendleburys and the Wolstenhomes

Ralph Pendelbury = Dyna Allens in 1594

Francis (1745–1820)

James Wolstenholme (1754–)

James ——— James

Richard = Rebecca
(–1831)

Henry
(1823–88)

Tom
(1810–63)

Thomas
(1859–1900)

Ann = Joseph Barron
(–1854)

Nathan
(–1861)

James
(–1864)

Alice
(–1861)

Nancy
(–1861)

Thomas
(–1862)

Betty
(–1849)

> Heirs and Assigns for ever as Tenants in Common and not as joint
> Tenants ...

The terms of his will were clear. When Richard died, his fourth share of the cottages would pass automatically to his heir(s). Tom, as Richard's oldest son, should, therefore, have smoothly inherited his portion when Richard died intestate in 1831. This, however, was not to be the case because Richard's three surviving brothers (Tom's uncles) Thomas, James and Nathan began to argue among each other, and with Tom, about how Richard's quarter of the rent ought to be distributed. The dispute must have been the talk of Radcliffe, for eight of the people drawn into the arguments still lived there. The row involved the whole family: five uncles, one cousin, four aunts and Tom's brother Henry. Fighting Tom's corner most fiercely were his Aunt Ann (with her husband Joseph Barron), Uncle James and Cousin James (Wolstenholme, his mother's brother and nephew) and, of course, brother Henry.

Joseph and Ann (née Pendlebury) Barron

Ann and Joseph Barron were Tom's principal supporters. Ann Pendlebury already had an illegitimate son, Thomas, when she married Joseph in Radcliffe in 1815. Their marriage was a happy one, as their correspondence shows, and Thomas quickly assumed the name of Barron. When her brother Richard Pendlebury died in 1831, Ann (and Joseph) took his young son Henry (Tom's brother) into their care. Twelve letters written from the Barrons to Tom between 1837 and 1851 reveal the warmth and the sense of responsibility that the couple felt towards both Tom and Henry.

Joseph started his working life as a whitster (like Tom's father Richard) before becoming a glass-worker and a successful businessman. He and Ann began their married life in Radcliffe Bridge. Joseph was one of the founders of a glassworks at Worsbrough on the banks of the Dearne and Dove Canal and later moved to Hunslet (Leeds) and then to Mexborough, Castleford and Thornhill Lees.[1] Joseph worked for John Kilner (of Kilner Jars fame) before setting up the Don Glass Bottle Works in Mexborough. His manufacturing networks were close: his son Joseph married Mary Hartley (of Hartley's jams) and his daughter Ann married John, son of the Kilner glassworks founder. Ann (Pendlebury) Barron died in 1854 and Joseph in 1856. Joseph died intestate; his only surviving next of kin were named as his children Joseph, Hannah Kelly and Ann Kilner, confirming that he was not the father of Ann's son Thomas.[2] His estate was valued at under £800.

The bottle business passed to his son Joseph and his stepson Thomas. The latter was particularly successful, establishing the Phoenix Glassworks in Mexborough which at its height hand-produced 200,000 bottles a week. On his death, the glassworks passed to Thomas's six sons; they closed in the 1920s.[3] During the latter part of the nineteenth century, Thomas and his many (at least eleven) children came to dominate Mexborough society. It was said that, 'On the occasion of one family bereavement the Parish Church was filled with relatives alone ... the Barron species would keep a large-sized village in healthy swing.'[4]

The Wolstenholmes

Tom's other most vigilant supporters in the Swinton rent dispute were the Wolstenholmes, 13 of whose letters to Tom have survived. James Wolstenholme senior (brother of Tom's mother Rebecca) was born into a Radcliffe family of cotton weavers in about 1785. He married Ann Cherry in June 1805 and lived in Stand Lane, Pilkington (a couple of miles from Radcliffe) with their four children who all worked in the cotton industry. In 1851, James, now aged 63, was still working as a hand weaver and his son (Cousin James) had married and left home.

Father and son Wolstenholme were close to each other, and Tom to both of them. Tom sent tobacco to his Uncle James and cigars and newspapers to Cousin James. This letter from Cousin James to Tom, written in May 1848, gives a flavour of the warmth of their relationship.

> ... I have no doubt you will be wondering, what is the cause of this delay in neither hearing one way or the other, but the reason I will explain to you, it was Friday when your Uncle brot it and my Father forgot to post it in Manchester on Saturday, and he has forgot again this morning, but I will promise you certain on Thursday so that you will get it on Saturday, it is rather neglectful to forget
> it a second time, but we are pulling down a heavy Engine ...

The 'Uncle' referred to here was James Pendlebury with the next instalment of the Swinton rents. The 'Engine' in this letter was probably a mechanised loom, and its mention suggests that the Wolstenholmes employed a number of people to work for them. Their correspondence certainly gives the impression that they were comfortable financially; in 1844 James junior reported that their business was 'brisk'.

The three quarrelsome Pendlebury brothers

Thomas Pendlebury was undoubtedly the villain of the piece, and his son Francis little better. Thomas was the oldest of Francis Pendlebury's four sons, baptised in Radcliffe in December 1771. It was probably a shrewd move on his father's part not to name him as his executor (as convention would have suggested) but to appoint his second oldest son, James, to this role.

It seems that 'Old Tommy' (as he was later described) enlisted in the navy in July 1795 when he was 23.[5] This was at a time when notorious naval press-gangs roamed the land, virtually kidnapping able young men, so desperate were they to find sailors to man the ships that were to fight Napoleon.[6] If so, it would have been a hard life and a tough fate for Tommy. In any event, he served for nearly six years before returning to Radcliffe to work as a cotton bleacher. In 1812 a Thomas Pendlebury (assumed to be Old Tommy) was charged with fraud but managed to secure an adjournment on the grounds that his co-defendant had failed to do the required paperwork.[7] Old Tommy was recorded in the 1841 Census returns as a 'journeyman bleacher' staying at the 'Black Cat' in Radcliffe (probably a public house associated with the Black Cat Colliery near Hampson Square[8]), a 'retired sailor' living in Hampson Square (1851), a 'pauper' in Bury Union Workhouse (1861) and a 'retired labourer' on his death certificate in 1862. He liked to drink. He married and had two children. He died of 'general decay' in the Bury Union Workhouse in 1862, aged 92.

Old Tommy's son Francis (1804–86) was not much better than his father. He, too, was no stranger to the courts and was probably the Francis tried for felony at Salford July Sessions on at least two occasions in 1832.[9] He married and had six children. By 1861 he was living with his eldest daughter Agnes in Little Lever, just outside Radcliffe. He worked as a carter, a brick-maker and agricultural labourer but by 1881 was an 'inmate' of Bolton Union Workhouse where he again described himself as a carter. He died in 1886, aged 82.

James Pendlebury (1782–1864) was a rather different character. A calico printer by trade, he lived in one of the cottages in Eton Hill Radcliffe before moving to Stand Lane, Pilkington, where he and his wife Martha had ten children. As his father's executor, he was responsible for collecting and distributing the Swinton rents. He found this an onerous task. At the age of 63, he was still keeping accounts and running around after his brothers. In May 1845, just after rent day when the dispute had flared up yet again, James Wolstenholme senior wrote to Tom:

... I should have wrote to you sooner than this but your Uncle James never came near till this morning, Friday and so I thought it was no use of me writing it till I had seen some way or other to be over this Morning and I give him a receipt for it, and he wants you as soon as you receive this to write to him and let him know you have received it, and I hope you will, and address him very courteously, because he has done better than expectation ...

James died at Radcliffe Hall in January 1864, aged 82.

Nathan Pendlebury (1783–1861), the youngest of the three surviving brothers, was careful to keep a distance between himself and the squabbles. He was a whitster (cotton bleacher) who lived for most of his life in Ringley Brow, Pilkington. He married three times, first to Martha Gregory (with whom he had six children), then to Margaret Jackson and, finally, to Mary Ann Heaton. His personal life was beset with sadness: he not only lost two wives but also five of his six children, four of whom died before the age of two. His recorded occupations seem humble enough – a whitster, porter, carter and, finally, a 'crofter' (a cotton bleacher) – but he seems to have been relatively prosperous. In 1826, for example, when he was living at 'Withings', the churchwardens collected just over 14s. from him in church rates (the average tithe paid being only about 3s.).[10] And it was to him that the Wolstenholmes appealed for help when James failed to take any action over the rents. Nathan died in January 1861, aged 78, at his home in Ringley Brow after being ill with bronchitis for four weeks.

The Swinton rent dispute

These, then, were the main protagonists in the Swinton rent dispute. On Tom's side were Ann and Joseph Barron and the two Wolstenholmes; and against him was Old Tommy, helped by his son Francis. Sitting somewhat uneasily somewhere in the middle were James and Nathan. On the sidelines were his three aunts Betty, Nancy and Alice.

This is what happened. When his father died in 1831, Tom's due share of the Swinton rents failed to materialise. It was probably in order to establish his legal entitlement to the money that he asked the parish clerk of Radcliffe to provide, first (in February 1833) a copy of his parents' marriage certificate and, second (in May 1834), a copy of his own birth certificate which named them as his parents (these are the earliest of the nineteenth-century Pendlebury papers to survive). Tom was forced to appeal to Uncle James (one of the two executors of his grandfather's will). When James failed to respond, he turned to the second executor, Mr Sutton (a grocer and draper living in Radcliffe), for help. Uncle Nathan kept his distance, as a letter from Joseph Barron to Tom (July 1839) reveals.

> ... we wrote to your uncle Nathan Pendlebury on the 14th of June
> stateing to him your desire to know what Money there was in Mr
> Sutton's hands belonging to you and wiere the will or a copy of the will
> might be seen we likewise informed your uncle Nathan of you writing
> several times to your uncle James and could not receave and answer
> and last of all to Mr Sutton, and he sent your own letter sealed up back
> again we have been waiting 4 weeks for an answer to our letter and
> received no answer we think they will not answer the above questions.
> It therefore know remains with you to do what you think proper your
> Aunt Ann thinks that you had better come by way of Castleford if you
> think of coming down ...

Aunt Ann was more than happy to do battle on Tom's behalf. She, of course, knew all about the affair, having already received a lump sum of £20 from the Swinton rents under the terms of her father's will. And she knew her brothers only too well. A couple of years later, Joseph passed on her advice that Tom should come in person to Radcliffe as quickly as possible to stake his claim.

> ... your aunt desires to inform you that the property belonging to your
> Father was left to him and his haeirs for ever your aunt thinks it is
> high time you come down to see about your property or you will lose
> it and if you come down this Spring call at Castleford before you go to
> Radcliff and your aunt can give you better information how to go about
> your property ...

The problems were presumably sorted out, but only temporarily, because the wrangling started up again four years later. If the three uncles had wanted to exclude Tom from a share of the rents they could not have devised a better system. The arrangement was that the rent money was to be shared out at the Black Bull in Swinton twice a year, on the first Tuesday in May and the first Tuesday in November; anyone not there in person at the time the money was distributed forfeited his share. This was fair enough for the locals but hard on Tom in London. Henry had explained the system to Tom in April 1843 in a letter cited earlier. Joseph Barron added a postscript stressing how important it was that Tom attend the distribution of rents.

... I hope you will take the hint given from your Uncle and Aunt
Hampson from Radcliffe respecting you coming down at the time
specified, that is the first Tuesday in May and the first Tuesday in
November at the Black Bull Inn Swinton, that being the time when
they receive the rents. Please call at our house before you go to
Radcliffe ...

By now Uncle and Aunt Nancy Hampson had also been drawn into the
dispute. Nancy, like her sister Ann, had inherited £20 from the Swinton rents
from her father. She lived with her husband in Pilkington and worked as a baker.

Tom, however, seems to have missed more than one deadline that year. He
wrote to Joseph Barron three weeks after the November 1843 rent day to ask
how he might still claim his money. Joseph replied

... In your letter dated Nov. 24th you wish to know what steps to
take for your share of rent due to you. Your aunt says that uncle James
Pendlebury told her the last time she was at Radcliffe that if no one was
there at the time of drawing the rents you would get no money, and it
now appears to be the case. Your aunt thinks you had better let it rest
for the present, till you can come down yourself or send your aunt to
make a proper arrangement, it is your own fault in not writing sooner
to us, we could (have) ordered some way if you had given us time ...

Joseph's irritation was beginning to show: if Tom could not come up to
Lancashire or arrange for someone to represent him, he had only himself to
blame if he missed out on the money. Joseph may have lost patience by this stage;
or perhaps he and Ann were in bad health (there are a number of references in
his letters to himself, or Ann, being 'poorly'). Or he may have been just too
busy. It was in 1844 that he moved from Castleford to Thornhill Lees to work
for John Kilner and he had found the change stressful, as he wrote in January
the following year.

... I hope you will excuse me for not writing to you soonir one reason
is I have been in agition of leaving Castleford for some time I have
now brought the thing to a close and removed to Thornhill Lees and
working for Mr Kilner where I hope I shall more Peace of mind thin
I have had for many years of late you will here more of this when you
see Mr Kilner ...

The first Mr Kilner in this letter probably refers to John Kilner senior, who was working in Thornhill Lees. The Kilner family (notably Caleb, John Kilner's oldest son) was later to run a warehouse in London near to St Paul's Churchyard where Tom often worked.

From now on it was the Wolstenholmes rather than the Barrons who took the lead on Tom's behalf. Tom may have managed to be at the Black Bull for the following May rent day because James (junior) Wolstenholme wrote shortly afterwards '... I hope that you enjoyed yourself the short time you was in Radcliffe as I am sure you was heartily welcome ...' However, the dispute was not resolved. Tom's supporters were growing more desperate and decided to go *en masse* to plead his case before the intractable Uncle James, as a letter sent two weeks after the October rent day reveals.

> ... Nothing has transpired since my last letter about the rents, but some of us is going to visit your uncle James about them, and to see which way he is for acting. My father says he is determined that he will see you righted, but however we wont forget the 5th of next month, and if any thing transpires herewith I will let you know for I am sure you will be very anxious to know ...'

The 'some of us' referred to here might well have included James Wolstenholme senior and junior, up to four of Tom's aunts (Betty Gee, Alice Clarke, Nancy Hampson and Ann Barron) and, perhaps, Joseph Barron himself. A large-scale map of Radcliffe in 1848–51 shows how closely together these uncles and aunts (with the exception of Ann Barron) lived. Within a couple of miles of each other was: Old Tommy (Hampson Square and Bury Union Workhouse); James (Eton Hill and Stand Lane); Nathan (Withins and Ringley Brow); Alice (Chapel Field); Nancy (Green Street); and Betty (Water Lane). 'The 5th of next month' was the first Tuesday in November 1844 when the rents were next due to be distributed. At this meeting Uncle James was finally persuaded to hand over some money to James Wolstenholme senior to pass on to Tom. In May 1845, just days after the rent distribution, Tom received a letter from James Wolstenholme senior (it is the only letter from him to have been kept and perhaps marks the importance of the occasion).

> ... Enclosed I beg to hand you something which I have no doubt, will meet with a kind reception, not for the prodigious sum that it is, but merely as a perfect right, it is a post office order for £3 7s 5d, no one her having had any but your uncle James and yourself, the rent drawn

27 Map of Radcliffe, 1848–51.[11]

was £16 5s 0d and repairs £10 9s 1d so that there was £5 15s 11d left, and your Uncle James had the remainder after you had had yours ...

The postscript gave a breakdown of income and expenditure under the heading 'This is a general list of what I call expences':

	£	s.	d.
Mr Watson	2	5	4
Servants for Liquour	0	7	0
Repairs and Expences	7	10	5
Property Tax	0	3	4
House Tax	0	3	0
	10	9	1
Rent drawn by James Pendlebury	16	5	0
Expenses deducted	10	9	1
Leaves in Hand	£5	15	11

Sent the Sum of £3 7 0 *

The order having cost 6d.

The identity of Mr Watson is not known. The cottages seem to have been in poor repair, with nearly half the rent spent on repairs and expenses. The charge of 7s. for servants for liquor seems high: the first Tuesdays in May and November must have been merry affairs at the Black Bull.

Estimating the value of this rent money to Tom is not easy, but it is unlikely to have covered more than about four months' rent for his small house in Curtiss Hatch (assuming that Tom's maximum potential share of the Swinton rent was two payments a year of just under £7 and that his rent for his house was about £20 per annum). However, in reality the amount of money distributed can rarely have been anything like the full amount; Tom seldom, if ever, received his full share, as a letter from James Wolstenholme (May 1846) reveals.

... Enclosed I have wrote you a copy of the expenses altogether and shown you what a fourth share his of it, and I copied them from Bills your Uncle James had in his possession, and I have given him a receipt

---

* £3 7s. 0d. in 1844 is equivalent in terms of 2010 prices to £261 using the retail price index or £2,370 using average earnings.

of it. he has allowed you one pound for arrears, making altogether £2
2s 7d a very small trifle indeed ...

In short, Tom would have been lucky to have received three months' worth of
annual London rent money, at most, from his Radcliffe uncles. The money would
surely have come in very useful, but it was hardly a fortune.

This detailed letter also contains the first mention of Thomas (Old Tommy),
the oldest of Tom's Pendlebury uncles, and the prime troublemaker in the
Swinton saga. James Wolstenholme (senior) to Tom.

> ... Your Uncle Thomas is in the workhouse, and he has signed his
> share over to the parish, before they would accept him as an inmate of
> the house, and the Overseer was for turning him out on Wednesday
> Morning, if he did not get his share, but your Uncle James said he must
> not have a penny, nor Nathan either this time ...

Old Tommy would normally have been required to sign over any income,
including his share of the Swinton money, to the workhouse on admission,
but his brother James was prepared to do battle with both his brother and the
overseer to stop this happening. Old Tommy, however, was not going to give up
his struggle easily and a year later, just after the May rent day, he had another
row with the workhouse officials. James Wolstenholme (junior) described what
had happened.

> ... The row is over for another 14 months. Old Tommy went as usual,
> he told the Goverer of the Workhouse that he would go for an walk,
> and when he got there, as usual, began to kick up a shine, but James
> has now got better courage he sent for a policeman and as Thomas was
> glad to give up the row, he said he had never authorised the parish
> authorities to receive his share of the Rents and if your uncle James
> paid it over to them he would take him before the Magistrates, but
> however he has paid it over and the Governor says he shant let him out
> again on the rent day ...

This time, James Pendlebury had stood firm and called the police. Old Tommy
took fright and backed down, threatening to go before the magistrates to rescind
his agreement with the workhouse. This was all too much for law-abiding James,
who felt obliged in the circumstances to honour Tommy's promise and hand
over his share of the rent to the governor, although only after the governor had

promised to keep Tommy under lock and key on the day the rents were next due to be distributed. So Tommy's share on this occasion went to the parish authorities rather than to Tom and the others. It is little wonder that James was tired of the whole affair; but worse was to come.

Old Tommy was now determined to stop not only Tom but also his two younger brothers from getting their share of the rents. Eighteen months and three rent days later (November 1847), James Wolstenholme junior again wrote to Tom.

> ... I should have wrote before but I thought I would get all the news
> I could. Old Tommy has made the usual rendesvous at Swinton and
> is turned out of the Workhouse in consequence, and moreover he has
> been after a copy of the will from Chester, having had several people
> looking after it also, but at last they have found out there is one, so he
> is rather cooler now. For if there could have been no will found, him
> and his son Francis would have took all that your Grandfather left, but
> unhappily for him, rogue as he is, he could not do so ...

Old Tommy had now gone to the trouble of checking up on his father's will. Had Francis Pendlebury not made a will, his property would, under the laws of intestacy, have passed in its entirety, after his wife's death, to Tommy as his oldest son. Tommy could then have left it all to his own son Francis. However, Francis Pendlebury *had* made a will and one which had left the Swinton cottages to be shared equally between all four of his sons. It must have come as quite a blow to Old Tommy to discover that there was nothing he could do to stop the rents being shared out between himself, his two brothers James and Nathan, and his nephew Tom. The row had become very nasty indeed.

Tom received his November 1847 share of the Swinton rents a few months later from James Pendlebury via a letter from James Wolstenholme junior. '... I have sent you a copy of the receipt I give your Uncle and say that you can have them by you write as soon as you receive your money ...'

But Old Tommy was not finished yet. Six months later there was more trouble at the Black Bull in Swinton. When the rents came to be distributed in May 1849, James Wolstenholme wrote

> ... you will have [r]eceived the usual share of Rent allotted to you, I
> [p]osted it on Saturday last [an]d I had not time to write [soon]er, and
> we have no Sunday [d]elivery here, so I could write [n]o earlier, but has
> soon as you get the Money please to write immediately

Everything is going ... well here with as, I ... those Bull baiting
scu[m at] Swinton are at an end now old Tommy his come out o[f] the
Workhouse again, he b... when he has drawn and is to be turned over
to the P[arish] authorities they are making something out of him ...

Unfortunately, parts of this letter are missing, but it seems that Old Tommy
was back in the workhouse but had nevertheless once again managed somehow to
escape for the day so that he could be at the Black Bull to receive his rent share
which he had then handed over to the parish. James Wolstenholme's disgust
at the 'scum' in the inn is palpable but he now seemed more tolerant towards
Tommy. Perhaps Tommy really was trying to reform his ways; he was back in
Hampson Square, Radcliffe in 1851, described in the census as a 'retired sailor'.

The rent dispute continued to rumble on. A year later James Pendlebury
once again failed to pass on Tom's share of the rent to James Wolstenholme.
Was James avoiding him? James Wolstenholme to Tom, May 1851:

... I am sorry after this delay to inform you that your Uncle James
has not turned up a farthing as yet, and I am afraid that he does not
intend to do. but I will see him personally and ask him what he means
to do and then I will write again. I should have written long ago only I
expected him every day ...

Events were clearly coming to a head because when James Wolstenholme next
wrote to Tom (January 1852), attorneys had been called in, though to what
purpose is unclear.

... old James has been to let us see his also, and he instructed me to
write to you to say that he was very sorry to see his brothers going on
in this manner, but he says he can't stop them. The notices are served,
I believe by an attorney and I do expect that in future there will be
no more disturbance, but I should not like to swear there would not
be, for my belief is that that which gets hold surely he ought to keep
possession.
    Uncle James called there almost every day previous to the rent day,
but not since, when he does he won't forget, I assure you ...

'Old James' was now nearly 80 and had clearly had enough of this tedious
battle. He did not like the way his brothers (now Nathan as well as Old Tommy)
were behaving. The fact that James 'called there almost every day previous to

the rent day' suggests that the tenants had fallen behind with their rent. If so, the attorney may have been called in to serve either an order(s) for the payment of arrears or for an eviction.

An (undated) letter from James Wolstenholme provides the last word on the Swinton rents. After much persuasion, 'the rogues' had agreed to sell.

> ... You will almost think that we have forgot you, but such his not the case, we have been working at the rogues all the time, and now they are willing to sell, so you must write to me on receipt of this, to say if you are willing to sell or not, as the attorney for the purchaser wants to see a letter from you with instructions, else we told them we would be responsible for your share in it, so I would advise you to sell, as you would never have any prospect of getting a fair share otherwise, so if you think proper to sell[scratched out] you can either come down yourself to receive your share or I will transmit it to you. You know it will be a week or two before the writings are made out and the money paid, but I will write to you before the time comes ...

It is a pity that this letter is undated and that the uncles are not mentioned by name. The decision to sell may have been triggered by Uncle Nathan's death in February 1861 or by Old Tommy's in June 1862. Given that Tom died at the beginning of 1863, it is highly likely that he never received his fair share of the proceeds from the sale.

The end of the Radcliffe connection

This final letter about the Swinton rents is the last to survive from Radcliffe. It brings to an end the tangible link between London and Radcliffe, and between Tom Pendlebury and the eight surviving children of his grandfather Francis Pendlebury (1745–1820), parish clerk of Radcliffe. Of these eight children, only two broke free from Lancashire: Richard, who fought at the battle of Corunna; and Ann, who married Joseph Barron. Three sons and three daughters remained living in the Radcliffe area. Thomas, James and Nathan lived to the ages of 91, 89 and 82 respectively. Elizabeth (Betty), Alice and Nancy lived to the ages of 83, 86 and 79. Only Alice receives no mention in the Pendlebury letters: she married and lived in Chapel Field, Prestwich, before moving to Stand Lane, where she died in April 1861 of 'old age'. Nancy became dependent on parish relief and died at home in Green Street, Radcliffe, in 1861. Betty Pendlebury married Thomas

Gee and died in Water Lane, Radcliffe, in August 1849, of 'Old Age' after a stroke. Henry told Tom the news.

> ... I wright these few lines oping that they will find you all well as it leaves us all at present I have to inform you that your Ant Betty at Rattliffe was taking with a stroke on they 8 of this month and she nevr spoke more she was Bured on Friday ...

From now on Tom's life was fully taken up with his own family in London, with his wife Jane and her many relatives and with his children Rebecca Jane, Ann, Thomas, Thomas William and Emily Augusta.

28   Radcliffe Bridge looking north, 1854.[12]

CHAPTER THIRTEEN

'Take a light brown Rappee, flavour it slightly with Strong Liquor, Eau de Cologne and Port wine Lee': Tom as messenger, salesman, tobacconist, 1834–1851

T O M always knew how to enjoy himself. But amid the overcrowding, bustle and filth of the streets, London was an unforgiving place for anyone who was at all vulnerable. There was very little apart from the workhouse to help those who fell on hard times. Under the Poor Law Amendment Act of 1834, parishes were required to group together into 'unions' under Boards of Poor Law Guardians who set up workhouses in each union to which the destitute could apply for help. These institutions provided basic care for the homeless poor, including 'disorderly and profligate women', who had to work to pay for their care. Single pregnant women found on the streets, the very old and sick and 'idiots' filled these austere and forbidding buildings. Workhouses provided rudimentary shelter, food and medical care but were often regarded as worse than prison because the law required that conditions inside them should be 'less eligible' (that is, worse) than those outside. There was a workhouse in every neighbourhood in London, and Tom would have been ever mindful of the need to escape their clutches. It was essential for the breadwinner to keep his head above water.

Tom usually managed to find work. His often precarious employment was dependent upon links between Lancashire, Yorkshire and the South, improved sea, canal and rail links, and the vitality of London as a trading centre in products such as cotton and tobacco. Several key players in this story appear very early on in the Pendlebury documents: Robert Jaques, a master mariner; Robert Milner, a draper; Robert's brother Charles, a tobacco manufacturer; and Thomas Milner, an importer and businessman. Tom worked for one or more of these men for at least 20 years. Their individual stories and their fortunes informed and shaped his working life.

Robert Jaques

References to Robert Jaques occur in letters written between 1836 and the end of 1850. Jaques was three years older than Tom, had a private income, and married late in life. Though born in London, his father came from the small Yorkshire village of Easby Abbey which was only seven miles from Hunton where Robert and Charles Milner were born. At the age of 17, he began working for the East India Company and served as a midshipman aboard the *Marquis Camden* and the *Berwickshire* (1823–26) and then as a 5th mate and 4th mate aboard the *Sir David Scott* and *Lord Lowther* (1827–30).[1] After leaving the East India Company, he continued as a seafarer; by 1841, he was described as a master mariner and, later, as a 'gentleman'. He married at the age of 42; his wife was Eliza Pettitt, the daughter of William Pettitt of Mount Hall Farm in Essex, and their wedding, and the birth of their first daughter in 1848, were announced in *The Times*. He and his new wife moved to Addington Place, Camberwell, which was only half a mile away from where Tom lived but worlds away in terms of the kind of people who could be found there. It was a street of 28 houses occupied by mainly professional people. Here resided, among others: a master baker employing two men; a surgeon; a linen draper; two professors of music; an artist in painting and one in watercolours; a female professor of dancing; a school mistress and eight scholars; two dissenting ministers; a general medical practitioner; a police constable; two merchants; a superannuated surveyor of taxes; an oil broker; a commercial traveller in drugs; a wine merchant; a working silversmith; a landed proprietor; a captain in the royal marines; a proprietor of houses and fund holder; a dealer in cotton, linen and woollen manufactures; and a commission merchant (born in Germany). Jaques himself was described as a master mariner and employed a French governess (Euphrosine Aly), a groom, a cook and a housemaid.

As a master mariner who had worked for the East India Company, Jaques was a seaman of some skill. It is not clear whether he was a passenger or a working mariner when Tom travelled with him on the *Java* to Bombay in 1836 but he was probably sufficiently qualified to have commanded the ship. Six years later, in August 1842, this notice in *The Times* appeared.

FOR MADRAS, calling at the Cape for passengers, to sail the 10th August, and embark passengers on the 15th, the well-known teak ship

MARY ANN, 500 tons, ROBERT JAQUES, H.C.S. Commander; lying in the West India Docks ...

Jaques sailed ships to the Indies on a number of occasions and the *Mary Ann* had sailed the previous year to the Cape and Madras, though under Tarbutt's captaincy.[2] Tom may have gone on a second long voyage with Jaques in 1840 or 1841; and Henry Pendlebury, too, may have sailed with him in 1844 when one of the letters mentions him being missing at sea.

In charge of ships sailing between London and the East Indies, Jaques made an ideal partner for Robert, Thomas and Charles Milner who had business interests in the cotton, lead and tobacco industries and who, like him, came from north Yorkshire families. Their activities were based in the St Paul's Churchyard and Cannon Street areas of London.

29 St Paul's Churchyard c.1820. St Paul's Churchyard, which skirted St Paul's Cathedral in the City of London, was a bustling commercial street. This view is from Paul's Chain to Watling Street. Robert Milner's drapery shop, where Tom worked at times, was about half-way along the colonnade on the right.

Robert and Charles Milner, Thomas Milner

Robert Milner was born in Hunton, a small village near Richmond in north Yorkshire, in about 1808 where his father Charles was a farmer. He came to London some time in the early 1830s and set up a drapery business (Bailey, Milner & Company) in St Paul's Churchyard. By 1836 this business was already well established. In 1841 he employed five assistants, two maids, a housekeeper and a porter, all of whom lived with him in a house in St Paul's Churchyard. In about 1849, he retired and moved back to Hunton. There he lived alone (he never married) with a manservant and, later, a housekeeper. His letters to Tom reveal him to have been a genial man and a kindly employer.

Robert's younger brother Charles Milner was also born in Hunton. He, too, moved to London where he married Isabella Scott, the daughter of an earthware manufacturer; his brother Robert acted as best man. He soon moved to Barking where he described himself as a tobacco manufacturer (in 1851) and as an 'agent for American producer' (1861). He was granted the freedom of the City of London in October 1856.[3]

Very little is known about Thomas Milner. He was probably related to Robert and Charles; the 1841 Census records him as a 'lead merchant' living in Shoreditch with Mary Milner who appears, confusingly, not to be Robert and Charles's sister Mary Milner who was recorded in the same census as living at Peters Hill, an address used by Tom to collect his mail in 1842; she married James Fisher, a draper, later in 1841. In any event, Thomas Milner and Robert Jaques worked in partnership together trading under the name of Chas Milner & Company at 16 Cannon Street until the dissolution of their partnership in 1849.

Messenger

Tom was used to finding work wherever he could. In 1833, two years after his father's death, he was selling 'dark wine quarts' for Joseph Barron at 'Mr Milner's', while on his marriage certificate in August 1837 he described his occupation as 'messenger'. He appears to have worked in this capacity initially for his uncle Joseph Barron, who lived in Yorkshire, running errands and making arrangements for him in London. Joseph's agent, Robert Bool, passed on instructions in an undated letter.

... We are quite satisfied with Mr Cralebs affair and Mr Philpot can keep the money until I come to town. Please to tell Mr Charley the fishmonger to send four sammon from three to five pounds weight

each, please to send them off on Friday morning so that they may be
at the Swinton station on Friday night next. Hoping you are all well,
give Mr Barron's respects to Mr Charley and accept the same, tell the
fishmonger that Mr Barron will make all right with him when he comes
next time to town...

Neither 'Mr Charley' nor 'Mr Craleb' has been identified but 'Mr Philpot' was
a manufacturing agent living in Broad Street, not far from St Paul's. 'Swinton
station' probably refers to the boat stop on the Dearne and Dove Canal (opened
in 1804 and a busy thoroughfare by the 1830s carrying mostly coal plus lime,
iron, timber and corn). The railway did not come to Swinton until 1840.

By June 1834 Tom was working regularly for the Milner/Jaques partnership.
He wrote to Gussy '... I am going to Islington every day till Wednesday and
shall not be home before nine o'clock ...' Two years later (June 1836), he
was on board ship, working for Jaques. '... I am in better spirits now we are
getting under way to sail on Tuesday evening, and I have good hopes to be home
within the time stated ...' In August 1836 he set sail for India aboard the *Java*.
His responsibilities during this year-long trip are never described in his letters
to Gussy, although he confirmed that he was working for Jaques and another
master, as extracts from his long letter (already cited in full) show.

> ... i am happy to say that i have got my friend Charles with me witch
> makes me much more comfortable and we mess together. Charles es
> sister will call upon you in course of the week ...
>
> ... i am sorry to say that my friend Charles is not much company
> for me for he has been so verry ill all the voayge he is a mear skeliton
> but he seems to be getting better every day but to make amens he has
> scalded his foot wich has made him keep his bed a fortnight longer i beg
> of you my Dear to give his kind love to his sister but not to tell her any
> thing to make her uncomfortable ... i am sorry to say that Mr Jaques is
> as unhappy as he can be but my other master that is companion is a mad
> but a jolly good fellow and he cheers us up at times ...

'Charles' was probably Charles Milner who was about the same age as Tom
and who later became the tobacco manufacturer who supplied Tom with the
merchandise for his shop. 'Charles es sister' was probably Mary Milner and
Tom's 'other master' may have been Thomas Milner, Jaques's business partner.

Tom made at least one more long voyage with Jaques, although the details
are now lost. Soon after 1837, for example, Tom sent a note to Caroline Barnard

(Gussy's mother): '... You may think it strange of me directing to you, but when it is directed to a wife they very seldom put it in the post, but open it for a lark, therefore I have sent this by the pilot vessel ...'

Tobacconist and salesman

By 1841, Tom was regularly describing himself as a tobacconist, but his work involved much more than just selling tobacco from a small corner shop. He was probably some sort of travelling salesman for the Milner-Jaques tobacco business, promoting and supplying cigars and snuff. His work took him to different parts of England, Scotland and abroad, and he travelled by sea and on land. Although the Pendlebury letters provide teasingly small glimpses of Tom at work during the early 1840s, they do show that he was constantly on the move. The first two extracts are taken from Tom's letters to Gussy and the third from a letter sent by Uncle James Wolstenholme to Tom.

January 1843 (reply to Post Office Folkestone Kent)
  ... I think Mr Elgar is in better spirits than he was, and if he continues so I shall be home on Friday evening for I can assure you I would sooner be at home. You may think trudging about a pleasure but it is not to me in this case ...

January 1843
  ... We arrived at Canterbury on Sunday evening after riding all day outside of the coach, but I'm sorry to say that our travelling seems of no use, so I think I shall return by the steamer on Wednesday evening if we go to Folkestone. But if we go to Folkestone I think we shall go straight on to Antwerp, and then I cannot ascertain what time we shall come back, but I shall vote for coming home ... I am quite well and as jolly as a sandboy. I tell you not to write to me as we are not at one place long enough to receive the post ...

August 1844
  ... The Indians you spoke about, I think I would not send them if they are so very ill cracked and shaken for fear they should break and the directions which I give you I think it is wrong, it is Long Millgate not Short Millgate as I think I told you ...

'Mr Elgar' was probably John Elgar, a seaman who lived in Jane Street, near St

Paul's Churchyard. The 'Indians' were cigars and 'Long Millgate' was a street in Manchester in an area of poor housing and mills.

In 1846 Tom was travelling again. He visited Manchester, Liverpool and Glasgow. All this travelling was becoming wearisome, and he could not wait to get back home to London.

December 1846, from Cousin James Wolstenholme to Tom

   … You will perhaps think I have forgot you, we received your kind epistle from Liverpool, and I do assure you that we should have been

30   Tom's letter to Gussy, 1846

very glad to have seen you indeed. I have sent the oat cakes at the time you said your friend would be in Manchester, I hope they are duly received by your Mrs. for I presume you would be travelling at the time ...

December 1846, from Tom in Glasgow to Gussy

... I know sit down to a few lines to you this being the first operrtunity i have had i am know 4 Hundred from home and know not when i shall get away but i think on Saturday if possible I have been traveling ever since i left home and nearly froze to death whe had six horses to draw us through the snow, and i was quite froze to the Box of the coach but i do not mean to come home the same way i shall come by sea for i am sore with siting ...

And a couple of days later

... I am happy to think you have not ventured out this disagreable weather I hope you are quite well, I shall expect to see you tomorrow evening if the weather is fair not else you must come in and ask the porter for me as I shall verry likely not be up I have been very ill since thursday last give my love to mother Carrey and Soaphy ...

St Paul's Churchyard and the Cannon Street area

When in London, Tom's work was concentrated in St Paul's Churchyard, Cannon Street and Peter's Hill where could be found the draper's business of Robert Milner, the warehouses of Charles and Thomas Milner and Robert Jaques, and the tobacco business of Charles Milner and Company. His walk to work took him from the crowded dirty streets of Bermondsey, across Blackfriars Bridge, jammed with people, horses, carts, carriages and rubbish, and right into the overcrowded and noisy commercial heart of London. It was in St Paul's Churchyard that Tom had once snatched a few moments from his busy life as a messenger to write his heart-felt love letter to Gussy (June 1834).

The name 'St Paul's Churchyard' conjures up an image of a quiet corner of London where a young man might choose to sit and write a gentle letter to his sweetheart (as Tom did in 1834). However, in reality the Churchyard was a bustling place full of traders, merchants, warehouses, small manufacturers and shops. Robert Milner's drapery business was set on a busy commercial street.

31   Fall of houses in St Paul's Churchyard, 1852.[4] In 1852 the premises of Messrs Morgan
& Co., Shawl Makers and Warehousemen, collapsed after nearby excavations for a new
road. Next door to him was a building belonging to Messrs Cooke, Sons & Co., Manchester
Warehousemen. Robert Milner's shop was nearby, although he had retired to Yorkshire by the
time of this disaster.

142

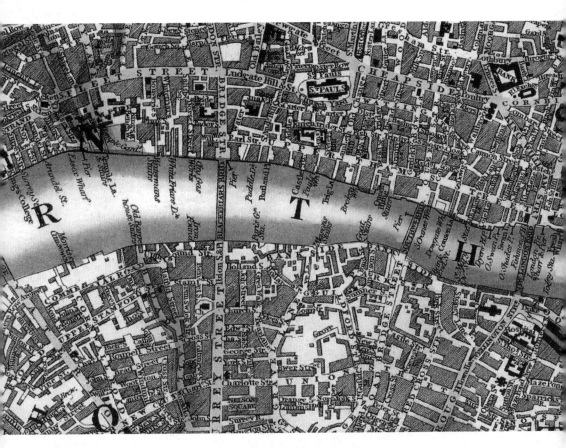

32   Map showing area around St Paul's Churchyard, the Thames and parts of Bermondsey and Lambeth, 1846.[5] The area around St Paul's lay at the hub of London's trading activities although, by the nineteenth century, virtually all commercial river traffic was located further downstream. Tom spent much of his working life within these busy commercial streets: Robert Milner had his draper's shop in St Paul's Churchyard and it was there that Tom wrote a love letter to Gussy; the Milners and Robert Jaques had warehouses in Cannon Street (to the right of Watling Street) where Tom worked for many years; John Kilner had a warehouse in Upper Thames Street and the Barrons walked there on one of their visits to London; Billingsgate fish market can be seen on the north bank of the Thames to the right and Smithfield Cattle Market was situated just off the top left of the map. Tom's journey home would have taken him across Blackfriars Bridge, past the tanneries to Brad Street (bottom left), a distance of about one and a half miles. South of the Thames, New Street (where Jane Pendlebury-Little-Chapman lived with her son Thomas) can be seen just south of New Cut (famous for its market); Bear Lane (home of Sophia and Archie van Dornick) is just to the right of Great Surrey Street; Nelson Street, home of Henry Pendlebury (and, when it was later renamed Kipling Street, home too to Elizabeth, Thomas and their daughters) lies in the bottom right corner near to the tanning yards of Bermondsey's Leather Market. Addington Place, where Robert Jaques lived, is shown in the bottom left corner. Nearly all the London events described in this book took place within these one and a half square miles.

33 'Ludgate Hill – a block in the street, 1872'.[6] Ludgate Hill, along with its continuations Fleet Street, the Strand and Whitehall, was the main west–east route through the city, leading all the way from Westminster right up to the front of St Paul's. It was a very busy thoroughfare.

34 City improvements, Cannon Street West, 1854.[7] Tom worked in warehouses in Cannon Street, which led into St Paul's Churchyard.

His neighbours included: a baker; five milliners; a cutler; a cheese-monger; a coalman; a merchant with his family, a clerk, a commission agent and his family, and 54 warehousemen; a wine merchant; a ribbon manufacturer; numerous warehousemen; two builders; a banker; another merchant with his family, several servants and over 50 warehousemen; a merchant of the Manchester Irish and Scotch Warehouse; a surgeon; a stationer; and 29 draper's assistants living in one building with four servants and four porters.

By great good fortune, an image of Robert Milner and his draper's shop has survived from 1836, the very year that Tom was working for him in St Paul's Churchyard.[8] In that year, Robert was the principal witness at the Old Bailey in the trial of Sarah Slow for fraud. Sarah had taken just one too many risks in her attempt to defraud his shop. She first bought a cheque from Robert for

£8 and then added the figure 'o' to the amount to make it appear as £80. She next cashed the cheque at Robert's bank (William Alers Hankey) and spent the money on various linen and other goods. She certainly had some nerve – or was rather stupid – because she used some of the money to buy a 'challi' dress from one shop and then tried to claim a refund for the dress at another shop. Challis was a soft, fine and lightweight wool cloth, not unlike cashmere; and a dress made of this type of material would have been a luxurious and expensive item and certainly not the sort of clothing that someone like Sarah would have been expected to wear. Sarah's audacity led finally to her downfall. She returned to the shop where she had originally bought the challis dress and sought to repeat her fraud by buying a new cheque for £8. But the shopkeeper, who had heard all about her first deception, recognised her, not least because he spotted the challis dress she was rather recklessly again wearing. This was a big trial. A total of 11 witnesses were called. Sarah was found guilty and sentenced to deportation.

Robert Milner began his witness statement with the words, 'Ours is a house of extensive business – I suppose there might be fifty ladies in the shop at the same time ...' He explained that his was a busy shop that issued many cheques. He chose his words carefully: '... when I first saw the prisoner, my impression was that she was not the person; but after I heard her speak, I said she was – I have not the least doubt in my own mind that she is the same person; but I do not swear it positively ...' Poor Sarah in her expensive stolen dress was doomed to fail as soon as she opened her mouth and spoke.

Tom also worked at numbers 14 and 16 Cannon Street, and it seems that these were commercial warehouses rather than residential addresses because they are not listed in the 1851 Census. The area was busy and noisy, like so much of London. It was also near Billingsgate Fish Market and less than half a mile from the great cattle market of Smithfield where fresh meat from the country was brought into the city to feed London's masses.

The smell of Smithfield Market

Statistics about the London meat trade are staggering. By 1842, 175,000 cattle and 1.4 million sheep were regularly brought each year from the surrounding countryside into the city. They were driven on foot from the outskirts and the rail terminals to Smithfield. In 1849 over 100,000 cattle were arriving by rail, usually to Euston, from where they were driven through the streets for two miles to the market. Tom, working just down the road from Smithfield, would no doubt have experienced some of the disgust expressed by Dickens, through Pip, in *Great Expectations*: '... So, I came into Smithfield; and the shameful place,

35 A drawing of Smithfield market.

being asmear with filth and blood and fat, semed to stick with me …'[9] In *Oliver Twist*, another description of Smithfield, this time of the journey of Oliver and Bill Sykes through the market, reads

> … It was market-morning. The ground was covered, nearly ankle-deep, with filth and mire; a thick steam, perpetually rising from the reeking bodies of the cattle, and mingling with the fog, which seemed to rest upon the chimney-tops, hung heavily above…the hideous and discordant dim that resounded from every corner of the market; and the unwashed, unshaven, squalid, and dirty figures constantly running to

and fro, and bursting in and out of the throng; rendered it a stunning and bewildering scene, which quite confounded the senses.[10]

Maker of snuff

With Tom travelling the length and breadth of the country, his wife Gussy was left to run their tobacconist's shop in Curtiss Hatch. It would have been normal for her to sell tobacco, cigars and snuff over the counter, even though she was not officially given an occupation on either the 1841 Census return or on her death certificate. She may have also helped him make snuff.

Making snuff was a highly skilled art, lying somewhere between cookery and alchemy. Among the Pendlebury documents are two sheets of paper, undated, which list 21 different recipes for making snuff together with tips on making and storing this valuable substance.

> Colour for Returns: sprinkle it with yellow Ochre mixed in water

> To Ripen Snuff: bury any quantity in Jars two or three feet in the ground for one month or more
> … Sprinkle it with Treacle and water, and Italian juice

Tom and Gussy were manufacturing snuff in almost 'industrial' quantities for distribution to other retailers. That this was the case is confirmed by the names of five firms in the St Paul's and Cannon Street areas that are listed on the back of these recipes. Two of these businesses are known to have sold tobacco products: Warburgs (Somerset Street, Whitechapel) was owned by Simeon Warburg, a cigar manufacturer of some repute; and Hubbards of Farringdon Street was a tobacconist.[11]

Some of Tom's recipes for making snuff

Strasbourg	*Macabau*	*Etrenne*
Six pounds Brown Rappee	Twelve pounds best dark	Nine pounds coarse Dutch
Six pounds Black Rappee	Rappee/fine grain/	Three pounds Black Rappee
Six pounds Fine Dutch	One 100 Drops of Otto of	Six pounds of Tonquin Bean
Three Drops of Orris Root	Roses and	A quarter of an ounce of
Eight Drops Rhodium	10 Drops of Sandal Wood	vanilla, and
Ten Drops Bergamot and	Put it through a fine sieve	Half an ounce of volatile
Twenty Drops essence of	and let it stand, in about	salts, dissolve and liquor
violet.	fourteen days bottle it off.	it in hot water.

Hardhams 37.
Nine pounds coarse Dutch
Three do. Black Rappee
One ounce and a half of vola
tile Salts, dissolved in hot
water, sufficient to liquor it.

Another.
Coarse light Dutch, flavour
with Strong Liquor - See
Recipe for Strong Liquor.

Etrenne.
Nine pounds coarse Dutch
Three Do. Black Rappee
six ounces of Tonquin Bean
a quarter of an ounce of
vanilla, and half an ounce
of volatile Salts, dissolve
and liquor it in hot water.

Another.
Take a light brown Rappee
flavour it slightly with
Strong Liquor, Eau de Cologne
and Port wine Lees.

Paris Rappee
Six pounds Dutch carrotte
four do Black Rappee

Princes Mixture
Ten pounds Black Rappee
Two Do. Good Dutch
Sixty Drops of Otto of Roses
Ten Do. Sandal Wood
Three Do. Ambergris, and
Three Do. of Millefleur

Another.
Dark Brown Rappee
scented with Otto of Roses

Gibbons Mixture
One pound princes mixture
One Do. violet Strasbourg
One Do. Tonquin Rappee
One Do. Brown Rappee
Twelve drops of essence of
Bergamot, and mix them
well together.

Tonquin Mixture
Let some Tonquin beans
stand in some best do
Rappee, for one week, then
sift it through the same
divider

Balsam

36 Some of Tom's recipes.

Gibbons Mixture

One pound princes mixture

One pound violet Strasbourg

One pound Tonquin Rappee

One pond Brown Rappee

Twelve Drops of essence of
     Bergamot

And mix them well together.

Wellington

Six pounds Dutch Carrotte

Four pounds Black Rappee

Six Drops of Sandal Wood

Eight Drops of Ambergris
     and

Six Drops of Otto of Roses.

Another

Take a light brown Rappee
     flavour it slightly with
     Strong Liquor, Eau de
     Cologne and Port wine
     Lees.

Flavour for Cigars

Cascarilla Bark

Dr Ruddiman's

Two pounds Dutch Rappee

Six pounds Black Rappee

Six pounds Brown Rappee

Twelve Drops of Rhodium

Twelve Drops of Sandal Wood

Twelve Drops Otto of Roses.

Princes Mixture

Ten pounds Black Rappee

Two pounds Good Dutch

Sixty Drops of Otto of Roses

Ten Drops Sandal Wood

Three Drops Ambergris and

Three Drops of Millefleur.

Cobourg

Six pounds Brown Rappee

Eight Drops of Rhodium

Four Drops Millefleur and

Four Drops of Ambergris

Ingredient	Meaning[12]
Rappee	A strong snuff made from a dark, coarse tobacco
Orris Root	The root of the Iris, used to scent snuff and also to strengthen and bind the scent of more-expensive violet. It encouraged sneezing.
Rhodium-wood	Used to scent snuff
Otto of Roses	A perfume made from an essential oil extracted from rose flowers.
Tonquin bean	The seed of a tree (*Dipteryx odorata*), native of Guiana. Its peculiarly agreeable smell was used to scent snuff.
Carrotte	A roll of tobacco from which snuff could be freshly grated.
Port wine Lees	The waste from the production of port.
Cascarilla Bark	The dried, bitter, aromatic bark of the cascarilla and a common ingredient in incense and in flavouring tobacco.
Ambergris	Also known as grey amber; a wax-like substance secreted in the intestines of some sperm whales. Initially dark and foul-smelling, it becomes solid and fragrant after much seasoning by waves, wind, salt and sun.

Then, between 1849 and 1851, Tom's world turned upside down. Robert Milner retired to Yorkshire, the business partnership of Charles and Thomas Milner was dissolved, and Tom lost his tobacconist's shop. Robert Jaques, too, seems to have retired to lead the life of a gentleman. At about the same time, Tom's personal life changed beyond all recognition. Gussy died, he remarried and, at the age of 41, became a father for the first time. The story now turns to Gussy's last days; and then to Tom's second wife, Jane Harding.

CHAPTER FOURTEEN

Miasmas and cholera:
Gussy, 1849

THERE is no doubt that Tom loved Gussy. He declared to her (1836) '...
Believe me my dearest Gussey to be yours while life remains ...', and he described himself as her 'constant and true lover'. In another letter, he addressed her as 'My Ever Dear and long lost Augusta' and ended with the words '... My Dear girl please not to fail writing if you have time for news from you will be as good as gold to me my love. Belive me to be your true and affectionate lover ...' Their marriage was a close one. Tom took Gussy to see his relatives in Radcliffe, and the Barrons and the Wolstenholmes approved of her. James Wolstenholme referred to her in 1844 as 'your highly esteemed wife' and was saddened when on one occasion Tom did not bring her with him to Radcliffe: '... I only regret that you did not bring your mistress with you as we should have been very glad to have seen her ...' And in 1844 Joseph Barron wrote (perhaps with a hint of disapproval) to Tom:

> ... we feel a little surprised that you did not Make our request known
> to your Wife about her coming down to Castleford to stay a few Weeks
> with us we hope you will have talked the matter over before know we
> hope she will soon come to see us ...

Both families spent time with her when they visited London.

Gussy took part in the nights out in London with Sophia, Bill, Archie, Tom and his brother Henry. She was close to her sisters and to her mother. But she never had children, and the letters hint that she was not always in the best of health. '... And we should be very glad to se your mistress but we think that she is a very poor traveler ...' (1844), and '... PS We were very sorry to hear of your Mrs. illness but hoping by this reaches you she will be recovered ...' (1844). Not even the best of constitutions, however, could have protected her from the cholera that rampaged through the streets of Bermondsey.

The story of the cholera epidemics in London, with four serious outbreaks between 1831 and 1854, has often been told. For many years, people had thought the disease to be caused by the dreadful smells and gases that were prevalent in most of the areas where cholera raged: the so-called 'miasma in the atmosphere'. However, the work of one man, an epidemiologist and statistician, identified the true cause of the disease as drinking water that had been contaminated by the fetid sea of overflowing cesspits that lay beneath London or which had been drawn from the insalubrious Thames. In 1853 Dr John Snow proved conclusively that drinking contaminated water drawn from the Broad Street Pump in Soho led directly to the severe outbreaks of cholera in the surrounding streets.[1] Although it would be many years before his work was fully accepted, growing public concern over the stinking Thames and the sewage problem did eventually lead to the regulation of the water companies and the gradual construction of a sewerage system.

Such reforms came too late for Gussy. Living in the low-lying area of what had once been Lambeth Marsh was not a good place to be when cesspits bubbled up to the surface and drinking water was pumped from the Thames directly below sewage outlets. Four weeks before her death, *The Times* newspaper reported (1 August 1849) that

> ... the districts on the south side of the river still form the field on which the disease [cholera] is most active. The deaths from it, which in this region were in three previous weeks, 93, 192, 443, rose last week to 514 ... The districts which show the greatest mortality are Bermondsey, where 64 deaths occurred last week, Newington, where there were 66, St. George (Southwark), where there were 70, and Lambeth, where there were 111 ...

Twelve days later, a detailed and horrific description of the area around Vauxhall Bridge, about a mile from where Tom and Gussy were living, appeared in the same newspaper.

> LAMBETH
> ... Here were deposits, which had been left by the tide, of a most offensive nature – such as dead dogs and cats, human excrement, and other obnoxious matters, emitting a most offensive odour ... At the corner of [Princes] street is a large building, in which article bones and kitchen stuff are used, which lie in Mr Hunt's yard until they become putrid, and cause the most obnoxious and unhealthy stench which it is possible to conceive ... Lower down ... is the boneyard of ... a dealer

in what are called 'green-bones' – namely bones which are taken by the butchers from the meat while it is still in its raw state; these bones are taken to Mr. Hunt's yard to the extent of several tons daily, and as they lay sometimes for weeks before they are used, of course they become putrid and emit a most poisonous effusion, which almost renders it impossible for a stranger to pass through the street without vomiting. In this street there are also several other equally injurious and obnoxious trades carried on, such as grease-makers, manure manufacturers, soap-makers, etc. ... There is no greater proof required than the registrar's returns, which shew that the cholera was 500 per cent worse in this borough than in any other part of the metropolis ...[2]

The statistics confirm how heavily the incidence of death from cholera was concentrated in Tom and Gussy's neighbourhood. Figures for deaths from cholera reported to the General Board of Health and published in *The Times* for the month in which Gussy died (August 1849) show that deaths in Lambeth, Southwark and Newington peaked at 247, almost as many as all the other London districts put together.

Just three days before Gussy died, the following report appeared in *The Times*.

... Of 6,194 persons who have died of cholera in London since September, 1848, 3,524 died on the south side of the Thames ... The mortality last week increased in the districts of St. George, Southwark, Newington, and Lambeth; it broke out with extraordinary violence in Greenwich ... The classes which have the greatest claim for public succour are not idle habitual paupers, but the hard-working artisan ... In a disease which so often attacks in the night, and is fatal in 24 hours, the poor have to procure orders before they can be treated. Unless some change be made in these simple administrative arrangements ...[3]

Gussy died at home at 2 Curtiss Hatch on 25 August 1849 of Cholera *Asiatica*. Her end was swift, coming just 14 hours after a doctor had been called.

Tom was devastated by Gussy's death. His cousin James Wolstenholme sent him his condolences four days later.

... We are extremely sorry, to hear of your Beloved Wife's death, through that dreadful malady Cholera, you see we know not when the Son of Man cometh, nor in what form, and how necessary it is for to be prepared for his reception, you must console yourself and not mourn at God's doing, she has already done that we all have to do sooner or later, but I hope we shall all meet again in a better and happier state and be made partakers, alike, of the Fruit of the Heavenly World.

Therefore Cousin, console yourself as I said before to the state you are left in and be sure to write on receipt of this with full particulars.

This devout non-conformist expressed his feelings in the way that came most naturally to him. His compassion and sadness shine through these simple words.

Tom's brother Henry's words, sent two months after Gussy's death, also resonate down the years. Written over 160 years ago, they still have the power to move.

... I wright these few lines to you oping that they will find you in good ilth as it leaves us at present. i received your parsel containg they Pin and they Broach and they Lock of Hear of your Dear Agusta, wich i shall put it in a fraim in leter it Gussy 1849 fror they remberince of them that as gone to they appy relmys abuve where whe all shall meet in unety i hope and nevir to Part no more ...

DEATH'S DISPENSARY.

OPEN TO THE POOR, GRATIS, BY PERMISSION OF THE PARISH.

37 A cartoon from the 1860s depicting people drawing water from a polluted water pump, one of the principal sources of cholera infection.

CHAPTER FIFTEEN

Pork sausages, grouse and family quarrels: the Hardings in Wiltshire, Liverpool and London

I N J U L Y 1850, a little under a year after Gussy's death, Tom married again. His new wife, Jane Harding, brought with her a large family of in-laws: a mother, three sisters, three brothers and six nephews and nieces. Tom also secured a plentiful supply of high quality pork, sausages and bacon because all the Harding men were pork butchers.

Tom and Jane probably met through the tobacco business. Jane's oldest sister Eliza was married to Charles Pascoe who was a butcher turned tobacco manufacturer living in Mitre Street, only four streets away from Tom and Gussy's tobacconist shop in John Street. It seems highly likely that Tom and Charles knew each other well through their business and that Tom met Jane when she came to London to see her sister Eliza.

Gussy had probably known her too. This would explain how Tom came to marry Jane less than a year after Gussy's death and why they chose the same church – St Margaret's, Westminster – for their marriage. Tom's best man was William Brunswick who lived in Buckingham Row, just a short distance from Strutton Ground where Tom had lived as a child and close to Charles Street where Gussy had once lived with her mother and sisters. Tom and his best man were exactly the same age and had a great deal in common. William had also been recently widowed and he, too, quickly married again: his second wife had the rather wonderful name of Olive Moth (a laundress who lived in the same house); and Tom acted as his best man.

Tom and Jane's marriage seems to have been very much a London affair, with none of his Lancashire relatives present. Even his brother Henry was taken by surprise. More than three months after the event, he was still unclear as to the identity of Tom's new wife. He wrote '… for i am comming to they exibiton but more to see you then enithing and your Wife but you never tould me who she was or wether i new er or not …' Tom did not, moreover, rush up to Radcliffe

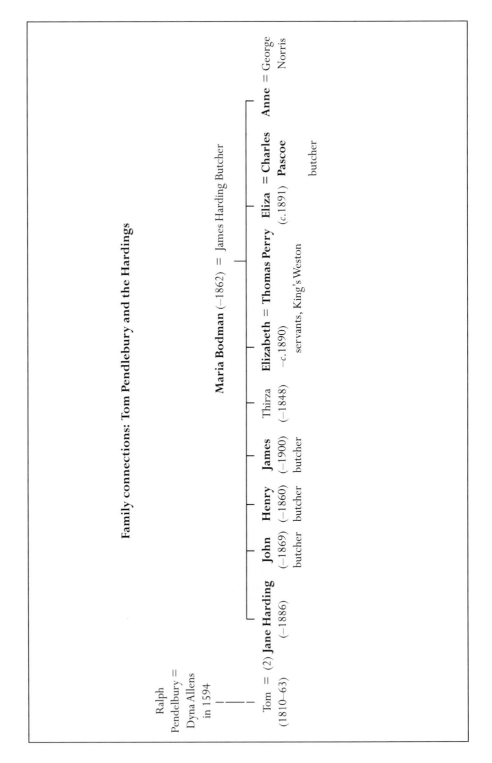

Family connections: Tom Pendlebury and the Hardings

Ralph Pendelbury = Dyna Allens in 1594

Tom = (2) **Jane Harding** (1810–63) (–1886)

Maria Bodman (–1862) = James Harding Butcher

John (–1869) butcher

Henry (–1860) butcher

James (–1900) butcher

Thirza (–1848)

Elizabeth = **Thomas Perry** –c.1890) (c.1890) servants, King's Weston

Eliza = **Charles** (c.1891) **Pascoe** butcher

Anne = George Norris

to show off his new wife: his cousin James Wolstenholme had still not met her ten months later: '... I hope Mrs Pendlebury is well and child also, and is glad to hear that you have got a partner for life this time ...' The 'child' was Rebecca Jane, born in spring 1851. In August 1851, over a year after the marriage, Joseph and Ann Barron and Henry's wife Elizabeth finally had the chance to meet Jane when they came down to London to visit the Great Exhibition and stayed with her and Tom in Brad Street.

The Hardings from East Knoyle

Jane came from East Knoyle in Wiltshire, a place very different from the mills of industrial Greater Manchester where Tom Pendlebury had been born and also very different from the murky streets of Lambeth where he now lived.[1] East Knoyle was set in a landscape of hills and rolling fields, with a church dating back to the Norman Conquest, thatched cottages and an ancient mill. It was an area of manor houses, farms, modest holdings, tenant farmers and labourers that looked to Hindon on the main turnpike London–Exeter road for its famous market and fairs.[2] By the time Jane was born, Wiltshire had become known as a source of good bacon and this reputation was to grow during her lifetime. The Harding men, all butchers, dispersed to London and Liverpool as soon as they were old enough to take full advantage of a butchery trade built upon Wiltshire's fine reputation as a pork, sausage and bacon producer.

It was into this agricultural community that Jane Harding was born in 1829, the daughter of James Harding and Maria (née Perman or Bodman). James was a butcher and died young but not before he and Maria had had nine children, all christened in East Knoyle between 1817 and 1831. Jane's mother Maria continued to live in East Knoyle all her life. She was described as an 'annuitant' (a person living on a pension) in 1851 and as a 'house proprietor' in 1861. She regularly visited her children in London, Liverpool and King's Weston, and died in February 1862 at Jane and Tom's home in Brad Street.

Tracing Jane Harding's Wiltshire roots is particularly difficult, given the uncertainties so typical of many early family records: non-standardised phonetic spelling of names, people's lack of precision about the year in which they were born, and the local predominance of families with the same surnames, first names and even occupations. For example, Jane's mother Maria's estimated year of birth appears variously as 1799 (Census 1841), 1788 (Census 1851), 1798 (Census 1861) and 1788 (death certificate 1862). Jane's sister Eliza's married name appears as Passco, Bassco, Pascoe and Passes, with her birth place of East Knoyle given on one occasion (by a London census enumerator) as *Noil*. Harding, moreover, was a common surname in Wiltshire. Another large family, many of whom were butchers and therefore presumably in some way related to Jane, lived in Hindon, three miles from East Knoyle. This family appears to have been related to the wealthy James Harding who was born in East Knoyle but who died in 1822 in Piccadilly, London. Finally, by coincidence, there was a second person with the same name (Maria Harding) and about the same age as Jane's mother living 20 miles away in Trowbridge: she too had a son named William; she inherited two cottages from her husband in 1840; but he was a grocer called Daniel Harding who appears to have been unrelated to Jane.

Eight members of Jane Harding's family feature in the Pendlebury correspondence: her mother Maria; her brothers Henry, James and John; her sisters Eliza, Elizabeth and Anne; and her sister Elizabeth's husband Thomas Perry. They were a close group. When Jane's brother and sister, Henry and Eliza, got married in July 1838 to Elizabeth Pascoe and her brother Charles, the two couples arranged a joint wedding at which each man acted as best man for the other. Both grooms, Henry Harding and Charles Pascoe, were butchers. Then when Jane's sister Anne, who lived nearby in Lambeth High Street, married George Norris (a smith) in May 1846, her sister Elizabeth and her brother-in-law Charles Pascoe witnessed the ceremony.

There were pork butchers galore. Jane's three brothers were all in the trade. James, for example, was a butcher who moved to Liverpool and married twice. His first wife, Letitia Fordham, was the daughter of a farmer and butcher. He had eight children and died a successful master butcher at the age of 78. John, too, moved to Liverpool where he worked as a butcher and he, too, married into the Fordham family of butchers. His wife Mercy was Letitia's sister and by 1861 he was an established sausage maker in Everton with two sons and three servants. After his death at the age of only 38, his wife Mercy continued the family business and in 1871 employed two men. Finally there was Henry. Henry was another pork butcher. He set up house at Rose Place, Liverpool, for his second wife, his young daughter, his brother John and his sister Thirza (who died of consumption at the age of 24). Henry was the black sheep of the family. A heavy gambler and drinker, he died of 'suffocation whilst intoxicated', alone, in a Liverpool boarding house in 1860.

Three of the girls escaped the meat trade, Jane herself, Eliza and Elizabeth. Although Eliza's husband Charles Pascoe was a butcher when she married him, he quickly exchanged pork for tobacco by becoming a tobacconist. It was Elizabeth, however, who broke most decisively away from the family mould by marrying Thomas Perry and living for much of her married life in service at King's Weston, Bristol.

Elizabeth and Thomas Perry

Elizabeth and Thomas worked together for the wealthy Miles family in King's Weston, where Thomas was a groom and Elizabeth a house servant. Their surroundings made a stark contrast to the Waterloo area of London where Tom and Jane lived. King's Weston House was a fashionable place in its heyday, visited by Jane Austin and described by her approvingly in her novel *Northanger Abbey*. By the time the Perrys began to work there, it was owned by Philip Miles, the man who financed much of Bristol's railways and docks and was Member of Parliament for Bristol from 1837 to 1852. He kept a large household. In addition to his six brothers and sisters, there were numerous servants: a governess, two grooms (one of them Thomas) and 14 servants (including Elizabeth). Census entries reveal that there were at least 35 adults, in addition to the house staff, living on the estate and employed in its running. These included: five gardeners, a laundress, seven labourers, a carpenter, two farm bailiffs, a gamekeeper and an under-keeper, a monthly nurse and an ordinary nurse, two dressmakers and several other servants.

Thomas Perry's first letter from King's Weston to Tom in London dates to early 1852, when he was already engaged to Elizabeth.

Dear Thomas,

I received the Glass safe on Friday for which I am greatly obliged It is a very good on, I can get my Name put on in Bristol Elizabeth sends her kind love to all she is quite well I should have writen before but I expected some of our people was coming to London to morrow but they dont know when they are coming now as their is a dispute in the house I shall send something by them but will let you know

Your Most Respectfully Thomas Perry

The reference here to 'a dispute in the house' probably referred to a disagreement between the people 'upstairs' rather than 'downstairs', as it seems to have interfered with plans for them to come to London.

The second letter was sent about five months later and five weeks before his wedding to Jane's sister Elizabeth.

Dear Tom,

Elizabeth informs me you lost my address when I was in Scotland. I thought it must have been something of that occured as I did not here from you. I hope this will find you all in good health as it leaves me at this time I hope the baby has got better of the Hooping Cough. I should like to be in London this week to see the Old Duke Buried I should think it would be a grand sight.

I have been back from Scotland about 5 Weeks I did not come through London or I should have called on you I saw Henry in Liverpool and found them all well. We have some very wet weather here for this last 3 weeks almost drowned out but folks have begun Hunting this fortnight and I think they have been wet through every day since I should soon get tired of that sport. I cannot say when I shall come to London again not before next summer I think.

Please to give my kind respects to Ann and Mrs Pendlebury and all friends and accept the same from your affect Friend

Thomas Perry

Hoping to hear soon

It was Tom and Jane's daughter Rebecca Jane who had whooping cough. 'The Old Duke' was the Duke of Wellington who died in December 1852 and was buried in St Paul's Cathedral. Three of Thomas's brothers-in-law (Henry, James and John Harding) were living in Liverpool by this time. 'Ann' was Jane's sister in London. Thomas had been in Scotland with Philip Miles who had hired a hunting lodge for the shooting season. Thomas Perry clearly had little liking for the sport.

In June 1853, Thomas Perry wrote again. The Miles family was planning another trip to Scotland, this one to begin a few days before the start of the grouse season on 12 August.

Dear Tom,

I received your kind letter and was glad to hear you was all well I cannot brag much about ourselves at Present for we have both a bad cold but Please God I hope we shall be right again. I cannot say wether I shall come to London before the beginning of August If I do it will be the beginning of July to send the dogs to Scotland we go ourselves the 6 or 7 of August you was saying you had a parcel for Elizth if you would be so kind as to take it to 44 Belgrave Square and ask for the Hallroom Maid we should be much obliged and I will write and tell her about it.

The weather is changeable here just now but they are cutting down the grass. I should like for you to drop in and have a Pipe with me this Afternoon.

I suppose you was at Ascot one day I should like to see the Soldiers Encampment it will be a grand sight for a good many.

Elizth will write to Mrs P soon hoping the Children are well Our kind love to all and accept the same yourselves, from your Affect

Brother & Sister

Thomas & Elizth Perry

PS We was sorry to here the news of Emma's death and it appears Henry is in a bad state of Health

They send the boxes away from Belgium on Monday afternoon

Number 44 Belgrave Square was the London home of the Miles family. The 'Soldiers Encampment' at Ascot was probably a muster of troops waiting to be sent off to the Crimea, where war with Russia had just begun. It was Henry Harding who was in a bad way, and it was his first wife Emma who had just died. It is clear that the Miles household, complete with hunting dogs, planned to set off for Scotland to arrive in time for the 12th of August.

The fourth letter, sent from Scotland in August 1853, reveals their destination – Lochindorb Lodge, in Invernesshire. Thomas wrote again from there three weeks after their arrival.

Dear Tom,

You will think it unkind of me not writing as I promised before this time but the old saying is better late than never thank God I got to my journeys end safe and I am quite well hoping this will find you all the same I had a letter from Elizth she is as well as can be expected but her Mother was poorly when she wrote but I Hope she will soon get better I suppose she will soon be going home with Elizth.

I hope you have got into something before now London is a dear place for anyone to be out of employment. We had a beautiful Passage over, arrived here on the Thursday night about 11 tired enough we are getting some good sport it is a good season for grouse I expect we shall stop here about five weeks longer but do not now which way we shall go home yet I should like for you to be here for a few weeks I know you would enjoy yourself the weather is very fine.

I sent you a paper yesterday which I hope you will receive what are you backing for the Ledger I think Sittinbourne will not be a long way from the winning post. Please give my love to Mrs P. and all inquiring friends and except the same yourself Meantime I remain your affect and well wisher

Thomas Perry
Lochindorb Lodge Nr Grantown Inverness-shire

'Mother' was Maria Harding. Lochindorb Lodge is set in an area renowned for
its wild scenery, heather moorland and lochs, grouse shooting and trout fishing
and was just the sort of place that the wealthy Miles family would rent for the
hunting season. They may even have owned it; they were certainly rich enough.

Not all the staff went with the Miles family to Scotland: Thomas Perry's wife
Elizabeth (Jane's sister) stayed behind. The fifth and final letter to survive from
the Perrys was written by her to her mother and is undated. It reveals her to
have been less literate than her husband.

My Dear Mother
You will think I foogot you But I often think of you hoping this will
find yo Better then last time I heard thank yo this Lines as at this time
– Let me know whin you hear from Jane I hope James wife will get
over him You will if please you.

Dear Mother, this is short Letter But I will Send a longer about this
as I know you Been opping to hear from me I now conclude with true
and my kind love to you

from your affectinit dauter E Perry

38 King's Weston House in the early 1800s.[3]

The 'James' mentioned in this letter has not been traced.

Thomas and Elizabeth worked at King's Weston House for at least another ten years. When their family grew too large, they moved out of the big house and into the village. Soon after, they left King's Weston and went to nearby Bedminster where they ran the railway station. Thomas became the railway station master, two of his sons the booking clerks and a third the telegraph clerk.

The Harding brothers and the disputed legacy

Tom seems to have struck up a genuine friendship with Elizabeth and her husband Thomas Perry. He also appears to have been on good terms with Jane's three brothers. Henry, who was a heavy drinker and gambler, freely confided in Tom about his gambling activities.

> Dear Brouther,
> I arived home last night and was happey to heir by your letter that Mother arived to London seaf – I ham happey to Inform you that after a splendid stleger at Wetherby that Heroine wone by a neck – as for B Doctor for Chester i do not fancy him as he do belong to a betting man and it is hard to kno what they do mene with him but i think he cannot win even if they do wont him to do. I have back Confessor Hothorpe and Hippolytus for it.
> hoping all is well with kind love to you, Jane and to all the family from your
> Affecent Brouther

He added a postscript

> NB I wish you wood go to som of the betting list houses and ce if they ar betting on Milnthorpe steeple chase and right by return of Post to let me no all pertlers [particulars]

The St Leger was indeed run at Wetherby but 'Heroine' is not listed as a winner.

John (who shared a house in Liverpool with Henry) also wrote to Jane about Henry's betting (year unknown).

> Dear Sister
> I receved your letter and was glad to hear that Mother arrived safe … Henrys Horse wone on Friday it was about 11 o'clock last Night

Before he came Home Mrs told me this morning that he is Going up
to London about Next Wednesday or Thursday … The Horse Has to
run on the 29th of this Month she will win that if she gets fare Play the
rider is such a roge

say nothing …

Gambling was widespread in England by the 1850s, particularly among
working-class men in the north of England and in London.[4] Both Tom and
Thomas Perry also liked to have a bit of a flutter, as this note from Thomas to
Tom shows: '… what are you backing for the Ledger I think Sittinbourne will
not be a long way from the winning post …'

But, for Henry, gambling was more than just a pastime. Along with the
drink, it had come to rule his life. He had good reason to try to drown his
sorrows. He lost his first wife (Elizabeth Pascoe) after a year of marriage when
he was only nineteen and his second wife, Emma (Roberts), died when he was
just 32, leaving him with a baby a few months old. His tragic death in a Liverpool
boarding house and his considerable debts led to the bitter row about Jane's
father's legacy, a dispute that came to dominate the final years of Tom's life.

The dispute over the legacy concerned Jane's mother Maria's attempts to
save her husband's property from falling into the hands of Henry's debtors. The
argument hinged around whether or not her husband had left a clear statement
that he wished to leave his estate to her and her heirs 'in perpetuity'. Had he
done so, this would have allowed her not only to benefit from his property
during her own lifetime but also to pass it on to all her children, including
Jane, when she died. If he had not, then Henry, as the oldest son, could have
laid claim to his father's estate and would have been entitled to leave it to
whomsoever he wished. Unfortunately for Maria and her surviving children, it
appeared that James Harding's intentions had not been made clear, despite his
wife's protestations to the contrary.

It all came to a head with the death of Henry in May 1860. Henry owed
money, and his debtors demanded that they be paid out of his estate. The first
reference to this dispute is found in a letter written in April 1861 from John
Foot to Maria Harding.

… Your son James called on me the other day stating to me that theare
is some Little repairs whanting doing at the Cottages you live in I
whant you to get to know what it will cost to put the same in repaire
and forward it to me as it wase your Son Henry's wish for you to Stay
in the Cottages after his Death the Same cottages being his Personal

Property at his Death comes to his Children after
>   pleas to let me know if the above correct by returne of Post
>   you will much oblige John Foot

John Foot, it seems, was already acting both as the administrator and as the beneficiary of the property that he claimed Henry had inherited from his father. Foot was a brewer and inn-keeper who had lived for most of his married life in Carr Lane, West Derby, just outside Liverpool; and Henry had probably run up both drinking and gambling debts with him. Foot's letter to Maria worried her so much that she made an exact and careful copy of it which she sent to Jane in London two days later with a covering note: '... you see the letter foot send

39   Jane Pendlebury's letter to John Foot, 1861.

so I have nofi to do with it all and I am but purely myself Do let me know hem is none and I will write more next time ...'

Jane was furious and wrote back to John Foot in splendid, spirited and no uncertain terms (letter undated).

> Sir,
>
> Hearing my Mother have writing to you concerning repairing the Cottages She have made up hir mind to sell them therefore I request you to foward the writings of the Cottage as soon as convenient giving you to understand that my brother Henry and Yourself have no right with them as the Lawyer told him in my Mother presents that he could not put them in his will they are my Mothers property as long as she lives at his Deth coming to us Children not Henrys Children if you think proper to adopt some of my Brothers Children before his Deth is nothing to do with us what Debts there ware at Henrys Deth is nothing to do with my mothers Property should you not atend to this further proceding will be taking for the recovery of them and we will [rest of sentence illegible]...
>
> Yours Respectfully JP

The outcome of this dispute is not recorded, but it seems that Maria lost the argument because at about this time she moved from Wiltshire up to London. Although described as a 'house annuitant' in East Knoyle in 1861, she was living in London two years later at Tom and Jane's house in Brad Street. John Foot, moreover, did indeed 'adopt' one of Henry's children, at least temporarily. In 1861 Emma Jane Harding was living with him and his wife as a 'lodger', but by 1871 the poor girl had been relegated to the position of a 'personal servant'.

Tom and the Hardings

It is easy to imagine Tom being overwhelmed by the sheer size of the Harding family. He came from a very small family: both his parents died when he was in his twenties, and his close relatives consisted of one brother Henry in Yorkshire, an uncle and cousin in Radcliffe, and an uncle and aunt in Mexborough. With his marriage to Jane, Tom was surrounded by Hardings. His mother-in-law died at his house in Brad Street, several of his sisters-in-law lived nearby, and he enjoyed a close friendship with Elizabeth and her husband Thomas Perry. By the time of his death in 1863, he had at least sixteen Harding nephews and nieces to add to his eight Pendlebury ones.

Tom's background was so very different from that of the Hardings. He wrote fluently and was widely travelled. He came from a long line of educated and god-fearing Pendleburys, parish clerks and pillars of their local community. His mother's family, the Wolstenholmes, was literate and hard-working and his Uncle Joseph Barron was a well-respected business man and a non-conformist. Butchers, by contrast, had a reputation for being 'over-fat and over-full', plagued by boils, carbuncles and alcoholism.[5] The Harding brothers' behaviour was in marked contrast to that of the small-scale employers and weavers who formed the backbone of Radcliffe village life. But the Hardings could at least read and write after a fashion. At a time when many people, particularly women, still put their 'mark' rather than their signature on official documents, Maria Harding and her children were all sufficiently literate to be in the habit of writing letters, a skill no doubt learnt at one of the flourishing East Knoyle schools.[6]

The Pendleburys, however, also had their moments, not least 'Old Tommy' who was brought up before the courts, got into a fight at the workhouse and regularly got involved in drunken brawls. Tom, too, enjoyed nights out on the town with friends, a few drinks, a good cigar and the occasional flutter on the horses. Life could never have been dull in the Pendlebury-Harding household

CHAPTER SIXTEEN

Aboard the *Bombay*, bound for Australia, 1852

A N unusual letter was found among the Pendlebury documents. It was written by someone called George Little on the eve of his family's emigration to Australia. The letter is addressed to 'My dear Aunt' and written on paper headed by a fine engraving of King's Hill, a beauty spot just outside Plymouth. Unfortunately, the identity of the aunt remains uncertain.

Friday August 27th 1852

My Dear Aunt

I am happy to inform you I recieved your letter this morning and sincerely thank you for the enclosed I went on shore on Thursday 26th took a Buss to Devonport & Betsy and myself Visited the Dock Yard we went thro the Ropemakers Houses or Sheds which are 1200 feet long there are Two that sise the upper part is were they spin the Yarn and the lower part the Cables for Her Majesty's Ships we saw the machinery at work in both houses after which we went up a Mount called 'Kings Hill' a favourite place of George the Third upon top of which there is a kind of Summer house from which with the aid of a Telescope we had a fine view of the arbour, Carsan Bay, Sound, Breakwater, Stonehouse, Victualing Houses, Plymouth, Lord Edgecombe's Seat and Park in fact the country round for many miles and it is as pretty a place as ever I or any person saw, the diversity of scenery is so great I have had the pleasure of tasting the west Country fish and should very much liked you with us to have partaking with us I have also caught some horse Mackeral alongside, with crooked Pins to the surprise of a great many who laughed at me for my simplicity as they thought but they were astonished to see me catch in about 20 minutes more than some of them could in 1 hour I caught 4 and lost 1 making some of them who laughed at me with there Hooks look rather sheepish I skinned them and with two mackerall each betsy bought had a very good mess

THE BREAKWATER *From Mount Edgcumbe*

40 View from Mount Edgecombe, Plymouth 1852. The image at the top of George Little's letter paper.

for Tea. I have since bought some hooks and intend angling every opportunity.

Dear Aunt I have nothing more to say except that you must not forget to remember me to "Richard" I should have liked to have seen him before but you know I was rather tied but it is of no consequence I can wish him Good Bye through you and hope when next I hear of him he will have had much better fortune than of late from my heart I am sorry I know what it is to work for others and not reap any benifit myself, but I wish him and all, all they can wish themselves & believe me your affectionate Niece & Nephew and Children

G, E, J, F & Mary Ann Little

There is such a confusion of Sound and noise on board putting there Boxes & away you must excuse all Defects

I remain ever Yours Dear Aunt

G. Little

169

Ship Bombay Plymouth Sound

The enclosed is a piece of Myrtle from Kings Hill I do not know if it will grow.

Tell William 'tis a <u>Sprig of Myrtle</u>

Myrtle was thought to bring luck, good health and fertility.

George Bartholomew Little, the writer of this letter, was clearly an adept hand at catching mackerel, perhaps because he was always happy around water. Born in Rotherhithe in 1820, and later moving to Limehouse with his wife Elizabeth (Keys), he came from a family of watermen and had worked as a lighterman on the Thames. Lightermen were highly skilled, carrying goods rather than passengers along and across the busy river. George would have good reason to think that his work would be valued in Australia. In any event, he and his family did board the *Bombay* and survived the journey: he, his wife Elizabeth, and their three children – Jane (born in 1843), Frances (1847) and Mary Ann (1850) – all appear on the inward passenger list of the ship when it arrived in Australia.[1]

Theirs was to be a dangerous and eventful voyage. The *Bombay* set sail from Plymouth on 29 August 1852 (two days after this letter to his aunt was written) with 706 emigrants on board and arrived in Melbourne on 14 December. Two accounts of the *Bombay*'s voyage survive, one a diary kept by Richard Moffat and the other a journal written by Archibald Gilchrist.[2] Together, they provide a vivid picture of the excitement and dangers of a long voyage in a great sailing ship.

The *Bombay* had been built for the East India Company in 1800 and she was fast: her yardarms were over a 100 feet in length and she had three masts. The 'confusion of Sound and noise' described by George Little in his letter to his aunt was indeed great. In the two days before sailing, the crew took on board 25 sheep, 12 pigs, a cow, baskets of poultry, fresh water and vegetables. The voyage was rough and hazardous, with frequent storms. Within two days of leaving Plymouth, all the emigrants were sick, and the flying jib was blown to pieces. A month later, her gunsail boom broke free and fell into the sea. This was followed by the loss of the main top sail, the fore top gallant sail, a jib and one of the mizzen sails in gale-force winds so strong that portholes had to be screwed down. Heavy tempests and violent squalls, with great waves washing over the decks, were a common occurrence. In one particularly instance, there were '… boxes and dishes flying about in all directions. Some of the passengers, especially the women, were in great terror. Some never went to bed and those who did were like to be thrown out …'[3]

41 The *Ballengaegh* emigrant ship leaving Southampton for Australia.[4] The ship would have been similar to the *Bombay*, on which the Littles sailed.

Twenty-four deaths were recorded, mostly among the very young who were particularly vulnerable to illness. A mother of nine died with one of her children when she fell down a hatchway; a young boy was caught up in a fight between two men and had his ear severed; a rope came loose and felled a man to the deck, causing a severe shock to his brain; another man fell overboard; one jumped to his death; and one man died of consumption having been ill for more than three months. Moffat wrote somewhat disapprovingly '... but for all the deaths that we have on board we hear nothing but mirryment and laughter day after day ...'[5]

There was clearly a joyous side to this voyage. Twelve births were recorded, and a school was provided for the children who were given '... a great many very nice books ... plus slates, pencils and copy books ...' at the end of the voyage as a reward for their attendance.[6] Many adults learned to paint or make hats. Emigrants bought bacon, cheese and baking soda from an American ship that came alongside. There was always merriment to be had, with flutes and drums played late into the night. The women held a tea party on deck. There was a great sense of camaraderie: during one particularly heavy sea swell '... The dishes are tumbling about the deck in all directions, near night it got worse, the people were tumbling up and down the deck at every heavy lurch the laughter was terrible it was like a dance ...'[7]

The decks were washed down every day, the ship was clean and the emigrants generally in good health. There were also wonderful sights to be seen: great shoals of flying fish (one of which flew through a porthole to land on someone's bed); an albatross with a wing span of six feet; dolphins; pilot fish; cape pigeons and sea-crows; sharks and bottle-nosed porpoises.

The emigrants must have anticipated their future in Australia with some trepidation. Towards the end of the journey, the chaplain lectured the men on the necessity of being prepared for death and advised them that provisions and lodgings in Melbourne were very expensive. On arrival in Port Phillip Bay, the *Bombay* was delayed for several days at the quarantine station to allow the typhus fever that was on board to run its course. Once ashore, the Littles settled in Boroondara, in the eastern part of Melbourne; today, still, some of its local names – Kew, the Surrey Hills and Camberwell – testify to its immigrants' memories of England. Within three years of landing, George owned a house and land at Red Gum flat (an area that was later to have its own Camberwell Town Hall, Camberwell Road and Waterloo Street); he was working as a carpenter.[8] He died in 1885 at the age of 65, his wife Elizabeth lived to the age of 88, and his daughter Jane survived until 1904.[9]

The identity of the aunt to whom George Little's letter from Plymouth was addressed has not been established. It was most likely to have been Maria Harding, Jane Pendlebury's mother. She had a grandchild called William who was six years old and just the right age to be told about the sprig of myrtle. He lived with his parents Eliza and Charles Pascoe in Mitre Street, a couple of minutes' walk from Brad Street. The possibility that the addressee was Maria Harding is strengthened by the mention of the man Richard who was having such a hard time working for others. Jane's Uncle Richard was a gardener and, later, a porter. He lived with his wife in the Wiltshire village of Frampton Cotterell but appears to have been childless; and he is thought to be the 'Richard' whom Jane cited as her father when she married a second time in 1865. He was quite likely to have visited and stayed with the Pendleburys or the Pascoes in London.

In any event, it seems likely that George Little and his family were well known to the Pendleburys. The Little family came from a long line of watermen living in Rotherhithe, and Tom would have known many of the men who made their living on the big ships that sailed between London and the colonies or on the multitude of smaller boats that carried passengers and goods backwards and forwards across the Thames. He had voyaged to India on at least one occasion and worked for many years for the mariner Robert Jaques. His best friend Archie van Dornick was also a mariner and his brother Henry had been a waterman (albeit in Yorkshire).

The Littles emigrated at a time when it was all the fashion to do so. An announcement in July 1851 that gold had been discovered in Clunes, Western Australia, had triggered a mini gold-rush. The dream of a new, healthy and prosperous life appealed to many families struggling to survive the overcrowding and poverty of London. Even Tom considered emigrating at about this time. His employment was becoming increasingly precarious and he was struggling hard to make a living.

CHAPTER SEVENTEEN

'London is a dear place for anyone to be out of employment': Tom's last years, 1851–1863

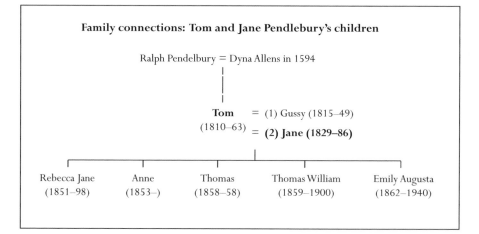

Family connections: Tom and Jane Pendlebury's children

Ralph Pendelbury = Dyna Allens in 1594

Tom   = (1) Gussy (1815–49)
(1810–63) = **(2) Jane (1829–86)**

| Rebecca Jane | Anne | Thomas | Thomas William | Emily Augusta |
| (1851–98) | (1853–) | (1858–58) | (1859–1900) | (1862–1940) |

Gussy's death at the end of a hot August in 1849 marked a turning point in Tom's life. The story has already been told of the cholera outbreak that killed her and of how, within a couple of days of her shocking and sudden death, Tom lost his tobacconist's shop, his home and his job. The months immediately following Gussy's death and before his second marriage to Jane were difficult ones for Tom.

In September 1849 Tom was in mourning and homeless. He stayed briefly at 1 John Street, the home of his former landlady and family friend Mrs Skirving, before moving in with his friend William Brunswick in Westminster. Overcome with grief, he can have taken little interest in the notorious case of the Miniver Place murder that spellbound most Londoners that autumn. Three weeks before Gussy died, Frederick and Maria Manning had murdered their lodger at Miniver Place, a street that lay in the heart of the Leather Market area of Bermondsey, only a few streets from Tom's 'patch'. Maria and Frederick were both arrested in the days before Gussy's death. The trial captured the imagination of the people, and large crowds attended their execution in November at Horsemonger Gaol, just minutes from where Tom and Gussy had lived.[1]

Eleven months after Gussy's death, Tom married Jane Harding and nine months later, at the age of 41, he became a father for the first time. Marriage to Jane brought him four children and an energetic and lively crowd of in-laws; but it did not bring him steady employment.

Getting by on odd jobs

Unfortunately for Tom, the partnership of Charles Milner & Company, based at 16 Cannon Street, was dissolved in 1850, soon after he had lost his tobacconist's shop. Thus ended the long-standing business arrangement between Robert Jaques and the Milners. This was bad news for Tom who had been regularly employed in one capacity or another by these men for at least 17 years.

From now on until his death in 1863, Tom was in and out of work several times. He was unemployed again for a while at the end of 1849, but by October the following year was once again doing odd jobs for his old master Robert Jaques. Four letters from Jaques to Tom have survived from this period, all written from Clarence Square, Brighton, where several 'house proprietors' let rooms and some of the tenants were, like Jaques, ex-East India Company employees. Jaques' instructions to Tom were, as always, written in a concise manner, with never a 'please' nor 'thank you' and with never an enquiry into his well-being. Tom's description of him in 1836 as 'unhappy' seems to have been well justified.

October 1850

Tom – I want you to call at the Saracen's Head Aldgate to morrow (Saturday) & pay for my Linen Box. Put the enclosed direction on it & send it down to Camberwell by the "Parcels Delivery Company" – Go early in the forenoon – so that it may be delivered the same day. If you see Mr Coleman ask him for a bottle of "Tincture of Myrrh" for me. We shall be up on Tuesday next as I arranged with you. Yours etc. Robert Jaques

November 1850, from Brighton:

Tom,

Meet me at the London Bridge Station at 1/4 past 8 o'clock tomorrow (Wednesday Evening) Yours etc.

December 1850, from Jaques at 41 Clarence Square Brighton

Dear Tom,

Call at Hodges (the Coachmakers) as soon as you receive this and

42   London Bridge, 1872, from the Southwark side.[2] This bridge dated from the 1830s, but this was the site of the original Roman bridge over the Thames, and also of the great multi-arched medieval bridge. For centuries it was the only bridge in the London area and was always congested with traffic and pedestrians.

get the front fall of the curtain for my dog cart and send it down to me. Book it at the London Bridge Station. If there is a small parcel (underlined) for Mrs Jaques left by Mrs. Lear, make one parcel of the two. I shall be in London some day next week, but shall write you a line. If there are any letters forward them. Call on Ambrose and tell him to earth up the celery in the back garden ready for frost, all here are going well,

I should like the parcel sent down tomorrow

December 1850

Tom, Meet me at the London Bridge Station tomorrow (Monday) at one o'clock

Aldgate was the ancient gate in the city walls on the east of London, and the 'Saracen's Head Aldgate' was a busy coaching inn on the road to Cambridge. The 'Parcels Delivery Company' was the London Parcels Delivery Company that was amalgamated with Pickfords, Carter Paterson and Beans Express in 1912. 'Tincture of Myrrh' was used in a diluted form as a remedy for mouth ulcers, thrush, sore gums and tonsillitis. The instruction that Tom was to meet him at London Bridge Station on Wednesday evening showed great confidence in the postal service: Jaques was able to write to Tom on Tuesday evening in the expectation that Tom would receive the letter in time to meet him the following evening. 'Hodges the Coachmakers' has not been traced, but Mrs Lear was a dressmaker living in Kennington (not far from Addington Place) and Ambrose Brown was a gardener who lived in Dulwich Hill, Camberwell.

The domestic nature of these final surviving instructions from Jaques probably reflect the fact that he had by now given up his seafaring adventures in favour of a more settled home life. He had married comparatively late in life, in his late thirties, and from now on he referred to himself as a 'gentleman' without adding a specific occupation. When he died in January 1869, his effects were valued at less than £450. He had a life insurance policy worth £300 and left two silver cups, one engraved with his initials 'R.E.W.', to his two daughters, both of whom were now married and living close by him in Camberwell.[3]

Tom was also doing odd jobs for Robert Milner, whose letters to him were warm, friendly and informative, in marked contrast to those from Jaques. Robert was very fond of Tom. The letter he wrote in November 1849 (addressed to Tom at 14 Cannon Street) is worth citing in full. It not only paints a fine picture of how an urbane man such as Robert Milner viewed retirement in the rural backwater of the tiny and unremarkable village of Hunton. It also shows

> Brighton Fridays
> Oct: 25. 1850
>
> Tom —
>
> I want you to call at
> the Saracen's Head — Aldgate —
> to morrow (Saturday,) & pay for
> my Linen Box — Put the enclosed
> direction on it & send it down
> to Camberwell by the "Parcels
> Delivery Company" — Go early,
> in the forenoon — so that it may
> be delivered the same day —
> If you see Mr. Coleman ask
> him for a bottle of "Tincture
> of Myrhh" for me — We shall
> be up on Tuesday next as
> I arranged with you
> Yours &C
> Robert Jaques

43 Robert Jaques' letter to Tom, 1850.

the high regard in which Robert held Tom. His letter is more like one written between equals than between master and employee.

Dear Tom,

This village is one vast nest with a very few exceptions of Rouges, Poachers and Whores - so that game is in all directions completely destroyed over the range that I hoped to have seen my friend Bag a good score I have not tasted a Bird or game of any sort so far; all the outskirts are now doubly preserved by the Duke of Leeds, Aylesbury, Wyvill and others of the nobility - it cannot be had at present without paying more for it than you can get in London – I hope you are jolly and well as also Mr Churchman, Harry Higgs, Barney etc. – How goes on the ('Antimanacutory') Barneys mixture; I often fancy you having a dip – 'Don't drink gin or anything before dinner, keep off the Lasses and keep your 'old man square'

What the Devil has been the weather with Mr Coleman - I have only heard of him once and that to the effect he had been bad – let me know how he is – and give my warmest regards to him – Leonard will enclose you a letter at any time My trunk is coming down – put me in 2 lbs Bacca a piece of Brown rappee and a bit of bigger head that flat hand pressed stuff.

How is Alderman Brown and Mrs, Skitten Dick etc.

I have 10 doz at … Please to put in my trunk any thing you see about belonging to me – I want a piece of Band or Box cord 10 yds long – for in this poor, lost, miserable half Hovel the Devil me care sort of place can you get any thing but quim

Farmers down in this part are failing like fun – all are going to the Dogs Corn is only worth 4/9 to 5/– Bushel Potatoes go at 2/– Bushel, Best Butcher's meat best pork crops, legs mutton Pork at 5½ none higher other cuts 4 to 4½ - the very finest new milk 2d per Imperial Quart, the best finest fresh butter 10½ [a] lb for 16oz. – it has till this week been 8 to 8½ [a]lb –The finest geese in their feathers 3/9 to 4/3 the fact is there is no money, I had to send miles to get change for a fiver – wanted change for 6d in coppers yesterday, all the Bloody place could not muster it without taking down part in farthings and part in spice for the young ones – I take devilish good care to live well it is cheap: coals 7/9 to 8/6 a ton, sticks for nowt

The Duke of Wyvill owned Constable Burton Park, a magnificent hall and estate

44 Robert Milner's letter to Tom, 1849 (first page)

lying just outside Hunton. Mr Churchman was the Clerk of Charles Milner & Company and Henry Higgs was probably an accountant who lived in the City. 'Barneys Mixture' was a blend of tobacco from Virginia. Mr Coleman has not been traced, but 'Leonard' was Leonard Campbell, a tobacconist who lived in City Road in 1851 and is mentioned in another letter, again in relation to trunks, letters and tobacco. Alderman Anthony Brown was a fishmonger elected for the Billingsgate Ward in 1824, and Chamberlain in 1844; he lived about half a mile to the south of Tom, in Kennington. Thomas Skitten was a porter who lived in Lambeth. 'Rappee' was strong snuff made from a dark coarse tobacco and 'quim' was slang for a prostitute Milner was presumably talking here about nearby Richmond or Catterick rather than the small sleepy village of Hunton.

The description of farmers 'failing like fun' was a reference to the agricultural crisis which was uppermost in people's minds in 1850 when Milner wrote this letter. A banking crisis, followed by economic depression, the failure of harvests in Europe and the spread of potato blight led to the Great Famine in Ireland. In England, cheap foreign corn (following the repeal of the Corn Laws in 1846) caused a prolonged agricultural depression. The corn prices Milner cited were very low indeed.

Robert Milner continued to find more jobs for Tom to do. Between February 1852 and December 1853, he sent Tom several letters asking him to pack up his London belongings into boxes to send to Hunton.

From Hunton, February 1852

Dear Tom,

We got safe home on Friday night please tell Charley that I will write him to tomorrow for to day I am so busy with matters I have not time.

please to drop me a line and say how and when the Box was addressed to.

Best respects to all

I will write to you again after the Box arrives

July 1852, from Hunton

Dear Tom,

Yours I duly recd and am happy to say the Box is safe to hand tho' in a very Broken State – I have left the following things behind and which have named to Charley in his letter and will you be kind enough to pack them – I have said nothing about the whip, which you please take care of for me till next you hear.

Your Bacon comes of next week – please give the enclosed to Leonard or leave it as directed.

If any shawl is not at Charley's I will have left it at the Belle Sauvage, also one packet Stuff – will you please enquire and drop me a note.

With best respects to Mrs Barnes Same to Jane

From Yours Truly, Robt Milner

Your Bacon will come with Charley's ham but I will write you when sent off.

Let Leonard have his note as soon as possible as he may have something to enclose

'Charley' was Robert Milner's brother Charles. The 'Belle Sauvage' was a well-known inn near St Paul's Churchyard. 'Mrs Barnes' was Eliza Barnes who lived in the same house in Brad Street as Tom and Jane and whose husband was a Custom House Officer.

Tom also did some work around this time for Charles Milner and carried out small tasks for his uncle Joseph Barron. Whether Joseph paid him to do so is unclear, but the formal tone of two letters suggests that he did.

November 1851, from John Turner:

Dear Sir, I am instructed by your Uncle to write to you, and to inform you that the Hamper containing the Hams were forwarded from here last Saturday according to the directions herein specified so that if they have not already reached their destination you had better enquire of Pickfords' or Chaplins for them, the Invoice is enclosed inside the Hamper ...

A week later:

Sir,

After receiving yours this morning I went up to the Station and found that the hamper was duly entered and forwarded on the 1st Inst. from Swinton Station, how it is that you have not got it yet appears to be a query as we have sent goods since to London which has got to hand. They were sent by the Midland and therefore it will be no use you going to the Great Northern, you must go again to Pickford's in Wood Street and I think you will find it as they have wrote from this Station about it

John Turner, born in Rotherham in 1816, was living in Newbridge, Swinton, with his wife and two children in 1851, a 'Book Keeper at the Glassworks'. Ten years later, he was described as a 'Glass bottle manufacturer' and staying at a boarding house in London near to St Paul's Churchyard. His fellow boarder was Samuel Blunn, another glass manufacturer for whom Henry was working in 1851 (see above). Joseph Barron knew him well (see above). 'Mr Turner' appears on several of the envelopes sent to Tom in the 1850s, suggesting that he played a full part in the Yorkshire–London trading network.

The first of these letters was sent to Tom 'Care of Mr Brown Store Cannon, City London' and redirected to Tom's home in John Street. Pickfords had a warehouse by the Regents Canal in Camden Town and kept huge stables with over 300 horses to transport goods from the railway stations to individual customers.[4]

At Christmas 1852 Tom treated himself to a good Havana cigar (or, to be precise, '2½ Havanas at £1 each on 20th December from Charles Milner & Co.'). But he was soon out of work again. It was at this time that he was thinking about emigrating to Australia; money must have been very short for him as he seems on this occasion to have been unemployed for a while because he was still out of work a little later in the year. Thomas Perry to Tom: '... I hope you have got into something before now London is a dear place for anyone to be out of employment ...'

Very little is known about what Tom was doing during the last ten years of his life when he usually described himself as a 'warehouse man'. His and Jane's second daughter, Ann, was born in 1853 and their first son, Thomas, in 1858. The only document to survive from this time (other than letters about the disputed Harding legacy) hints at financial troubles. It is a notice summoning Tom to a meeting of the Loyal Pride of the Thames Lodge No. 3903 of the 'Manchester Unity of Independent Order of Oddfellows, to be held at the "Lord Nelson" in Nelson Square, Bermondsey, on 24th June 1854'. The Oddfellows was a friendly society originating in Manchester and particularly popular in Lancashire. 'An insurance company, savings bank, associated status grouping and trade union all in one', its aims were charitable.[5] Tom probably joined the Oddfellows as an insurance against sickness and unemployment. His invitation to the meeting noted, however, that he was 7s. in arrears with his contributions.

The year 1858 must have been a particularly difficult one for Tom and Jane. It later became known as the year of the 'Great Stink' of London. During the exceptionally hot summer, the sewage of nearly three million people fermented in the Thames and the stench was so unbearable that the curtains of the House of Commons had to be soaked in chlorinated lime to dampen down the smell. Parliament was finally persuaded to support a new sewerage system, which was completed in 1875. At the height of the 'Stink', baby Thomas caught whooping cough which developed into pneumonia. He died aged only six months. Tom and Jane paid the local undertaker, James Smith of 12 Cornwall Road, Lambeth, the sum of £1 15s. for '... a 2 foot 3 covered coffin finished two and one row of nails, 2 pairs of handles, plate of Inscription, pillow and mattress. Single hearse conveyance, driver with fittings ...'

Tom and Jane had two more children, Thomas William, born in 1859 (who later went to Industrial School and learned to play the saxophone and euphonium, see below) and Emily Augusta, born in 1862.

In June 1861, a great fire broke out in Cotton's Wharf in Tooley Street, about a quarter of a mile from Brad Street. It started in a bundle of hemp and developed into the largest blaze since the Great Fire of London in 1666.

45 The Great Fire in Southwark: scene at Cotton's Wharf on Sunday morning at two o'clock.[6]

It quickly spread to adjoining warehouses which contained highly combustible items such as tallow, sugar and saltpetre. The London Fire Engine Establishment deployed almost its entire force of 80 full-time fire-fighters, but the fire burned for two full days. It was an extraordinary sight. It is easy to imagine Tom and Jane with young Rebecca, Ann and Thomas William and some of their Harding cousins, joining the crowds that climbed onto the rooftops and thronged the banks of the Thames to watch the amazing display of fire, explosions and plumes of smoke stretching along the crowded riverfront.

Tom's illness and death

Jane's battles to secure her father's legacy for her mother Maria came to a head around this time. The story of the dispute, and of how Maria lost her home and other cottages in East Knoyle to her son's creditors, has already been told. Sometime towards the end of 1861, Maria came to live in Brad Street with Tom, Jane and their three young children. She was far from well; she had been suffering from bronchitis for many years and finally died of an acute attack of bronchitis at the Brad Street home in February 1862. The small house tucked against the Waterloo railway arches must have been in turmoil during those gloomy February days. With at least four daughters at her bedside – Eliza, Elizabeth, Anne and Jane herself – and three grand-children in the house – Maria's death marked the end of an era for her family. If Tom was present, did he have a sense already of his own mortality? His death lay just 13 months ahead, and he would have been already suffering from the effects of the lead poisoning that was tightening its hold on his system. He, too, would have been far from well.

Tom died at home in 10 Brad Street, of lead poisoning, on 10 March 1863 aged 53 years, and with Jane by his side. His last days cannot have been easy. Lead poisoning was an insidious and painful condition. It nearly always resulted in severe stomach pains which were often accompanied by swollen joints and sometimes by paralysis, shaking, memory loss and dementia. The condition was not uncommon in Victorian England and its causes, symptoms and treatment were already widely understood in medical circles. In 1839, Des Planches had published his highly respected two-volume *Lead Diseases: a Treatise* in which he described in detail the symptoms and treatment of the illness and identified its various causes. He concluded that workers exposed to lead dust or fumes were in even more danger than those who handled solid lead.

Tom was certainly exposed to lead in everything he did. He was surrounded by the stuff, at home and at work. It was everywhere: in water pipes, paint and the polluted dust discharged by the factories that lined the Thames in Bermondsey. The Pendleburys lived right in the heart of the demolition, construction, welding, plumbing and painting (the paint was lead-based) that was part and parcel of the redevelopment of buildings, roads and railway lines. For over 20 years (from 1840 to 1863), his home lay in the small collection of streets around what is now Waterloo East station: in Catherine Street, John Street, Curtiss Hatch (Roupell Street) and Brad Street. During this time, Waterloo East and Waterloo Bridge stations were built and whole streets redeveloped. Add to this the work that began in the early 1860s on digging the new sewerage system, and his streets ranked among the most unhealthy, noisy and dirty places in London.

Tom also handled lead in his daily work. He shaped large quantities of finished lead when he was a tobacconist during the 1840s as part of the process of making commercial quantities of snuff. Snuff was routinely wrapped in lead before being buried in the ground to ripen; and the ceramic jars in which it was afterwards stored were usually lined with lead. White lead was also used to adulterate snuff and to colour the cord-like fuses sold by tobacconists.[7] Then, towards the end of his life, he worked in a warehouse for a lead-works. This was the occupation stated on his death certificate, and he may have been working there for many years because he referred to himself consistently as a warehouseman for much of the 1850s and in 1861 and 1862. Warehouses in general were bad enough even without them storing lead. The 'Manchester' warehouses (so-called because they stored large amounts of Manchester's goods), for example, were notorious for being very dirty, smelly and polluted by gas; they were places where there was a high rate of mortality from phthisis (tuberculosis) in particular and respiratory diseases in general.[8]

Tom, therefore, was heavily exposed to lead for at least 20 years on a daily basis at home and at work. He was also a heavy smoker; and tobacco smoking is now known to make people more vulnerable to poisoning by lead. As Tom's health began to fail, so his money troubles grew and there was no family wealth to provide a safety net. His quarrelsome Uncles Tommy, James and Nathan in Radcliffe, and Jane's poor drunken brother Henry, had made sure of that.

As Tom lay dying, however, he could look back on an eventful life lived in exciting times. Born in a small Lancashire cotton town at the beginning of the century, he had lived long enough to witness the defeat of Napoleon and the rise of the British Empire. The Crimean War had been fought and the Indian Mutiny quashed. Working hours for factory children had been restricted, electoral franchise extended, and slavery abolished in the British colonies. Free trade arrived with the repeal of the Corn Laws. Livingstone discovered the Victoria Falls, John Speke reached Lake Victoria, Florence Nightingale nursed in the Crimea and writers wrote books, Charles Dickens, the Brontë sisters and Elizabeth Gaskell among them. The first public libraries were established, Marx and Engels composed the Communist Manifesto, and Charles Darwin published his *On the Origin of Species*. The Houses of Parliament were built, Big Ben installed and Balmoral Castle completed. Brunel built railways, the first propeller-driven steamship arrived, the penny post brought letter writing within the reach of the masses, and telegraph cables were laid all the way to America. William Fox Talbot invented the first instantaneous camera, museums and galleries were opened, and the first cigarettes arrived from America. The list of innovations and novelty is endless.

The Pendlebury correspondence contains little or no reference to affairs of such moment. There is the odd mention of the state of the cotton or glass-working businesses, the price of food or a visit to the Great Exhibition of 1851. For the most part, however, the talk is of family affairs: health, food, drinking, having a bet on the races and disputes over money. However, Tom could not help but be profoundly affected by what was happening around him as he lived and worked at the cusp of Victorian enterprise. He travelled to India at least once and worked in the commercial heart of London for mariners and entrepreneurs who built their businesses on the trade between Manchester, London and the colonies. His activities as a tobacconist and snuff maker kept him in touch with all the developments in the tobacco and cigarette trade as trade with Virginia burgeoned. He lived in one of the most overcrowded and rapidly changing parts of Lambeth, cheek by jowl with new railway lines and stations, the boats that plied the Thames and the factories that sprung up around to process the goods brought in from afar by those boats. His friends were mariners and warehousemen, his family dressmakers, shopkeepers and servants to a wealthy member of parliament.

Tom had his personal setbacks. His father and mother died when he was a young man; he lost his wife to cholera, and his first son to whooping cough. He was out of work on several occasions and he was cheated of his father's money. But he was enterprising and resilient. He kept in touch with relatives in Lancashire and Yorkshire, the Wolstenholmes and the Barrons in particular. He made life-long friendships with Carrey and Sophia Barnard, Bill Day, Archie van Dornick, Elizabeth and Thomas Perry, and with many others too. Although one employer, Jaques, may have been a miserable man, another, Robert Milner, was genial, amusing and intelligent company. Then there was his brother Henry, who was close, affectionate, loyal and fun. Tom liked his cigars, a drink with friends, and a bit of a flutter on the horses.

Perhaps Tom was a bit of a 'fixer'. He knew his way around London (and much of England too) and happily made arrangements for all kinds of things to be transported about the country, whether it was ham, fish or wine for the Barrons, cigars for the Perrys or boxes of books for Robert Milner. Everything that is known about him points to a kind-hearted, savvy, adaptable and reliable man who was never without a bit of a twinkle in his eye. He may have died poor but he left behind the kind of personal legacy that his wife Jane and his young children – Rebecca, Ann, Thomas and Emily – had good reason to celebrate.

46 Outside Richard Rowlett's rag store, Broadwall, *c.*1877.[9] Broadwall was just round the corner from New Street and The Cut. It suffered badly in the Lambeth floods in 1877. The woman holding the baby was a lace-maker; and the man on the right was an odd-handyman and a local comedian who had helped his neighbours in Princes Square to safety as flood waters rose to a height of four feet in first-floor rooms.

CHAPTER EIGHTEEN

'One vast poor family ... children in the street ... women gossiping at the Doors': Jane Pendlebury, 1863–1886

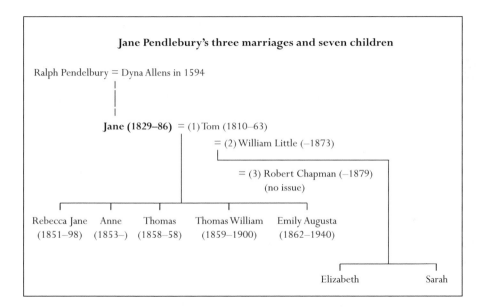

Jane Pendlebury's three marriages and seven children

Ralph Pendelbury = Dyna Allens in 1594

Jane (1829–86) = (1) Tom (1810–63)

= (2) William Little (–1873)

= (3) Robert Chapman (–1879)
(no issue)

Rebecca Jane	Anne	Thomas	Thomas William	Emily Augusta
(1851–98)	(1853–)	(1858–58)	(1859–1900)	(1862–1940)

Elizabeth   Sarah

W H E N Tom died in 1863, difficult times lay ahead for his wife Jane. She now had four young children to bring up on her own, including a two-month-old baby daughter. Apart from the emotional trauma of losing a husband, the death of the breadwinner was a dreadful blow when little more than the workhouse stood between staying alive and complete destitution on the unforgiving streets of Victorian London. Luckily, Jane was a strong and resilient woman.

Jane stayed on in Brad Street for a couple of years after Tom's death. Then, in April 1865, she remarried. Her new husband was William Little, a labourer by trade and 12 years younger than her. Somewhat curiously, Jane gave the name of her father not as James but as Richard Harding, deceased, a cooper (a person who made or mended barrels and casks). This was probably her Uncle Richard who lived just outside Bristol. He had no children of his own and may have unofficially adopted her, given she grew up in a large and fatherless family. Tom's brother Henry Pendlebury had done something similar when he named his father as Joseph Pendlebury (after Joseph Barron) rather than Richard Pendlebury.

Jane moved into 17 New Street with her new husband and the two Pendlebury children who were still young enough to live at home: Emma (aged nine, recorded as 'Emma P. Little' in the 1871 Census) and Thomas (aged 12 and recorded as 'Thomas P. Little'). New Street was to be Jane's home for the remaining 21 years of her life. The house was owned by Emma Paine (who lived six doors away from Tom and Jane's former home in Brad Street) and let on a lease to Robert Chapman, a watchman with a wife and one child. A copy of his tenancy agreement to rent the house for £26 a year has survived from 1858. Shortly after, Emma Paine moved to 6 Bear Street, two doors along from the house once occupied by Tom's first wife Gussy's sister Sophia and her husband Archie van Dornick. It was probably no coincidence that Emma's husband John was a pork butcher like so many of Jane's family. In these streets around Waterloo and The Cut, families and friends formed an exceedingly tight-knit community.

Robert Chapman, the lessee of the New Street house, continued to live there for the rest of his life. In addition to sub-letting rooms to Jane, her new husband William Little and the two Pendlebury children, he also sub-let to another family and to three lodgers. By 1871, the house had become even more crowded. The eight adults and six children now living there included Thomas and Emma Pendlebury Little and two new arrivals born to Jane and William: Sarah (born 1865) and Elizabeth (born 1866). When Robert's wife Sophia fell ill with bronchitis in 1872, it was Jane who nursed her and was present at her death. In the following year, William also contracted bronchitis and, again, Jane nursed him and was present at his death. Now, twice widowed, Jane still had three children entirely dependent upon her, two Littles and one Pendlebury. Thomas had by great good fortune been plucked from this almost Dickensian scene by the School Board for London to be sent as a boarder to a school for neglected and destitute children (see below).

Jane struggled to make ends meet. She probably took in washing, as she was known to have done later, and may have helped Robert Chapman's daughter Emma Sophia who soon moved into the house with her husband Edward Stevens (a ship's steward and son of a mariner) and their three children. Most likely she acted as a housekeeper or carer to Robert who was 11 years older than her. He and Jane had lived in the same house for over 15 years and she had nursed his wife so it would have seemed natural for her to look after him. She married him in 1878 and was with him when he, too, died, in 1879, of bronchitis and dropsy. On his death certificate, Robert's occupation was given as 'Horse Keeper'. A horse keeper was usually someone paid to feed the horses used by the London carmen, and it is possible that it was through his contacts that his step-son Thomas Pendlebury later found work as a carman in London's east end.

In August 1878, six months after her third marriage to Robert Chapman (and ten months before his death), there was a big celebration at 17 New Street. Five children from the house were baptised on the same day at the local parish church of St John Horsleydown. They were Jane's two children by her second husband William Little (Sarah and Elizabeth aged 12 and 10) and the three children of the two other lodgers, Edward and Emma Stevens (Chapman's daughter and son-in-law). What a party it would have been. There were Jane's other children by her first marriage to Tom: Rebecca Jane with her husband Henry Blanchard and their four children; Ann with her husband Henry Griffin and their two children; nineteen-year-old Thomas who had just started work as a carman; and Emily who was in service in Chelsea. Add to these her sister Eliza Pascoe, who only lived two streets away with her three adult children and their families. In addition, her sister Elizabeth Perry with husband Thomas and all seven of their children might even have travelled up from Bristol for the occasion. Then there were friends: Gussy Pendlebury's sister Sophia and her husband Archie van Dornick, whom Jane and Tom had known so well, lived nearby. And if Tom's brother Henry and his wife Elizabeth were still living in Nelson Street Bermondsey, they too would have come, adding another 11 children to the party. And one of those children, Elizabeth, was already married with a young daughter and now heavily pregnant with another. And this was just the Pendlebury side. Once the family and friends of the Stevens, plus the four other lodgers, were included, the event would have been more like a street than a house party.

In 1881, having lost three husbands and born seven children, Jane Pendlebury-Little-Chapman was living at 17 New Street with her youngest daughter Elizabeth. Her occupation was given as 'laundry woman (washing)'. Laundry work was an awful occupation. Exposure to heat, steam and the clothes of the sick, combined with the constant standing, mangling and ironing, were known to lead to bronchitis, anaemia, varicose veins, ulcers and uterine disorders.[1]

Jane died at home of uterine cancer in October 1886, cared for by her step-daughter Emma (daughter of her third husband Robert by his first wife Sophia) who was present at her death. Coming from a large family of butchers,

47   Washerwoman,
*c.*1880–1914.[2]

she was never without people around her. By 1886 she had three daughters, one son, sixteen nephews and nieces and thirteen grandchildren, including Jane Elizabeth ('Kit') and Emily Florence ('Em'), besides several stepchildren.

New Street no longer exists. In Jane's day, it lay in a nest of small streets just south of the Old Vic Theatre, built upon the damp grounds of the southernmost limits of Lambeth Marsh. The *Booth Notebooks* contain a description of the street and the area written soon after Jane's death.

> ... Mitre Street, Caffyn Street (late New Street) ... poorer than they used to be: a few fairly comfortable [houses] remaining but the majority poor and very poor: Caffyn St is the poorest ... a boy in a fit in Caffyn St with the whole neighbourhood out of window & in the street to look at him ... the bulk of the inhabitants both work & sleep in the district ... the inhabitants make one vast poor family whose lives are well

known to one another. There is more street life than even in the East, more children in the street and more women gossiping at the doors.[3]

Lambeth Lower Marsh Market

In the same *Notebooks*, Charles Booth has left a vivid description of the New Cut and Lambeth Lower Marsh Market, 'the common meeting place and market street' that was just five minutes' walk from Jane's home in New Street. It was 'always busy, though busiest on Friday & Saturday night and Sunday mornings ...' There could be found an enormous variety of produce on sale, including: loaves, meat scraps, pork chops ('first rate'), half cooked chickens ('not appetising to look at'), uncooked sheeps' heads, eggs (Best and 'Special line'), ducks, whole skinned rabbits, bunches of radishes, lemons and good cucumbers. Booth was fascinated by the fish barrow where cod, cods heads, whiting, Pollock and plaice

48   Sunday morning in the New Cut, Lambeth, 1872.[4]

were auctioned off to a crowd composed entirely of women. The rump steak was good and plenty of mutton chops were to be had. The costers' barrows along the north side sold fish and fruit and barrows of flowers, fuchsias, geraniums and small bedding plants in wooden boxes. There were barrows full of old keys and ironwork and haberdashery. Booth finished with the words '... but the glory of the Lower Marsh is by night. It is shy and quiet by day'.[5]

A report in the *Daily News* in January 1872 offers an even more colourful picture of the market on Sunday mornings.[6] All kinds of remedies were on offer, including 'a penny stick of some green substance, like sealing-wax, will make many scores of plasters on brown paper, warranted to cure warts, bunions, and corns'. Tooth extraction was available from a 'dental professor [who] wears

49 Street traders in the New Cut, 1893.[7]

a velvet cap, ornamented with about a hundred long-fanged double-teeth'. A baker's shop displayed '… most tempting jam tarts and puffs … [and] plum composition, a kind of compromise between cake and pudding, sold in large blocks'. Among the least salubrious objects on sale must surely have been the '… piled heaps of dirty women's clothing, upper and under, which female auctioneers are selling by a process known as a "Dutch auction"'.

Jane was a warm-hearted and gregarious woman. She was not well educated but she was strong and quick to defend those she loved. She would have been a well-known local figure, gossiping outside her front door or bargaining for clothes in New Cut market, and part of 'one vast poor family whose lives are well known to one another'. Thomas Pendlebury, Jane's son by her first marriage to Tom, spent his childhood and the early years of his married life in this close-knit community and it is to his story that this account now turns.

CHAPTER NINETEEN

'[T]he boys ... marching towards Addlestone, headed by their Brass Band and carrying their flags and banners': Thomas Pendlebury at Industrial School

THOMAS Pendlebury was only three when his father Tom died of lead poisoning in 1863. He grew up in the crowded house in New Street with his mother Jane, his stepfather William Little, his two sisters and, by 1867, his two new half-sisters. It was a tough, hand-to-mouth, existence in the poverty-stricken streets of Lower Lambeth Marsh, an area notorious for street crime, prostitution, overcrowding and pollution. Jane was poor, and her new husband William can have earned very little as an unskilled labourer. How Thomas felt about his new stepfather and two baby half-sisters can only be imagined. It may not have been easy for him, even though having a step-parent was a common enough occurrence in a neighbourhood where life expectancy was short. At least he did not end up in the workhouse, as many fatherless children did. With luck, he may also have managed to avoid being drawn into the petty crime that was rampant among the street gangs in the area. However, he did appear to be sufficiently 'at risk' to qualify for a place in one of the newly established Industrial Schools. On 18 July 1871, therefore, Thomas arrived at the Surrey County Industrial School for Boys in Byfleet, Surrey, sent by the School Board for London (SBL).[1]

Industrial Schools

Industrial Schools were intended to help those children who were destitute, but who had not as yet committed any serious crime, by removing them from their bad environment, instilling in them the habit of work and teaching them

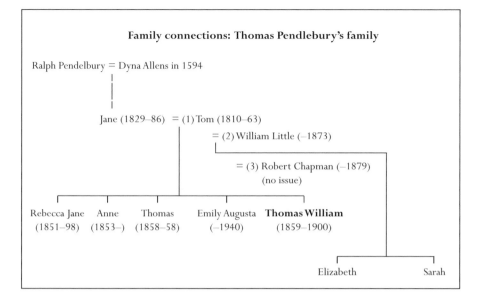

Family connections: Thomas Pendlebury's family

Ralph Pendelbury = Dyna Allens in 1594

Jane (1829–86) = (1) Tom (1810–63)

= (2) William Little (–1873)

= (3) Robert Chapman (–1879)
(no issue)

Rebecca Jane | Anne | Thomas | Emily Augusta | **Thomas William**
(1851–98) | (1853–) | (1858–58) | (–1940) | (1859–1900)

Elizabeth | Sarah

basic education and employment skills. Their early history and the part they played in the development of early state education have been well documented.[2] By the time Thomas was sent away, Industrial Schools were targeting children under the age of 14 who were found begging, destitute, orphaned, living on the streets or in the company of thieves. Parents, step-parents or guardians could also apply for a place at one of these schools on the grounds that a child was beyond their control.

Some of the first schools set up to meet the demand for Industrial School places were privately run, including the one that Thomas was later to attend. In 1871 the SBL appointed two Industrial Schools officers to investigate cases of child destitution in inner London and to bring before the magistrates those children they deemed suitable for Industrial schooling. It was through the intervention of one of these SBL officers that Thomas was brought before the magistrates to be sentenced to a period at the newly established Industrial School at Byfleet, in Surrey.

This intervention may have been the saving of Thomas. Without it, he would have been unlikely to have received any kind of education. Attendance at school between the ages of three and thirteen did not become compulsory until 1876, and when Thomas was growing up educational provision in London was very patchy, being mostly provided by religious and charitable foundations, and by the workhouses. Large numbers of children never went to school and even after the SBL set up its own schools, truancy remained high among those who did.

In 1873, for example, in the two schools nearest to where Thomas lived, the total highest attendance on any one day was 284 children out of 335 on roll (Webber Row) and 397 out of 522 on roll (Marlborough Street, New Cut); and it presumably fell far lower at other times.[3]

It was for children from neighbourhoods such as Lower Lambeth Marsh that the Industrial Schools were primarily designed. In the words of the London County Council

> ... The children who were brought before the Industrial Schools
> Committee were of the very lowest type. The streets [of London]
> swarmed with waifs and strays who had never attended school...
> children slept together in gangs...in empty boxes and boilers...in empty
> packing cases...covered over with tarpaulins and old sacks ...[4]

The SBL preferred these schools to be in country areas such as Byfleet, where Thomas went, so that inner-city children could enjoy a healthier lifestyle far removed from their sad homes. Each such school was expected to have its own board of management to oversee the spending of a grant from the authorities of 7s. per pupil per week.

The Industrial Schools were boarding schools that operated to a strict timetable between six in the morning and the children's usual bedtime at seven in the evening. There were set times for the classroom, learning a trade, housework, religion, meals and play. The schools aimed to provide an elementary education and training in a skill that would provide future employment. Everything was underpinned by a firm moral and Christian training, and in the early days the schools were regarded as semi-penal institutions and the children like prisoners. Corporal punishment was severe and solitary confinement not uncommon.

The SBL inspectors struggled to improve the initially very basic education of reading, writing, spelling and arithmetic. They recognised, however, the importance of the industrial training (including, for example, tailoring, shoe-making, bread-making, farming, market gardening, carpentry, plumbing, house decoration and, sometimes, blacksmithing) that could not only feed and clothe the children but also provide them with employment once they left school. In the belief that 'Listless idleness cannot be tolerated as it fosters vice and discontent, and is the foe of happiness and health', children were in their view best kept constantly busy.[5] When they were not eating or in bed asleep, children were expected to be in the classroom, at work or at drill, doing physical exercise or organised games and play. Cricket and football were encouraged.

Finally, there was the music. Nearly every boys' Industrial School had its own band; the SBL encouraged band practice not only as an excellent way to prepare boys for the army (many Industrial School children later joined band regiments) but also as a way of recruiting people to play in London's burgeoning parks and public gardens. Thomas's school provided nearly all these activities, including a flourishing school band. As an adult, he put his musical skills to good use when he played in the Carmen's Union Band.

The writer of the London County Council report sums up the spirit of enlightenment and social engineering that characterised both the SBL and, later, the Inner London Education Authority.

> ... Many of the children [in Industrial Schools] are taken from the lowest classes of society; from parents, one might even say ancestors, often steeped in vice, crime and immorality ... [Some of the children are bad] but none of them is so bad as to be absolutely irreclaimable ... Notwithstanding their inherent faults and failings, these little people are in reality very attractive and interesting...the majority of them are absolutely sharp-witted and intelligent ... [and having had to fend for themselves produce] an almost incredible story ...[6]

Thomas at the Surrey County Industrial School for Boys, Byfleet

Thanks to the vision of these Victorian educational and social reformers, Thomas swapped the mean streets of Lower Lambeth Marsh for the countryside of Surrey. Although the regime in Byfleet was more akin to a modern-day boot camp than a rural idyll, the intervention of the SBL was probably the making of Thomas. Thomas must have appeared extremely neglected to have caught the eye of the school inspector. Truancy on its own would not have been enough to earn him a place at an Industrial School. The SBL sent only 180 London children to Industrial Schools during the whole of 1871 (the first year of the scheme). It is possible, of course, that Jane 'worked the system' and pushed him forward as being beyond her control. It would not have been beyond a strong and resourceful woman like her to fight for her children as best she could. She would have heard on the Bermondsey grapevine all about the work of the new SBL inspectors and she may have seized upon a cheap way of feeding her only son and giving him a better future at little cost to herself. Although parents were expected to pay something towards the cost of their children's stay at Industrial School, the majority of London parents paid only 1s. 5½d. a week.[7]

Jane would have seen this as a good investment, particularly if Thomas and his new step-father were arguing.

It must have come as quite a shock to Thomas to find himself being brought before the magistrates and sentenced to four years in an institution far from home in an area where most people still worked on the land. He arrived at the school on 18 July 1871 and stayed there until his discharge on 10 November 1875 when his sentence expired.[8] Fortunately, a number of documents about the school still survive from that period, thanks to the scrapbooks of Alfred Wells. Wells was already the secretary of the school when Thomas arrived and he became its superintendent in 1872. He kept scrapbooks of newspaper cuttings, postcards, pictures and photographs. It is through these, and the school's visitors' book, that a picture of Thomas's schooldays emerges.

The school's manager was John Leyland, a Manchester born man. He seems to have approached the school primarily as a businessman rather than as an educationalist because, although the 1871 Census records him as 'Head' of nineteen boys, his occupation is given as 'Income from Land and Houses'. Thomas was one of the first intake of boys sent by the SBL, and the school had just moved to new premises. One SBL boy (Doughty) was already there, another (Hanson) arrived on the same day, and two others (Page and Ford) joined a few days later. Numbers quickly built up to about 200 children, many of whom had been sent by the SBL who, in 1874, gave the school a £500 building grant in return for securing 50 beds.[9] By the end of 1871, the school extended over 250 acres and was employing its boys on the land and in tailoring, shoe-making, carpentering and other useful occupations.[10]

The SBL's assistant inspector, Henry Rogers, visited the school four months after Thomas's arrival and found something lacking. He noted that although the boys looked well and healthy, and were well behaved and making progress, 'The standard of education is not at present very rich'.[11] A month later, he conducted his first official inspection. The teaching was still unsatisfactory in his view, but otherwise he generally liked what he found.

> ... Visited the School and examined the Boys ... I find all going on
> well, with fair promise of good work in the future, under favourable
> conditions. The rooms, dormitories have been constructed on principles
> of well-tried experience and knowledge of the work – and I can
> have but little doubt that in a short time the Institution will earn its
> reputation as a successful and well-conducted school.
> The educational work is not yet placed on a satisfactory footing.

But I trust that the engagement of a well-qualified schoolmaster will produce a better result...

Six months later, the situation had improved considerably. Sydney James, another SBL inspector, noted that

... The Institution appears to be in good working order and well organised and likely to be among the first and best of our Farm Schools when its arrangements are completely developed. I have examined the first Three Classes. They have done very fairly considering the circumstances of the day being intended for a holiday and the Boys naturally excited and anxious to get through and be done with it ...

When Henry Rogers visited the following year he found the school '... very much improved in every respect since my last visit ... I am glad to find that the general standard of education has been much raised ... I have had very good exercises from the elder Boys ...' Sydney James, too, was satisfied with what he saw on a subsequent visit, though he felt the playground to be inadequate. '... The Boys have done very well in Reading and Writing from Dictation and in their Copy Books. The Ciphering is very fair as to standard but is rather hasty and incorrect ...'

This was the last SBL inspection to be recorded during Thomas's stay in Byfleet. Classroom teaching, it seems, had improved but was not outstanding. Seven months after Thomas's departure, an SBL inspector noted that, 'No "Standard" is used in the School nor is their "Code" recognised by Inspector – if ever enforced by the School Board, it will probably be found that Standard Four will not be exceeded, nor, as at present appears, would it be useful to do so ...' Standard Four (of six Standards of Education) meant that most children could: read a few lines of poetry or prose; write a sentence slowly dictated once, by a few words at a time, from a reading book; and master the compound rules of arithmetic, including common weights and measures.[12] Thomas, it seems, had a good chance of leaving school with a solid grounding in the basics of literacy and numeracy.

The SBL Inspectors were not the only people to visit the school. Magistrates and all kinds of local dignitaries were regularly entertained. Without exception they found the boys to be happy, healthy and cheerful, and the dormitories to be clean and well arranged. However, space seems to have been a problem, with calls for a separate dining room and larger dormitories. One magistrate commented (October 1872) that '... In the bedrooms the beds appeared to be far too closely packed together, there being but a few inches between bed and bed, some additional sleeping seems absolutely necessary, though the rooms as far as they go are light and airy'. For Thomas, of course, such a level of overcrowding would have been nothing new. He was used to sharing a couple of rooms in New Street with his mother, step-father and four younger sisters.

The comments in the visitors' book concentrate on the classrooms, dormitories and chapel, with little mention of the industrial training and farm work that occupied so much of the boys' time. Fortunately, the scrapbooks of Alfred Wells fill this gap. Wells painstakingly cut out and kept press cuttings from the local newspapers on Industrial Schools in general and on the Byfleet school in particular.[13] Equally carefully he preserved postcards, pictures and photographs that he mounted in another scrapbook which he compiled fourteen months before Thomas left the school.[14] His material tells a rosy story of school bands, treats at the vicarage and cricket matches.

In the year 1873, for example, the *Surrey Advertiser* reported various treats for the children including an annual summer event to celebrate their manager John Leyland's birthday. On that occasion, 226 children marched to a field, led by their band, and, after a cricket match, enjoyed a large meal of tea and cake. Visits to the rectory became a regular annual event, with a cricket match against the village followed by a 'substantial meat tea' and the distribution of hymn books and bibles. Cricket matches against the village and Wandsworth Industrial School were encouraged. The outings seem to have become far more ambitious in the years immediately after Thomas's departure. There was, for instance, a ploughing match in 1876. Christmas 1878 was a jolly event, with bread, meat, pies, puddings and copious draughts of milk. A week later, a feast of buns, roast pork, baked potatoes, plum pudding and nuts was laid on by the rectory. This particular feast, however, came at a cost: the newspaper reported that the reverend and the rector, family and friends, gave a musical entertainment '... interspersed with readings of an amusing and suitable character'.

And every time the children went out *en masse*, their band led the way. Mr Penny was their bandmaster, and they made a grand sight, as a newspaper described: '... the boys of the Home were seen marching towards Addlestone, headed by their Brass Band and carrying their flags and banners ...'[15]

Accounts such as these paint a glowing picture of ruddy-cheeked boys revelling in innocent pleasures, but there may have been a darker side to the school. A long article published in the *Weekly Times* seven years after Thomas had left paints a different picture. The reporter was openly critical of the school's manager, Mr Leyland. He drew attention to the fact that the school was without the customary board of management and wrote of Leyland's 'shrewdness of

50 Shoes made and worn by the boys, Surrey Industrial School.[16] Copyright, Surrey History Centre

business' that drove him to increase numbers to boost his profits. Leyland, he reported, cultivated 50–60 acres of ground which provided sufficient food not only to feed the staff and boys but also to sell commercially. Although tailoring and shoe-making ran at a loss, Leyland grew enough rose bushes to provide nine tons of rose leaves to sell to a distiller and he kept the boys hard at work distilling large quantities of rose water in his rose distillery ('a pretty ornamental building, serving to hide the Industrial School from his residence'). The reporter implied that Leyland even made a profit from the 7s. a week per boy that he received from the authorities as the boys grew nearly everything they ate. And he took a particular dislike to a 'sort of porridge made of rice and vegetables' that the boys were eating for dinner on the day he visited.

The reporter maintained that he had heard of no planned outings, seen no swings or indeed 'anything to indicate that there is a desire to give the boys any pleasure'. He saw a mother visiting an eleven-year-old who had lost his finger in a chaff-cutting machine accident ten days previously and commented, perhaps somewhat cynically, 'A hand with four fingers may pick a pocket, but not so easily wield a spade'. Contrast this with his picture of Leyland, living in his comfortable mansion, '... seeming to have no association with the School except in the sense that a Cuban planter has an association with the occupants of his negro quarters'. Leyland, fulminated the reporter, was intent on maximising his profit and employed an 'Ogre' with a whip in her hand to keep the boys slaving away in his rose gardens during the busy summer months. In his view, the boys were little different from prisoners because they would be arrested by the police and returned if they absconded. Finally, somewhat grudgingly and perhaps to protect himself from an action for libel, he admitted that the school had never been associated with any scandal. Nevertheless, he concluded, the boys 'certainly did not strike me as looking particularly happy'.

Two weeks later, the *Weekly Times* printed a spirited defence of the school written by the school's superintendent Alfred Wells, he of the scrapbook fame.

Wells confirmed the commercial success of the rose-water distillery but said that 'the Ogre' was a figment of the imagination. 'Treats' abounded. The school had 11 of the best swings in Surrey, a football pitch, bagatelle, games such as draughts and solitaire, and 'a magnificent dissolving view apparatus' that had cost £90. He seemed to be particularly indignant about the reporter's attack on the boys' diet. On three days of the week, he said, the boys had 6 ounces of cooked meat (not 5) and a pound of potatoes; on three other days they ate a pint of soup, 6–8 ounces of bread, 2 ounces of cheese and three quarters of a pint of coffee; they had fish once a week when it was available. The rice and vegetable soup so derided by the reporter was in fact a highly nutritious concoction consisting of:

51 Thomas Pendlebury's school report, 1875.

40 pints of rice with onions, carrots and turnips *ad libitum* boiled in with 80 pounds of beef which was hashed to provide the next day's dinner. Eaten with the bread this formed a wholesome and satisfying meal. In fact, this was probably a much better diet than Thomas would have expected at home in Lambeth.

The truth, of course, probably lay somewhere between these two accounts. Industrial Schools were intended to be tough places. Some of the children were very deprived.[17] Illness and 'deficiency in intellect' were as much of a problem as bad behaviour and truancy. What is remarkable about the system set up by the SBL is that every girl and boy attending an Industrial School under their auspices was listed by name in the appropriate committee report. In Thomas's last year at school (1875), 2,557 children were named, with the performance of each assessed as 'good', 'medium' or 'poor'. Thomas scored a 'good' both in terms of his health and of his conduct, as did most of his contemporaries.

When Thomas left, his schoolmaster gave him a glowing reference, dated 10 November 1875 and sent to Jane in New Street.

> Surrey Certified Industrial School
> Byfleet Surrey
>
> During the time I have known Thomas Pendlebury I have found him to be obedient and obliging. He has discharge the duties of a monitor in the School for some time past & I have always found the class in good order when he was present. He appears to have abilities that (if properly used) will fit him to become a useful member of Society. In leaving this School he has my best wishes and if at any time a word from me can do him any service I shall be ready, willing, & happy to give it.
>
> [signature illegible] Master

Thomas left school with one skill that was to bring him great enjoyment in later life: it could only have been at Byfleet that he learned to play brass instruments. Luckily Alfred Wells included a picture of the school band in one of his scrapbooks dated to September 1874 when Thomas was still at the school. Aged about 15, it seems likely that Thomas is one of the older boys pictured holding either a saxophone (mid-centre of the photo) or a euphonium (at the back on the right).[18]

When Thomas was discharged from school, he returned to London but probably not to New Street. The SBL only allowed their discharged boys to live at home if, in their view, the parents or relatives were 'sober, respectable' and could provide them with their own bed in a bedroom, not a living room.[19] Jane may not have been able to manage this. The house in New Street was still

52   School Band, Surrey Industrial School, *c.*1874.[20] Copyright, Surrey History Centre

crowded: although Sophia Chapman and William Little had died during his time away at school, Robert's daughter Emma, her husband and her three children had moved in and Jane still had Thomas's two young half-sisters to look after. She was probably also caring for an ailing Robert Chapman whom she was soon to marry.

The SBL's officers may have helped Thomas to find lodgings in Bethnal Green and employment as a carman: they routinely placed boys in employment and followed up their progress with their employers. From there, he transported goods by horse and cart between a ships' chandlers and the London Docks. It was there, too, that he met and married Elizabeth Hollamby in 1881.

CHAPTER TWENTY

Workhouse, brass bands and the dock strike, 1870s–1900

S OON after Thomas was discharged from the Industrial School in Byfleet, he met and married Elizabeth Hollamby. He took her back to New Street to live with his mother Jane until Jane's death in 1886. He and Elizabeth had seven daughters, one of whom was the grandmother of the present author.

Jane Hollamby and her daughter Elizabeth

Elizabeth Hollamby was not yet 18 when she married Thomas in January 1881 in the church of St James the Great, Bethnal Green. She was illegitimate and had been born in the workhouse of St George in the East in July 1863. This parish workhouse was situated between Prusom Street and Princes Street (now Raine Street) and extended over a large area. The workhouse records show that her mother Jane 'Holmby', aged 30, had been admitted to the workhouse on Sunday 31 May 1863 and that she discharged herself 12 days after the birth by her 'own desire'.[1]

Elizabeth's mother Jane had a sad history. She seems to have been the daughter of Maria and William Hollamby (a cabinet maker) and born in September 1839 in Medley Place, just off Bermondsey Street. By 1841, she had moved with her parents to Old Street; her sister Mary Ann was living with relatives and her brother James had been admitted to the Bermondsey District Infant Poor Establishment in Merton. Both her parents appear to have died before 1850, and the only Jane Hollamby recorded in the 1851 Census is of a nine-year-old girl living in a Sussex workhouse. Ten years later she appears as 'Jane Halme', a barmaid working in Mile End at the 'Bank of Friendship' public house in Beaumont Row. She presumably became pregnant while working here because the Bank of Friendship lay within the catchment area of the workhouse of St George in the East to which she was admitted to give birth to her daughter in 1863. Poor Jane and, later, her daughter Elizabeth, could neither read nor write and so their unusual name was regularly misspelt.

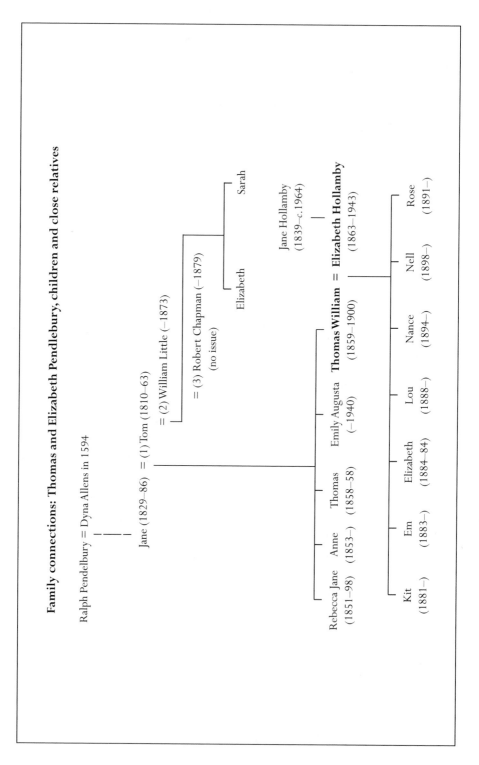

Family connections: Thomas and Elizabeth Pendlebury, children and close relatives

After her discharge with a young baby from St George's workhouse, Jane Hollamby disappears from the records. She may have died, although no record of her death has been found. In any event, little Elizabeth was taken in as a 'nurse child' by a woman called Mary Moody, wife of Thomas Moody, a leather-dresser ('Moody' appears later as 'Mondy' and 'Maudy'). Elizabeth lived with them in Woolf Terrace, Bermondsey (just off Maltby Street near Dockhead, right by the railway arches). There she lived in one room with her two 'parents' and their young granddaughter. It cannot have been a pleasant existence. Thomas Moody's work as a leather-dresser was a smelly and uncomfortable job which involved using a curved blade to scrape the fat and hair off animal hides that had been soaked in strong chemicals. But at least she had a family to care for her. She regarded Thomas Moody as her father: when she married Thomas Pendlebury in 1881, Moody gave her away, and she later gave his name as her maiden name rather than 'Hollamby' on her first daughter's birth certificate. Perhaps in similar vein, Thomas signed himself as 'Thomas Henery', presumably in recognition of the important part that his Uncle Henry Pendlebury (Tom's brother) had played in his upbringing. The Moodys later moved to west Leeds where Thomas Moody continued to work as a leather-dresser well into the early 1900s.

Elizabeth was pregnant at the time of her marriage to Thomas, and their first daughter was born five months later. Six more daughters followed over the next 17 years, of whom all but one (Elizabeth, born in 1884) survived into adulthood: Jane Elizabeth (known as 'Kit'), born in 1881; Emily Florence ('Em'), born in 1883; Louisa Annie ('Lou'), born in 1888; Rose Elizabeth, born in 1891; Annie Elizabeth ('Nance') born in 1894; and Ellenor May ('Nell'), born in 1898.

Thomas, carman and trade unionist

Thomas and Elizabeth had a large family of girls to feed and both worked hard, Thomas as a carman and Elizabeth as a needlewoman. A photograph found among the Pendlebury material is thought to be of him driving his two-horsed cart. The two horses in the image are typical of the heavy carthorses used to transport goods for breweries, distillers and coal merchants, and by carriers generally.

Charles Booth, that meticulous social commentator, analyst and reformer, had plenty to say about the carmen who worked in London at the end of the nineteenth century.

... With heavy traffic the pay and position of the driver primarily depends on whether he drives one horse or two ... a tradesman likes

53 Thomas Pendlebury with his cart and two horses.

to have his own cart and horse and his own man, for it is convenient in a hundred ways, besides being a source of pleasure at times on Sundays and holidays ... The main grievance in this trade concerns the length of the working day ... A week's work, inclusive of time occupied in the stable, will average from 96 to 100 hours ... The work, however, is seldom strenuous, and always involves more or less waiting ... For such long hours as prevail, the pay is low. There is perhaps no man's employment which yields so small a return per hour. To drive a cart demands but little skill, nor any exceptional intelligence ... for two-horse vans the pay varies from 22s to 26s with a few at 28s ...

Booth went on to note that

… Carmen are largely addicted to strong drink, but it is not supposed
that it plays any considerable part in their sickness and mortality …
The men suffer from rheumatism and bronchitis, and such illnesses are
the most prevalent and dangerous …[2]

The picture of Thomas Pendlebury driving his two-horsed cart was probably
taken towards the end of his life as he has the air of an older man. With two
horses, and (hopefully) in regular employment, his wages may have been towards
the top end of the range of a carman's earnings. Even so, however, there can
have been few home comforts for his wife and (eventually) six daughters.

The Pendleburys were no doubt affected by the Great Dock Strike of 1889
which began when the men working in the West India Docks came out on
strike in protest at the 'call-on' system and the very low hourly rates of pay.[3]
They were quickly joined by the stevedores and others and, six days later, the
docks came to a standstill. The dock owners introduced 'blacklegs', fighting
broke out, men were injured, and the strikers and their families endured great
hardship. Daily marches drew thousands of onlookers and supporters from all
over London, women joined with the men to support the action, church missions
opened soup kitchens, and strikes broke out in other factories and workshops
throughout the east end of London. The starving dockers and their families were
saved from capitulation by Australian workers who began to send money over in
large quantities from the beginning of September onwards. The employers were
forced to negotiate: the dockers won a small rise in their hourly rates though not
an end to casual employment. The strike did, however, bring about a dramatic
rise in trade union membership, from 750,000 in 1888 to 1.5 million in 1892.[4]

Thomas was probably already a member of the London Carmen's Trade
Union when the strike began. His union was set up in 1888 to represent the
carters of east London who travelled to and from the docks and warehouses
(the union was later renamed the National Union of Vehicle Workers until it
became part of the Transport and General Workers Union). If so, his earnings
would have plummeted during the strike. In any event, his sympathies would
have been with the strikers; and his strong and principled wife Elizabeth would
no doubt have been alongside him helping. It is not difficult to imagine him in
those eventful days of 1889, playing his euphonium in one of the bands that
led his fellow unionists on their marches through east London and, eventually,
victoriously on to Hyde Park.

His local branch, London Carmen's Trade Union Brass Band No. 13, had its
own set of rules tailored to the needs of its brass band. The rule book, which
has survived among the Pendlebury papers, set out 15 rules which stipulated,

54 Rule Book and Thomas Pandlebury's contribution card, London Carmen's Trade Union, 1896.

among other things, that the instruments belonged to the branch and were in the care of four trustees, two from the band and two from the branch. An elected committee of nine, four from the band and five from the branch, were responsible for regulating the business of the band. Practices were set for every Wednesday evening at 'The Ship', Long Lane, Bermondsey. The committee could expel a member for misconduct, systematic non-attendance, for being in arrears or 'if he shows such a stubbornness to learn, that the Bandmaster may consider him not capable of learning an instrument.' Anyone refusing to obey the bandmaster, or using 'profane language', was to be fined 2d. each time. Finally, those in arrears through being out of work or in distress could appeal to the committee. The rules were strict. In 1897, for example, a notice summoning members of the branch to attend a Special General Meeting ended with the words, 'For non-attendance a Fine of 3d will be imposed. Roll Call at 9 o'clock.'

The union subscription was set at 6d. a week in its first year, a not inconsiderable sum. Thomas never fell behind with his dues. One complete union rule book and several contribution cards survive. A loose sheet of paper records the dues (5s.) paid by Thomas from April 1895 onwards; he paid his last recorded amount (1s.) in November 1899, just a few weeks before his death.

Two sheets of band music have also survived. Both are for *The Tournament*, a quick march by Bonheur; one is the part for the saxophone horn and the other for the euphonium, that mainstay of military and marching bands. Playing in the band was an important part of Thomas's life: his youngest daughter remembered her father going every week to band practice in the first-floor rooms of a nearby public house.[5]

Thomas's action against the docks

Somewhere along the way things went sour for Thomas. He can never have earned much money from his long days driving his horses and cart between Bethnal Green and the docks. There were many mouths to feed, and his wife Elizabeth always supplemented their income as best she could by doing skilled needlework at home. She was already working as a collar-maker a couple of months after her marriage to Thomas and, by 1891, was a 'shirt collar holer'. A bill survives from this period which shows that, not unusually, the family relied on credit to buy essential items such as shoes. The document is undated but belongs to the 1890s; it is from a local shoe and clog manufacturer and lists as owing the sum of 10s. 5d. (7s. 6d. for the purchase of one pair of men's tan shoes and 2s. 11d. carried over from a previous purchase). Four separate payments of 1s. have been made, irregularly, towards paying off this debt.

The family's situation was to become even more precarious when Thomas had an accident at work. Exactly what happened in unclear, but the incident was sufficiently serious to justify him taking legal action against the docks. His union presumably provided him with legal advice and a solicitor. Five letters survive from his solicitor that refer to compensation for an injury without giving any further details. All were sent from Clinton & Co., Solicitors, of 59–60 Chancery Lane, headed 'Yourself and the Docks', and dated between June and July 1897. The fourth reads, '… The defendants have without prejudice made an offer of £25 to settle your claim for compensation, please let us know by return whether you accept this sum'. The fifth and final letter merely asks Thomas to call at the solicitor's office and there is no indication as to whether he accepted the offer of £25. Assuming his weekly wages amounted at most to 30s., the offer represents the equivalent of just over three months' pay. The fact that the docks were prepared to offer anything at all to someone who was not directly in their employment suggests a gross degree of negligence on their part and that Thomas was seriously injured. When he died in Guys Hospital a little over two years later, of 'Suppurative Peridonitis Toxaemia', his family maintained that his death was caused by his accident. If so, he spent his last years fighting a poisonously infected wound and was probably unable to work very much at all.

Thomas was only 41 years old when he died. Thomas's death brought an end to this family's male Pendlebury surname in London, a lineage that has been traced from Lancashire through Richard Pendlebury (who was wounded at the battle of Corunna) via Tom in London to Thomas himself. Like his father Tom, Thomas lived for most of his life in the same few streets. Tom's homes had been clustered around Waterloo East station and Thomas's lay a little further to the east in what is now Borough Market: New Street, Arthur Street, Downes Street, Stamworth Street and Rudyard Place, just off Kipling Street. Kipling Street was familiar territory to Thomas. His uncle Henry had lived in the same road in the 1870s when it was still called Nelson Street. The occupants of all these streets tended to be poor but respectable; they were neither the 'lowest class, vicious, semi-criminal' nor the 'very poor in chronic want' that Charles Booth found in some of the streets nearby.[6]

In other respects, too, Thomas's life echoed that of his father's. Like Tom Pendlebury, he could read and write, his father having learnt under the benign influence of his relatives in Lancashire and he under the auspices of the School Board for London. Both men made their living in the heart of London, Tom in trade, as a tobacconist and as a warehouseman, and Thomas as a carman in the London Docks. Both died a death hastened by the dangerous working conditions of the times: Tom from lead poisoning and Thomas from an infected wound.

55   Thomas, possibly on his wedding day in 1881.

There, however, the similarities end. Tom travelled to India, the Netherlands, Canterbury, Scotland and Lancashire. Thomas is not known to have ventured any further than Byfleet in Surrey, although it is hard not to imagine him taking his family up to Yorkshire to visit either Uncle Henry, Elizabeth and his many cousins in Wombwell or to west Leeds to see Thomas and Mary Moody, the couple who had been like parents to his wife.

Did Thomas, like his father, keep in touch with his relatives in Radcliffe? Perhaps not, for by the late 1880s the Pendlebury's Lancashire roots were probably too far in the past to have meant a great deal to him. His father had died too young to be able to tell him about how his grandfather Richard Pendlebury had fought at Corunna or to pass on tales about his great-uncle Tommy's fights with the workhouse. Perhaps Uncle Henry took over his role; he would have made a wonderful story teller.

Henry and his large family lived only five minutes' walk away from Thomas's home in New Street in the early 1870s. Given his generous nature and his closeness to his brother Tom, it is inconceivable that Henry did not keep in close touch with his young nephew. He was still alive when Thomas and Elizabeth Hollamby were married and when their first three children were born. He knew Jane (Thomas's mother) well. And when Thomas married, he entered 'Henery' (which was how Henry always spelt his name) as his second name (rather than his officially registered second name of William), suggesting that he thought of his uncle as the father he had never properly known.

There is good reason to think that at least some of Henry and Tom's children remained in touch. One of Henry's daughters, Elizabeth, who first came with the family to London in the 1870s, married a man from Bermondsey, Richard Dowdle, and had ten children. Their homes in parts of Bermondsey and Lambeth were never far from the places where Tom's children and grandchildren lived. They were linked, too, by work. Richard Dowdle was a carman from at least 1871 onwards and it may have been he who helped Thomas to find his first job in that trade in the late 1870s. Then, some 35 years later, Henry's granddaughter Ellen Dowdle worked in Pink's Jam factory at the same time as Thomas's two daughters, Louise and Rose, were also working in a jam factory (name unknown). Close in age, this group of second cousins – Henry's ten Dowdle grandchildren, and Tom's six granddaughters – must surely have had much in common.

There is a definite twinkle in Thomas's eye in the only picture of him that has survived.

CHAPTER TWENTY-ONE

Shirt collars and jam:
Elizabeth Pendlebury, 1863–1943

W HEN Thomas died in January 1900, he left behind a wife aged only 37 and six young daughters. Elizabeth (née Hollamby) Pendlebury had been brought up in poverty and was used to working. She started to earn money as a collar maker within a couple of months of her marriage to Thomas in 1881 and, although unable to read or write, brought her children up successfully at a time when there was no state safety net – other than the workhouse – to help those who could not support themselves.

The threat of the workhouse can never have been far away from Elizabeth's thoughts. She had been born in one of these forbidding institutions, and there were many dotted round the part of London where she lived. In Southwark alone, the enormous St Saviour's Union workhouse dominated Marlborough Street (next to New Street where Elizabeth began her married life), and others darkened Russell, Westmoreland and Mint Streets. They were to be found in Maid Lane (between Blackfriars and Southwark Bridges) and in Renfrew Road (Kennington). Directly across the river, they existed in Bread Street and Saffron Hill. Long after her death, her daughters still remembered vividly how she used to send them off every morning to walk across the bridge to the workhouse to get their breakfast. In times of difficulty, it seems that it was to the workhouse of her birth, St George in the East, that Elizabeth turned for help. It is not difficult to imagine the steps of those six young girls as they came out of Rudyard Place, turned right into Kipling Street and then left along Snowfields, cutting through Guys Hospital (where their father had died) to cross London Bridge. Once on the other side of the river they would have made their way along Lower Thames Street, past the Tower of London and the London Docks (where their father had worked and been injured) before reaching Princes Street and the scattered buildings of the workhouse, school and infirmary of St George in the East. There they probably headed for one of the kitchens attached to the complex of church and hospital buildings because help from the workhouse itself would have been restricted to those

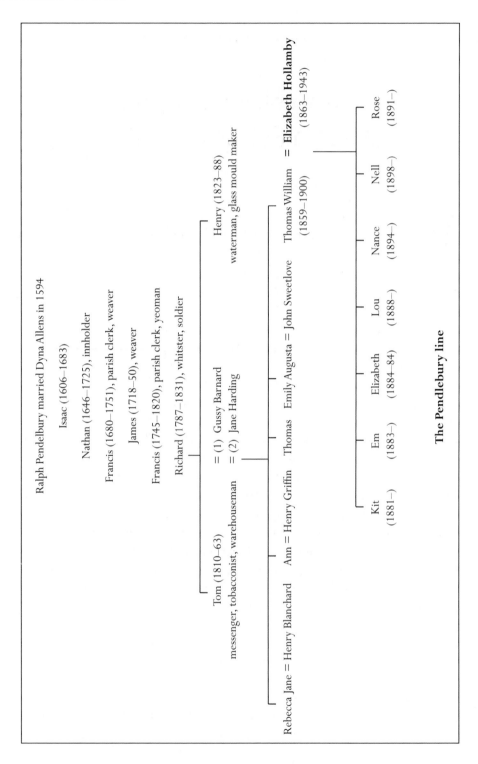

Ralph Pendelbury married Dyna Allens in 1594

Isaac (1606–1683)

Nathan (1646–1725), innholder

Francis (1680–1751), parish clerk, weaver

James (1718–50), weaver

Francis (1745–1820), parish clerk, yeoman

Richard (1787–1831), whitster, soldier

Henry (1823–88)
waterman, glass mould maker

Tom (1810–63)   = (1) Gussy Barnard
messenger, tobacconist, warehouseman   = (2) Jane Harding

Rebecca Jane = Henry Blanchard   Ann = Henry Griffin   Thomas   Emily Augusta = John Sweetlove   Thomas William   =   **Elizabeth Hollamby**
(1859–1900)   (1863–1943)

Kit   Em   Elizabeth   Lou   Nance   Nell   Rose
(1881–)   (1883–)   (1884–84)   (1888–)   (1894–)   (1898–)   (1891–)

The Pendlebury line

56   Rudyard Place, Kipling Street, 1936.[1]

living within its catchment area. Breakfast would have been a meagre affair – a little bread and milk, with jam or cocoa if they were lucky.

At some stage in the early 1900s, Elizabeth Pendlebury added a young foster child to her household of six daughters. Unofficial adoptions were commonplace at the time, and money usually changed hands, but whether Elizabeth received any payment for doing this is not known (the child was described as a 'visitor' in the 1911 Census). In any event, young Etheldreda (Ethel) arrived and stayed in the Pendlebury home until she reached the age of 21. She was called after the church where she was christened (St Etheldreda's Roman Catholic church in Holborn) and given the surname of her mother, Berringer. Ethel's mother Minnie was one of the daughters of the Pendlebury's local butcher, John Berringer. He moved several times during his life, but always to streets (Crucifix Lane, Snowfields and Bermondsey Street) within a stone's throw of New Street and Rudyard Place where Elizabeth and her daughters lived. Elizabeth would have bought her meat from Ethel's grandfather and probably knew Ethel's mother Minnie well. Minnie was almost the same age as Em Pendlebury and also did sewing for a living; she continued to live at her father's house in Bermondsey for many years.

Elizabeth also took in lodgers. In 1901 Harriet Smith, aged 24 and from Bermondsey, lived with the family in Rudyard Place (Kipling Street) and worked as a shirt collar machinist. Elizabeth made sure that her own daughters knew how to sew; by 1901 Kit and Em were earning money as shirt collar makers.

Sometime in the early 1900s, the family moved from Kipling Street to Hillingdon Street, which was an improvement, at least in terms of its surroundings. The former lay in the heart of industrial Bermondsey right next to the leather market but the latter (a collection of terraced two-storey houses occupied by 'many poor, many fairly comfortable' people[2]) was situated in a working-class residential area only a stone's throw away from Kennington Park with its Refreshment House (built in 1897) and a smart bandstand (erected in 1900).

But the first decade or so of the twentieth century was a difficult time for the Pendleburys as the rise in real wages fell way behind rises in food prices.[3] By 1911, only Em had married and left home and, with five daughters and a foster child to support, Elizabeth took in another two lodgers: Florence Hoare and her young son Frederick. The household now depended for its livelihood entirely upon men's clothing and jam.

Two of the girls, Louise and Rose, worked for a jam 'manufactory' as a 'pattern stopper maker' and a 'labeller'. Although it could be fun working outside the home, factory conditions at the time could be truly dreadful and the wages low.[4] One social commentator wrote that '... Many of them [the jam workers] work ten and a half hours a day, pushed and urged to utmost speed, carrying cauldrons of boiling jam on slippery floors, standing five hours at a time, and all this often for about 8/– a week'.[5] Their take-home pay was at best about 10s. a week but this could drop to as little as 3s. 6d. out of season. At the time of the 1911 Census, about 1,500 women and girls were employed in the Bermondsey factories making jam, biscuits, sweets, custard, pickles, tin-boxes, glue, vinegar and the like. The jam factories, all within easy reach of Kipling Street, included Lipton's, Southwell's, Pink's (which had a particularly bad reputation as an employer) and Hartley's. The latter employed over 2,000 employees and it would have been ironic had Lou and Rose worked for them because they were related, albeit very distantly, to its owners. Their first cousin twice removed (Joseph Barron, son of Joseph Barron and Ann née Pendlebury) had married into the Hartley jams family in 1838.[6]

In the sweltering heat of August 1911, the women in the Bermondsey factories went on strike against low wages and poor working conditions.[7] Their strike began with a march down Tooley Street, with women workers from Benjamin Edgington tentmakers, Pearce Duff custard makers, Shuttleworth's chocolate

57 Pinks' strike, Bermondsey, 1911.[8] Ellen Dowdle (Henry's granddaughter) worked in Pink's jam factory in 1911 and is probably among these strikers. So, too, may be her two second cousins, Louise and Rose Pendlebury

factory, Peek Frean's biscuits, Hartley's jams, and others, led by Pink's jam employees shouting, 'We are not white slaves, but Pink's slaves'.[9] The struggle lasted ten days and its outcome was a success. The women in all but three of 22 factories returned to work with increased wages and better working conditions.

Jam production was considered to be unskilled work reserved for those most desperate to earn a living. Sewing, by contrast, was seen as a more skilled occupation, although it was nearly as poorly paid. Elizabeth Pendlebury, her two daughters Kit and Nance, and Florence the lodger, all sewed for a living. In 1911 Elizabeth was working from home as a 'Gent's Linen Collar Button holer'; Kit was a 'Forewoman' for a linen collar maker; Nance was a 'Gent's Cap Cutter'; and the lodger Florence was a clerk for the same firm of linen collar makers. They were constantly on the watch for better pay, with Rose spending time in service in Ventnor (the Isle of Wight) and working at Fremlin's Brewers (St Katherine's Dock) and at Crosse and Blackwell's jam and pickle factory (demolished to make way for County Hall, headquarters of the London County Council). Full-time factory workers such as Kit, Rose, Nance and Florence could expect to earn between 11s. and 18s. or more a week.[10] An 'out-worker' (i.e. someone working from home) would have been lucky to have earned 6s. Clothes-making paid more than jam-making, but it was still a pittance compared with the 18–20s. a week that even a male casual labourer could expect to earn.

This, of course, was one of the problems with being an all-female household at a time when a woman's income was seen as a supplement rather than as a substitute for a man's: their income remained low no matter how hard they worked. Working mothers, somewhat unfairly, were blamed by some for the many social problems that beset the poorer neighbourhoods. John Hobson, for example, had no doubts that the 'average [female] London factory hand' was primarily responsible for the 'physical and moral deterioration of the race which we have traced in low city life'. Her wage-earning activities, he proclaimed, turned a baby into the 'street arab', who became the 'tramp, pauper, criminal, casual labourer, feeble-bodied, weak-minded, desolate creatures, incapable of strong, continuous effort at any useful work'.[11] It is to Elizabeth's credit that all seven of her girls avoided such a fate.

Elizabeth had no brothers or sisters of her own to support her, although Thomas and Mary Moody, the couple who had taken her in when she was a baby and whom she regarded as her parents, were still alive and living in Leeds in the early 1900s. Instead, she was surrounded by a large, and entirely female, group of her mother-in-law's relatives. There were the three daughters of Tom and Jane Pendlebury, all now married, Rebecca Blanchard, Annie Griffin and Emily Sweetlove; and the two married daughters of Jane and her second husband (William Little), Sarah Miller and Elizabeth Collier. Between them, they produced a total of 29 children, all of whom would have called her 'Aunt' and nearly all of whom lived very locally. Many of these women were very close, as the marriage records show. Rebecca's husband, for example, was best man at her sister Annie's wedding; Rebecca's sister-in-law signed the register at Sarah's wedding; and at Elizabeth's ceremony, her brother-in-law acted as best man and her half-aunt Jane ('Kit') Pendlebury signed the register.

It is not difficult to imagine Elizabeth at home working her treadle sewing machine while young Ethel and Frederick played at her feet. She always had food ready for Nell when she came back from school and for Kit, Rose, Lou and Nance when they returned weary from their work in the nearby jam and clothing factories. Their home at 70 Hillingdon Street was a crowded one by modern standards. The nine of them, eight females and one baby boy, lived in only three rooms and a kitchen.

Although Elizabeth never learnt to read or write, she made sure that all her girls had an education, were fed and clothed, and grew up with a strong sense of what was right and wrong. Her oldest daughter Kit, who was 19 when her father died, was the greatest possible support to her; her sisters adored her and regarded her almost as a second parent. The girls remained inseparable, even as adults. Five of them (including four who married) lived and died within the same square mile of her and of each other in the Camberwell area of south London. She lived with two of them in her old age and, right up until the time of her death in 1943, had tea with them all every Saturday. When she died at the age of 80, she was surrounded by her six daughters and by her foster-daughter: Ethel hitched a lift on a lorry and was dropped at the corner of Rye Lane so that she could be there at her death. In the front room of a house in Camberwell, all mourned the loss of a truly remarkable woman, fine mother and step-mother. The author still has the locket she wore when her photograph was taken in 1935.

58   Elizabeth Pendlebury, aged 72.

Conclusion

Families have deep roots. This writer can recall the stories told her about her great-grandmother Elizabeth Pendlebury, whose gold locket she still treasures. She remembers great-aunts Em, Kit and Nell, and can still imagine herself as a child tip-toeing through their darkened rooms, brushing with a shiver of apprehension against dusty heavy velvet drapes, a-wonder at their china dolls, porcelain tea sets, fine needlework and the ticking clocks on their crowded mantelpieces. She thinks of grand-mother Rose (her warm generous 'thin nanny') and dear kind great-aunt Nance and recalls trips to see Flanagan and Allen at the London Palladium, to visit Battersea Fun Fair and to buy Arthur Ransome books in a small bookshop in Dulwich village. She can still taste those special Yorkshire puddings, soaking in the drippings from her grand-mother's favourite 'H Bone' cut of beef. Of such small things are enduring memories made.

THE Pendleburys were never wealthy. None of them ever held either great office of state or hereditary title, nor owned splendid mansions or substantial wealth. Like the majority of the population, they sought to achieve health and prosperity for themselves and their children through work and family. In so many ways theirs is a story that is repeated countlessly through the ages. What especially distinguishes them is that documents survive to tell their tale today, thanks in part to their origins in Lancashire, a county that has a long tradition of well-preserved church and other records, to the excellence of the Victorian postal system, and to someone's hoarding instinct that allowed some of the many letters which passed between husbands and wives, mothers and daughters, uncles and nephews and brothers and sisters, fortuitously to survive to the present day.

Like so many Lancashire families in the seventeenth and eighteenth centuries, the Pendleburys' prosperity rose and declined with the fortunes of the cotton industry. From alehouse-keepers to small-scale cotton weavers working in their own homes, they advanced to become handloom owners in a position to employ other men to work for them. They learned to read and write, became churchwardens and parish clerks, men of modest property and pillars of the local community. By the beginning of the nineteenth century, however, their fortunes had begun to fail as the grip of the men with capital and ruthless machines tightened. Large families and low wages increasingly took their toll until the likes of Richard were forced to join the many other young and undernourished lads enticed into the armies sent to fight Napoleon. Like many, he was seriously wounded and pensioned off.

When Richard's son Tom settled in London, he, too, was following a pattern shared by so many of his contemporaries, drawn as he was to the capital by its seeming promise of employment and opportunity. He, typically, lived all his life within the same few streets and, again, typically, changed jobs frequently and found work wherever he could. He fell in love, travelled abroad, and mixed with seamen and traders. He worked for a tobacco importer, running errands, selling cigars and making snuff. His activities were based in the trading heart of London, near to St Paul's. He drank, smoked and gambled during regular 'flearups' with his brother Henry and friends; his first wife died of cholera, and he was himself poisoned by the lead contamination that infused the pollution of the inner city. He raised children, had money problems and rowed with his family over inheritance matters. What distinguishes him from his contemporaries, however, is that these details of his life, and his words and thoughts, are still known over 150 years after his death.

The life of his son Thomas was likewise unremarkable for his times. He lost his father when very young and was brought up by a step-father; he married a girl who had been born in the workhouse; and his work led to premature death. Like the majority of his fellow transport workers, he joined the early trade union movement that emerged from the bitter disputes in the London Docks. However, his story is distinguished in two respects from that of the boys who ran wild with him in the poorest streets of Bermondsey. First, he was rescued from possible destitution and crime by the School Board for London, that most remarkable instrument of Victorian social enlightenment, and sent to one of the very first Industrial Schools. Second, his experiences, like those of his father Tom, are documented. A school report and one slightly pedantic schoolmaster's hobby of keeping meticulous scrapbooks about the school and its brass band bring to life Thomas's schooldays. And his union dues cards and sheets of music commemorate his days as an active trade unionist.

The Pendlebury odyssey is the story of ordinary people, of the ebbs and flows of fortune, of the mastery of literacy, of the birth of children and the death of loved ones. It is ordinary in the sense that it is so similar to the stories shared by the ancestors of so many people alive today. The struggle to survive against sometimes almost impossible odds, the quest for personal and financial improvement and the importance of family shine through, from the progress of the early Pendleburys in Lancashire to the resilience of Tom in nineteenth-century London and the resolution of Elizabeth who, though born in a workhouse and widowed young, managed to raise seven girls on her own. It is through the lives of such people that the past whispers gently through into the present. A truly English odyssey.

References

Chapter 1: Radcliffe and Bury in Lancashire

1　J.P. Earwaker, 'An Account of the Charters, Deeds, and other Documents, now Preserved at Agecroft Hall, Co. Lancaster', *Transactions of the Lancashire and Cheshire Antiquarian Society*, vol. IV (A. Ireland & Co.: Manchester, 1986), pp. 200–20.

2　W. Farrer and J. Brownbill, (eds), *A History of the County of Lancaster*, vol. 5 (Constable: London, 1911), pp. 20–5.

3　H. Fishwick, *Pleadings and depositions in the duchy court of Lancaster time of Henry VII and Henry VIII* (The Record Society: Rochdale, 1896), pp. 3–7.

4　Ibid., pp. 99–108.

5　J.K. Walton, *Lancashire: A social history, 1558–1939* (Manchester University Press, 1987), pp. 7–19.

6　C. Horner, 'In the labyrinth: John Dee and Reformation Manchester', in C. Horner (ed.), *Early Modern Manchester* (Manchester Centre for Regional History, 2008), pp. 17–36.

7　A.G. Crosby, 'The regional road network and the growth of Manchester in the sixteenth and seventeenth centuries', in C. Horner (ed.), *Early Modern Manchester*, (Manchester Centre for Regional History, 2008), p. 3.

8　Walton, *Lancashire: A social history, 1558–1939*, p. 41.

9　J.F. Curwen, *The Later Records relating to North Westmorland: or the Barony of Appleby*, (Titus Wilson & Son: Kendal, 1932), pp. 378–80.

10　Ibid.

11　S. Bowd, 'In the labyrinth: John Dee and Reformation Manchester', in C. Horner (ed.), *Early Modern Manchester*, p.31.

12　S. Scott and C.J. Duncan, 'The mortality crisis of 1623 in north-west England', *Local Population Studies*, vol. 58 (1997), p. 14.

13　M. James, 'The Lancashire population crisis of 1623 – further comment', *Local Population Studies*, vol. 37 (1986), pp. 53–4.

14　Scott and Duncan, 'The mortality crisis of 1623', pp. 14–25.

15　James, 'The Lancashire population crisis of 1623 – further comment' *Local Population Studies*, vol. 37 (1986), p. 53.

16　*Lancashire Parish Register Society* (LPRS), (Lancashire On-Line Parish Clerks site, http://www.lan-opc.org.uk).

17　*Bury (St Mary the Virgin)*, (LPRS CDs 1, 10).

18　Walton, *Lancashire: A social history, 1558–1939*.

19　Ibid., p.22.

20　Camden's account was translated from Latin by Philemon Holland in 1610 and is available at http://www.philological.bham.ac.uk/cambrit (accessed 25 Sept. 2011).

21 Walton, *Lancashire: A social history, 1558–1939.*

22 Crosby, 'The regional road network and the growth of Manchester in the sixteenth and seventeenth centuries', p. 7.

23 Ibid., p. 33.

24 *Bury and Radcliffe Annual for 1910* (The *Times* Office, Bury, 1910), p. 79. Radcliffe Local Collection, A12 BUR.

25 Bowd, 'In the labyrinth: John Dee and Reformation Manchester', in C. Horner (ed.), *Early Modern Manchester*, p. 22. See also a contemporary account by Thomas Potts, *The Wonderfull Discoverie of Witches in the Countie of Lancaster* (Carnegie Publishing: Lancaster, 2003).

26 H. Brierley, 'Notes on Lancashire Parish Registers', in H. Fishwick and P. Ditchfield (eds), *In Memorials of Old Lancashire*, vol. II (Bemrose & Sons: London, 1909), pp. 191–203.

27 R.B. Outhwaite, *Clandestine Marriages in England, 1500–1850* (Hambledon Press: London and Rio Grande, 1995), p. 8.

28 Ibid., pp. 21–49.

29 *Radcliffe, 1557–1783* (LPRS CD 60/1).

30 http://www.buryparishchurch.com, accessed 25 Sept. 2011.

31 Walton, *Lancashire: A social history, 1558–1939*, pp. 47–9.

32 Crosby, 'The regional road network and the growth of Manchester in the sixteenth and seventeenth centuries', p. 13.

Chapter 2: The early Pendlebury innkeepers

1 M. Spufford (ed.), *The World of Rural Dissenters 1520–1725* (Cambridge University Press, 1995).

2 A. Roberts, 'Literacy and the spread of ideas', Turbulent Times, seventeenth-century Appleby (no date). (http://www.applebymagna.org.uk/appleby_history/ar6_turbulent_times.html#Part1Literacy, accessed 25 Sept. 2011).

3 Reproduced by permission of the Lancashire Record Office, WCW infra 1608.

4 Reproduced by permission of the Lancashire Record Office, WCW infra 1608.

5 J.P. Earwaker, *Remains, historical and literary, connected with the palatine counties of Lancaster and Chester*, new series volume 3, (Sims: Manchester, 1884).

6 Sources used for these meanings: C.W. Foster (ed.), *Lincoln Wills*, vol. 2, 1505–1530, (Horncastle: Lincoln, 1918), pp. 93-300); *Middle English Dictionary* (Ann Arbor: Michigan, c.1998); J.P. Earwaker, *Remains, historical and literary, connected with the palatine counties of Lancaster and Chester*; N. Cox and K. Dannehl, *Dictionary of Traded Goods and Commodities, 1550–1820* (2007), (http://www.british-history.ac.uk/source.asp?pubid=739, accessed 25 Sept. 2011).

7 Manchester Library and Information Service, MFPR 2097.

8 Outhwaite, *Clandestine Marriages in England, 1500–1850*, p. 22.

Chapter 3: Civil war and religious upheaval: Isaac Pendlebury, 1606–1683

1 Walton, *Lancashire: A social history, 1558–1939*, p. 26.

2 J. Healey, 'Economic fluctuations and the poor: some Lancashire evidence, 1630–80', unpublished paper delivered at the 2008 Economic History Society annual conference.

3 Ibid.

4 Walton, *Lancashire: A social history, 1558–1939*, p. 26.

5 S. Bull, 'A general plague of madness': The Civil Wars in Lancashire, 1640–1660 (Carnegie Publishing: Lancaster, 2009).

6 Ibid., pp. 217–25.

7 Bury and Radcliffe Annual for 1910, p. 79.

8 Ibid., p. 39.

9 E. Baines, History of the County Palatine and Duchy of Lancaster (Fisher Son & Co.: London, Paris and New York, 1836), p. 12.

10 Bury (St Mary the Virgin), (LPRS CD 10).

11 M. Gray, The History of Bury, 1660–1876 (Bury Times Ltd, 1970), pp. 10–11.

12 Bull, 'A general plague of madness': the Civil Wars in Lancashire, 1640–1660, pp. 66, 93.

13 Ibid., pp. 283–9.

14 Ibid., p. 298.

15 H. Fishwick, 'Lancashire and Cheshire Church Surveys, 1649–1655', Parochial Surveys of Lancashire, part 1, (Wyman & Sons: London, 1899), p. 26.

16 Farrer and Brownbill (eds), A History of the County of Lancaster, vol. 5, pp. 56–67.

17 Ibid.

18 Ibid.

19 R.T. Herford, Memorials of Stand Chapel (H. Allen, Prestwich, 1893), p. 13.

20 Fishwick, 'Lancashire and Cheshire Church Surveys, 1649–1655', pp. 29–30.

21 Farrer and Brownbill (eds), A History of the County of Lancaster, vol.5, pp. 56–67.

22 Radcliffe (St. Mary the Virgin), (LPRS CD 60/61).

23 Bull, 'A general plague of madness': the Civil Wars in Lancashire, 1640–1660, pp. 65–6, 401–5.

24 Reproduced by permission of the Lancashire Record Office, WCW infra 1683.

25 Reproduced by permission of the Lancashire Record Office, WCW infra 1683.

Chapter 4: From humble beginnings: Nathan Pendlebury, 1646–1725

1 Parish registers of St Mary the Virgin Radcliffe, Radcliffe (St Mary the Virgin), (LPRS CD 60/61).

2 P. Clarke, The English Alehouse: a Social History, 1200–1830 (Longman Higher Education: London, 1983).

3 E. Kennerley, 'Lancaster inns and alehouses, 1600–1730', The Lancashire Local Historian, vol. 5 (1990), pp. 40–51.

4 Farrer and Brownbill (eds), A History of the County of Lancaster, vol.5, pp. 56–67.

Chapter 5: Weaving, parish affairs and velvet breeches: Francis Pendlebury, 1680–1751

1 An excellent factual introduction to the Lancashire cotton industry can be found in J. Mortimer, Cotton Spinning: the Story of the Spindle (Palmer, Howe & Co.: Manchester, 1895)

2 Ibid.

3 N. Smelser, Social Change in the Industrial Revolution (Routledge & Kegan Paul: London, 1967), p. 56.

4 Lancashire Record Office, WCW infra 1821.

5 P.M. Smith, 'Churchwardens: An Introduction to the Nature of the Office', Churchman, vol. 114/2 (2000).

6 History of education and schools, author unknown, (http://www.devon.gov.uk/index/councildemocracy/neighbourhoods-villages/record_office/family_history_3/school_records/hoe_school_before_1830s.htm, accessed 25 Sept. 2011).

7 Gray, *The History of Bury, 1660–1876*, pp. 33–6.
8 Lancashire Record Office, WCW infra 1751.
9 Lancashire Record Office, WCW infra 1820.

Chapter 6: Parish clerk and man of property, Nathan Pendlebury, 1722–1796

1 Lancashire Record Office, WCW infra 1799.
2 Lancashire Record Office, WCW infra 1762.
3 Sentence of Consecration of Additional burial ground (Manchester Archives and Local Studies, L210/1/14, 18 Sept. 1787).
4 From an early parish magazine, personal communication, John Higson.
5 Mortimer, *Cotton Spinning: the Story of the Spindle*, p. 90.
6 Ibid., 79–80.
7 Ibid., 80.
8 Lancashire Record Office, WCW infra 1796.
9 Lancashire Record Office, WCW infra 1799.

Chapter 7: The changing face of Radcliffe, Francis Pendlebury, 1745–1820

1 Register of St Mary the Virgin Radcliffe.
2 Lancashire Record Office, WCW infra 1796.
3 K. Binfield (ed.), *Writings of the Luddites* (John Hopkins Press: Baltimore and London, 2004).
4 M. Bush, *The Casualties of Peterloo* (Carnegie Publishing: Lancaster, 2005).
5 Parish Registers of St Mary the Virgin Radcliffe, Radcliffe (St Mary the Virgin).
6 W. Radcliffe, 'Origin of power-loom weaving', Mortimer, *Cotton Spinning: the Story of the Spindle* (Palmer, Howe & Co.: Manchester, 1895).
7 A.A.W. Ramsay, *Sir Robert Peel* (Books for Libraries Press: New York, 1928), pp. 1–9.
8 Lancashire Record Office, WCW infra 1815.
9 Personal communication, Barry and Pam Gidney.
10 Lancashire Record Office, QSP 2342/48.
11 J. Dunleavy, 'Industrial Revolution and Religious Change', *Lancashire Local Historian*, vol. 4. (1986).
12 The Church Rate Book, St Mary's Radcliffe, 1826–1827 (Manchester Archives and Local Studies, GB127.L210/2/1/4).
13 1841 tithe map for Radcliffe (Lancashire Record Office, DRM 1/83).
14 J. Mortimer, *Industrial Lancashire: some manufacturing towns and their surroundings* (Palmer, Howe & Co.: Manchester, 1897).

Chapter 8: Wounded at Corunna, Richard Pendlebury, 1787–1831

1 Attestation record, Regimental Archives, Grenadier Guards (Regimental Headquarters Grenadier Guards document R201), p. 124, personal communication, Barbara Chambers. Details of the documents available can be found at http:// britisharmyresearchnapoleonicwars.co.uk/index.php?p=1_7_1st-FOOT-GUARDS-RESEARCH#ATTESTATION, accessed 3 Oct. 2011.
2 Personal communication, Barbara Chambers.

3 Personal communication, Barbara Chambers.

4 Attestation record, Regimental Archives, Grenadier Guards, p. 24, personal communication, Barbara Chambers.

5 Muster Rolls for the Regiment (National Archives (Public Record Office), WO12), personal communication, Barbara Chambers.

6 B.J. Chambers, *John Collett & a Company of Foot Guards* (2010).

7 C. Summerville, *March of Death: Sir John Moore's Retreat to Corunna, 1808–1809* (Greenhill Books: London, 2003).

8 Ibid., pp. 6–87.

9 Chambers, *John Collett & a Company of Foot Guards.*

10 Ibid., p. 209.

11 *The Times*, 2 February 1809.

12 Summerville, *March of Death: Sir John Moore's Retreat to Corunna, 1808–1809*, p.197.

13 The National Archives (Public Record Office), WO 121/96.

14 The National Archives (Public Record Office), WO 23.

15 Summerville, *March of Death: Sir John Moore's Retreat to Corunna, 1808–1809*, p. 217.

16 The National Archives (Public Record Office), WO 121/182.

17 Baptismal records of St Margaret Westminster 1823 (City of Westminster Archives, SMW/PR).

18 Index to Attestations, 1775–1817, for the 1st Foot Guards (Grenadier Guards), personal communication, Barbara Chambers.

19 Poor rate, highway and scavenger (Absey), (Westminster City Archives, SMW/E/9/627, 630,633 and 636).

20 Letters of Administration for William Barnard, 1833 (National Archives (Public Record Office), PROB 31/1319/1261), and the Pendlebury documents.

21 Adapted from Cary's New and Accurate Plan of London and Westminster, the Borough of Southwark and parts adjacent (http://www.ph.ucla.edu/epi/snow/1818map/1818map.htm, accessed 3 Oct. 2011).

Chapter 9: 'I niver throw dirty warter in any man's face', Tom and Gussy, 1836–1837

1 National Archives (Public Record Office), PROB 31/1319/1261.

2 *The Times* ('Ship News East India Shipping' section, 1837).

3 *Illustrated London News*, 29 Oct. 1842 (University College London, Special Collections).

4 S. Barnett, 'Java the sailing ship, 1813–1940' (http://www.tenbratpress.org, accessed 3 Oct. 2011).

5 Ibid.

Chapter 10: 'Murky' but the best place to live, Tom's London, 1833–63

1 M. Mayhew, *Illustrated London News*, 18 Sept. 1852.

2 G. Gibberd, 'The Location of William Curtis's London Botanic Garden in Lambeth', *Garden History*, vol.13, no. 1 (1985), pp. 9–16.

3 Ibid., p. 17.

4 H. Roberts and W.H. Godfrey, *Survey of London: volume 23* (London County Council, 1951), pp. 77–8.

5 Ibid., pp. 1–11.

6 Letter from Robert Milner to Tom, 22 November 1849.

7 H.A. Harben, *A Dictionary of London* (H. Jenkins: London, 1918). 'Fifty Years of the Glass Bottle Trade, Messrs. Kilner Bros.' Jubilee', *The British Trade Journal* (1 Dec. 1894).

8 Ibid.

9 G. Doré and J. Blanchard, *London: a Pilgrimage* (Grant & Co.: London, 1872, reprinted in 1994 by Dover Publications: New York), p. 120.

10 H. Roberts and W.H. Godfrey, *Survey of London: volume 23*, pp. 1–11.

11 C. Dickens, *Dombey and Son* (published in monthly parts ,Oct. 1846–Apr. 1848), Chapter 6.

12 Old Ordnance Survey Maps, London Sheet 76, Waterloo & Southwark 1872, Alan Godfrey Maps.

13 G. Doré and J. Blanchard, *London: a Pilgrimage*, p. 22.

14 M. Thoma, 2010. *History of Economic Thought Lecture 12* (2010), (http://www.economistsview.typepad.com/economics493/lectures, accessed 2 Oct. 2011).

15 R. Turvey, 'Horse Traction in Victorian London', *Journal of Transport History*, 26/2 (2005), p. 57.

16 I. Maclachlan, 'A bloody offal nuisance: the persistence of private slaughter-houses in nineteenth-century England', *Urban History*, 34/2 (2007), pp. 227–54.

17 R. Turvey, 'Horse Traction in Victorian London', p. 46.

18 Ibid.

19 M. Alpert, *London 1849: a Victorian murder story* (Pearson Longman: London, 2004), p. 16.

20 Ibid., pp. 12–13.

21 F. Engels, *The Condition of the Working Class in England, From Personal Observation and Authentic Sources* (Oxford University Press edn, 1993), p. 36.

22 H. Roberts, W.H. Godfrey, *Survey of London: volume 23*, pp. 1–11.

23 Ibid., pp. 69–74.

24 M. Alpert, *London 1849: a Victorian murder story*, p. 143.

25 Cary's New and Accurate Plan of London and Westminster, the Borough of Southwark and parts adjacent.

26 Old Ordnance Survey Maps, London Sheet 76, Waterloo and Southwark 1872.

27 Southwark Local Studies Library, inventory number P4414.

Chapter 11: Fun, 'flearups' and brother Henry

1 *Mexborough and Swinton Times*, 29 Oct. 1910.

2 J.T. Arlidge, *The Hygiene, Diseases and Mortality of Occupations* (Percival: London, 1892), pp. 531.

3 F.E. Tayler, *The Folk Speech of South Lancashire* (John Heywood: Manchester, 1901).

4 Personal communication, Pam and Paul Gidney.

5 F.E. Tayler, *The Folk Speech of South Lancashire*.

6 Bury Image Bank, image number: b13091.

7 http://www.users.tinyonline.co.uk/gswithenbank/curiousc.htm (accessed 3 Oct. 2011).

8 *Illustrated London News*, 19 July 1851 (University College London, Special Collections).

9 http://www.rotherham.gov.uk/info/200136/local_towns_and_villages/320/catcliffe (accessed 2 Oct. 2011).

10 F.E. Tayler, *The Folk Speech of South Lancashire*.

11 Personal communication, Barry and Pam Gidney.

12 'Fifty years of the Glass Bottle Trade; Messrs. Kilner Bros.' Jubilee', *The British Trade Journal*, 1 Dec. 1894.

13 Ibid., pp. 43, 47.

14 Copyright Wombwell Heritage Group.

15 Ibid.

16 Personal communication, Barry and Pam Gidney.

17 Ibid.

Chapter 12: 'Bull baiting scum' at Swinton, relatives and rent disputes, 1839 to the 1860s,

1 D. Ashhurst, *History of South Yorkshire Glass* (J.R. Collis Publications: Sheffield, 1975).

2 Personal communication, Barry and Pam Gidney.

3 J.R. Ashby (ed.), *An Everyday Story of Mexborough Folk* (Mexborough and District Heritage Society, 1994).

4 *Mexborough and Swinton Times*, 29 Oct. 1910.

5 National Archives, ADM 29/26/81.

6 E. Gaskell, *Sylvia's Lovers* (Oxford University Press, 2008).

7 New Bailey Session April 1812, (Lancashire Record Office, QSP LC27/18).

8 Map of Lancashire and Furness, 1848–51, scale 1:10,560

9 Lancashire Record Office, QSP LC27/18.

10 Church Rates Book, St Mary's Radcliffe, 1826 (Manchester Archives, GB127.L210/2/1/4).

11 Map of Lancashire and Furness, 1848–51, scale 1:10,560 (Crown Copyright and Landmark Information Group 2011).

12 Bury Archives, b16270.

Chapter 13: 'Take a light brown Rappee flavour it slightly with Strong Liquor, Eau de Cologne and Port wine Lee': Tom as messenger, salesman, tobacconist, 1834–1851

1 *A biographical index of East India Company Maritime Service Officers, 1600–1833* (Guildhall Library, London).

2 *Madras Almanac*, 1842.

3 Freedom Admissions Papers, 1681–1925 (London Metropolitan Archives, COL/CHD/Fr/02).

4 *Illustrated London News*, 17 July 1852 (University College London, Special Collections).

5 Adapted from Cruchley's New Plan of London, improved to 1846 (http://www.ph.ucla.edu/epi/snow/1846map/1846map.htm, accessed 3 Jan. 2012).

6 G. Doré and J. Blanchard, *London: a Pilgrimage*, p. 118.

7 *Illustrated London News*, 6 May 1854 (University College London, Special Collections).

8 Old Bailey Proceedings, t18360713-1435, (http://www.oldbaileyonline.org, accessed 3 Oct. 2011).

9 C. Dickens, *Great Expectations* (http://www.online-literature.com/dickens/greatexpectations/20/, accessed 3 Oct. 2011), Chapter 20.

10 C. Dickens, *Oliver Twist* (http://www.online-literature.com/dickens/olivertwist/22/, accessed 4 Oct 2011), Chapter 21.

11 Old Bailey Proceedings, t18670610-540.

12 The meanings of these ingredients have been found using Webster's Online Dictionary and links from that site (http://www.websters-online-dictionary.org, accessed 3 Oct. 2011).

Chapter 14: Miasmas and cholera, Gussy, 1849

1 http://www.ph.ucla.edu/epi/snow, accessed 3 Oct. 2011.
2 *The Times*, 13 August 1849.
3 *The Times*, 22 August 1849.

Chapter 15: Pork sausages, grouse and family quarrels: the Hardings in Wiltshire, Liverpool and London

1 A. Claydon, *The Nature of Knoyle: East Knoyle, the people and the place* (Hobnob Press: East Knoyle, 2002)..
2 D.A. Crowley, (ed.), *A History of the County of Wiltshire*: volume 11, (http://www.british-history.ac.uk, accessed 3 Oct. 2011), pp. 82–103.
3 Bristol Record Office, Image 40762/5.
4 H. Huggins, *Flat racing and British society, 1790–1914* (Routledge: London, 1999), pp. 23–4.
5 J. T. Arlidge, *The hygiene, diseases and mortality of occupations*, p. 141.
6 D.A. Crowley (ed.), *A History of the County of Wiltshire*: volume 11, pp. 82–103.

Chapter 16: Aboard the *Bombay*, bound for Australia, 1852

1 Index to Unassisted Inward Passenger Lists to Victoria 1852–1923 (Public Record Office Victoria, personal communication).
2 This information is drawn from two unpublished diaries of the voyage: A. Gilchrist, 'Diary', 1852 (MS 9252 MSB 459); and R. Moffat, 'Diary', 1852, (MS 13670 Box 4044/1). Both are held at La Trobe Australian Manuscripts Collection, State Library of Victoria, Melbourne, Australia.
3 R. Moffat, 'Diary', 1852.
4 *Illustrated London News*, 13 Apr. 1844 (University College London, Special Collections).
5 Moffat, 'Diary'.
6 Ibid.
7 Ibid.
8 Australian Electoral Rolls, Victoria 1856, South Bourke, Templestowe.
9 Edwards Family Tree (http://www.ancestry.co.uk, accessed 2 Oct. 2011).

Chapter 17: 'London is a dear place for anyone to be out of employment': Tom's last years, 1851–1856

1 M. Alpert, *London 1849: a Victorian murder story.*
2 G. Doré and J. Blanchard, *London: a Pilgrimage*, p. x.
3 Robert Jaques, 1869 (Principal Probate Registry).
4 T. Barker, and D. Gerthold, *The rise and rise of road transport, 1700–1990* (Cambridge University Press, 1995), pp. 44–5; R. Turvey, 'Horse Traction in Victorian London', *Journal of Transport History*, 26/2 (2005), p. 43.
5 D. Weinbren, *The Oddfellows, 1810–2010: two hundred years of making friends and helping people* (Carnegie Publishing: Lancaster, 2010), p. 17.
6 *Illustrated London News*, 29 Jun. 1861 (University College London, Special Collections).
7 J.T. Arlidge, *The hygiene, diseases and mortality of occupations*, p. 426.
8 Ibid., p. 172.
9 J. Thompson, *Victorian London Street Life in Historic Photographs* (Dover Publications, New

York, 1994 reprint of 1877 original), pp. 16–19.

Chapter 18: 'One vast poor family ... children in the street ... women gossiping at the Doors': Jane Pendlebury, 1863–1886

1   J.T. Arlidge, *The hygiene, diseases and mortality of occupations*, pp. 118–19.
2   TUC Library Collections, London Metropolitan University.
3   C. Booth (1903), J. Steele (series editor), *The Streets of London: the Booth Notebooks – South East* (Deptford Forum Publishing: London, c.1997), pp. 25–7. See also
    C. Chinn, *Poverty amidst prosperity: the urban poor in England, 1834–1914* (Carnegie Publishing: Lancaster, 2006), pp. 99–100.
4   *Illustrated London News*, 21 Jan. 1872 (University College London, Special Collections).
5   C. Booth, J. Steele, *The Streets of London: the Booth Notebooks – South East*.
6   E. Walford, *Old and New London*, volume 6 (Cassell, Petter & Galpin: London, Paris & New York, 1878), pp. 407–25.
7   Museum of London, Image 004745.

Chapter 19: '[T]he boys ... marching towards Addlestone, headed by their Brass Band and carrying their flags and banners': Thomas Pendlebury at Industrial School

1   Children sent to Certified Industrial Schools at the instance of the School Board for London up to, and including, 24th June 1876 (London Metropolitan Archives, SBL/1578).
2   School Board for London, Report with Regard to Industrial Schools, 1870–1904 (London Metropolitan Archives, SBL/1578).
3   School Board for London Reports, 1875 (London Metropolitan Archives, SBL/1570).
4   Ibid., p. 4.
5   Ibid., p. 18.
6   Ibid., pp. 21–2.
7   Report of the Industrial Schools Committee, 16.11.1875 (London Metropolitan Archives, SBL/1570).
8   Children sent to Certified Industrial Schools at the instance of the School Board for London up to, and including, 24th June 1876.
9   School Board for London, Report with Regard to Industrial Schools, 1870–1904, p. 14.
10 Kellys *Directory of Surrey* for 1882.
11 This quotation, and the others from the inspectors and visitors, are taken from Surrey Industrial School Byfleet Visitors' Book, 1869–84 (Surrey History Centre, 399/1).
12 Revised code of Regulations, 1872. R. Aldrich, *Lessons from history of education: the selected works of Richard Aldrich* (Routledge: Abingdon, 2006), pp. 148–9.
13 A. Wells, 'Scrapbook of newspaper cuttings relating to industrial schools in Surrey and elsewhere, 1874–1882' (Surrey History Centre, 7556/1). All the cited newspaper extracts come from this source.
14 A. Wells, 'Scrapbook' (Surrey History Centre, 7556/3, dated September 1874 in Well's frontispiece).
15 A. Wells, 'Scrapbook of newspaper cuttings relating to industrial schools in Surrey and elsewhere, 1874–1882'.
16 Ibid.
17 Report of the Industrial Schools Committee, 16 Nov. 1875, pp. 37–40.
18 Personal communication, Phil Parker Ltd.

19 Report with Regard to Industrial Schools, 1870–1904, p. 23.

20 A. Wells, 'Scrapbook'.

Chapter 20: Workhouse, brass bands and the dock strike, 1870s–1900

1 Stepney Board of Guardians, Raine Street Workhouse, Admission and Discharge Register (London Metropolitan Archives, XIII 233).

2 C. Booth *et al.*, *Life and Labour of the People of London, second series, Industry*, vol. 3 (Macmillan and Co.: London and New York, 1903), pp. 325–6.

3 T. McCarthy, *The Great Dock Strike of 1889* (Weidenfeld & Nicholson: London, 1988).

4 B. Browne, *The Rise of British Trade Unions 1825–1914* (Longman: London, 1979).

5 Personal communication, Geoff Cutting.

6 C. Booth, *The Streets of London: the Booth Notebooks – South East*, p. 91.

Chapter 21: Shirt collars and jam, Elizabeth Pendlebury, 1863–1943

1 http://www.arewerelated.co.uk/4images/details.php?image_id=424&sessionid=cfa6dd9ad c0f9939ce2b45d02ef6eb34, accessed 4 Oct. 2011.

2 C. Booth, *The Streets of London: the Booth Notebooks – South East*, pp. 25–7.

3 U. de la Mare, 'Necessity and Rage: the Factory Women's Strikes in Bermondsey, 1911', *History Workshop Journal*, Issue 66 (2008), p.70

4 Ibid., pp. 63–80.

5 Ibid., p. 69.

6 Personal communication, Jane Burkinshaw.

7 U. de la Mare, 'Necessity and Rage: the Factory Women's Strikes in Bermondsey, 1911'.

8 TUC Library Collections, London Metropolitan University.

9 U. de la Mare, 'Necessity and Rage', p. 76.

10 J.A. Hobson, *Problems of Poverty: An Inquiry into the Industrial Condition of the Poor* (Methuen & Co.: London, 1891, 1905 edition), p. 69.

11 Ibid., pp. 77–8.

Index